Padre Pio

The Wonder Worker

IMPRIMATUR:
Most Rev. Sean P. O'Malley, OFM Cap.
Bishop of Fall River, Mass., USA
May 13, 1999, Immaculate Conception

The nihil obstat and imprimatur are official declarations that a book or pamphlet is free from doctrinal or moral error. No implication is contained therein that those who granted the nihil obstat or imprimatur agree with the contents or statements expressed.

Fifth Printing 2009

ISBN: 978-1-60114-009-8

OUR COVERS: The latest Marian Shrines and Saints book portrays the principal loves and apostolates in the life of the newly beatified Padre Pio. First and foremost was his fame as the first priest to have the stigmata of the suffering Christ—his wounds in hands, feet and side. He suffered in union with the crucified Christ for fifty years, especially in the Mass, the unbloody sacrifice of Calvary. The crucifix is the very one he was praying before when he received the stigmata. To the left of the crucifix we see the Padre in the confessional for women. Tens of thousands came to his confessional to be reconciled with God and receive direction and encouragement in the arduous work of seeking personal holiness. To the right we see Padre Pio in prayer before the image of Our Lady of Grace. The building is the House for the Relief of Suffering, a monument to the great love and compassion Padre Pio had for his fellow man. The priest who suffered freely and continually throughout his entire life was inspired to build this great hospital to alleviate the sufferings of others—how he loved the poor and the suffering!

Padre Pio

The Wonder Worker

Franciscan Friars of the Immaculate
Our Lady's Chapel, New Bedford, MA USA

In Thanksgiving and Acknowledgment

The editor of *Padre Pio, Wonder Worker* is fully aware of how God dipped into the "bottom of the barrel" in giving him the opportunity and joy of singing the praises of Our Lady through the printed word. All credit and glory goes to God. When our Father gives a son/daughter the inspiration to do something in the way of an apostolic labor He is never stingy in giving him or her the talents, experience and expert outside help necessary to follow through. God inspires us and then expects us to move. It all comes down to, "If you love me TRUST IN ME!"

Along with absolute trust in God, all action must spring from prayer and sacrifice. There can be no possibility of success or fruitfulness in the spiritual order apart from prayer and sacrifice. Ours is a praying community in which all action springs from our contemplation. Sacrifice comes quite readily when one sees a whole page, laboriously typed, disappear by hitting the wrong key on the computer. With the help of the two computer-expert friars, one who did our cover and the other, who seems to know "everything" about computers, it all works out in the end for the greatest glory of God.

To our expert proof readers, to the spiritual children and apostles of Padre Pio, a number of writers who volunteered articles or permission to use past material, and to the Capuchin Friars of San Giovanni Rotondo who allowed us to use articles and illustrations from their publication, *The Voice of Padre Pio* (see page 202) and so many other people who have given their moral and financial support, etc., but above all —their prayers—our heart-felt thanks. God reward all of you and may Mary Immaculate, the Mediatix of all Graces draw you ever closer to her Immaculate Heart.

— Bro. Francis Mary Kalvelage, F.I., Editor

Editor's Introduction

The many gifts Padre Pio had, such as bilocation, miraculous scents, prophecy, reading hearts, healing bodies and souls, interpreting languages and many other charisms, rank him among the most extraordinary Saints in the two thousand year history of the Church. These charisms are not really sensational much less impossible to those who have the faith. Did not Jesus Himself foretell that His disciples would "do greater works" than those which He did? (John 14:12)

The title of this book is one which could be easily misunderstood. In our day of superman comics, it may seem a bit irreverent to give the title "Wonder Worker" to the humble saint of Pietrelcina. Yet the Church does not hesitate to call Saint Anthony of Padua, *thaumaturgist*, "Wonder Worker." The 13th century Franciscan had the reputation in his lifetime of working great miracles, even raising the dead to life, and is still noted for answering the prayers of his petitioners, even in finding the most insignificant lost article.

Perhaps the main objection to the title "Wonder Worker" may be that in stressing the miraculous and extraordinary in Padre Pio's life, the real spiritual giant, inflamed with the love of God is lost sight of. Then too, an overabundance of miracles, especially unauthenticated, exaggerated ones, weakens the evidence for the well established, genuine miracles. Sidney Wicks in his book, *The Friends of St. Francis,* points that out. "If you desire to weaken the evidence of the miraculous in a man, you 'inoculate' his story, as it were with a miraculous virus—that is to say, you insist that everything he did was miraculous. That of course turns him into a legend."

In reading the life of Padre Pio for the first time a reader might be tempted to think that some rationalist did "inoculate it with the miracle virus," thus destroying the many real, authenticated miracles and obscuring the warm personality and heroic virtues of a great saint. It could happen, and has happened in the past. In writing the lives of the saints, influenced by a wave of popular enthusiasm, some authors have competed with each other in relating the spectacular over the ordinary.

On the other hand, to discredit well–authenticated and documented miracles and the miraculous powers of Padre Pio would be equally wrong. Father Raphael Huber, O.F.M. Conv., points out in his book *St. Anthony of Padua:* "While some of the miracles attributed to St. Anthony may be only legendary, there are others which are based on such early and authentic documents that to deny their factual existence would be supremely rash and highly unchristian." St. Bonaventure, doctor of the Church, once said that all favors can be obtained through prayers which are addressed to St. Anthony. Why should we not cherish the same fond hope in regard to Blessed Padre Pio?

At this turning point of human history, as we arrive at the threshold of the third millennium of Christianity, when God providentially raised up Padre Pio to meet the many onslaughts against Christianity and the Church in our day, he is opening up a new front, so to speak, in the battle for souls. One can readily conclude that these times are apocalyptic, for God to raise up such a Saint as the stigmatic priest, Bl. Padre Pio, who in identifying with the crucified Savior makes Christ alive for this unbelieving generation. Padre Pio's living the passion of Our Lord especially during the Sacrifice of the Mass attracted hundreds of thousands to San Giovanni Rotondo. His worldwide popularity, transforming a poverty stricken, backwater town in Italy into a thriving center of religious activity and a pilgrimage center drawing millions from over the world; the building of a modern 1600 bed hospital-complex for the treatment of the poor on a rocky hillside, with the latest in medical treatment and equipment is unexplainable from a purely natural point of view. The charismatic gifts he received from God, the many souls he brought to God and the inspiration and the direction he gave to ordinary Catholics in seeking perfection is clearly of a supernatural order.

Saints are raised up by God, especially great Saints, to meet particular crises mankind is going through. In the thirteenth century the Holy Spirit raised up St. Francis and St. Dominic and their respective followers to renew and reform the Church. The same was true at the time of the Protestant revolt. God raised up St. Ignatius Loyola, St. Theresa of Avila and St. John of the Cross, who remained in the Church, to initiate a counter reformation. The Church and the world today are desperately in need of religious revival. The demarcation lines are being more clearly drawn each day between the anti-life, anti-family culture of death and the pro-family, pro-God culture of life. So common today is the subjectivism opposing objective truth that the public accepts the highest public official in the land lying on a Bible (perjury) indicating that very little is sacred any more. The same official has vetoed repeatedly a bill that would protect the most innocent and helpless of humans—babies in the process of being born.

Standing opposite to this high public official is the chief spokesman for the Church and Christianity, Pope John Paul II. In his recent encyclical *Fides et Ratio* he shows how the anti-life mentality of our age goes back to the rationalism of the 18th century which holds that human reason is supreme. What cannot be understood by reason alone, unassisted by Faith, simply is not worth considering. Miracles cannot be explained so they, along with metaphysics, the supernatural and even God Himself are not worthy of man "come of age" to take seriously. As to be expected the Holy Father consistently points out that the only way to find the truth is through Him who is "the Way, the Truth, and the Life." Human reason without the light of Faith and Grace is self-serving, in-as-much as man in his fallen nature seeks his own selfish ends.

But, one might ask the question, "Who is listening to the Pope?" With some 90% of young Catholic couples using some form of artificial contraception and yet many going to Communion on Sundays, they obviously do not consider that the Church has a right to form men's consciences as to what is right and wrong. The Pope inaugurated Eucharistic adoration in St. Peter's and encourages Eucharistic Adoration wherever and whenever it is opportune, while some two-thirds of Catholics no longer believe in the Real Presence of Jesus in the Eucharist. But with all that the Pope suffers from confused and unfaithful lay Catholics, how much more he must suffer from so many clergy and religious who defiantly do their own thing. With the burden of the whole Church on his shoulders and concern for all mankind, it is a wonder that the Pope is so optimistic about the future. He is optimistic because he is a man of faith, hope and charity. In the monumental battle for souls peaking in our times he sees that the ultimate triumph is with God and the people of God.

The Holy Father sees paragons of personal holiness as never before in the history of the Church. And he doesn't hesitate to recognize these men and women, who practiced virtue in a heroic degree, by beatifying and canonizing such holy souls as Padre Pio. The very life and accomplishments of the Holy Father and the Saints he honors illustrates what truly holy souls can accomplish in making this world a safer and better place to live in. But above all they are effective instruments in defeating Satan and winning eternal salvation for millions. The influence of a Padre Pio, as illustrated in this book, can play a decisive role in the conversion of many souls and in the establishment of the social Reign of Christ the King.

We have had enough of putting Christ out of every facet of human life in our secularized society. There are indications that young people are turning again to the spiritual for answers to the multitude of problems of our day.

Padre Pio's work did not end with his death, we are assured by him who said before he died that after death his work, and his intercession on behalf of mankind would be even greater than in life. The hundreds of thousands who attended his beatification ceremony in Rome on May 2, 1999, attest to the accuracy of this prophecy. "Blessed Padre Pio, martyr of the confessional and instrument of reconciliation with God, pray for us sinners."

Sunday, June 16, 2002: Canonization of St. Pio of Pietrelcina, Confessor, at St. Peter's Square, Rome.

Preface

Fr. Andrew Apostoli, C.F.R.

Pope John Paul II has beatified and canonized more men and women during his pontificate than all other popes of this century combined! He sees in their lives concrete examples of the working of the Holy Spirit in His role of sanctifying the faithful in Christ. As such, they are models to inspire us to grow in holiness. With St. Paul, each of them invites us: "Be imitators of me as I am of Christ" (1 Cor. 11:1).

In raising the faithful Capuchin-Franciscan priest, Padre Pio of Pietrelcina, to the honors of the altar, Pope John Paul II has provided us with an especially powerful witness to the working of the Holy Spirit in the Church today. The Holy Spirit sanctifies us precisely by forming Jesus in us. The greater the likeness of Jesus, the greater the degree of holiness! In Padre Pio's case, we have someone in whom the Holy Spirit formed a veritable living image of Jesus. What was said of St. Francis might equally be said of Padre Pio: "He had Jesus in his mind, Jesus in his eyes, Jesus in his ears, Jesus on his lips, Jesus in his heart!"

When God raises up persons of outstanding holiness, they are usually people both of their own times and for their own times. How true this was of Padre Pio! Like many a young boy from a little Southern Italian town like Pietrelcina, young Francesco (the future saint) was born of typically poor, hard-working, God-fearing peasant parents. When asked in later life what he was like as a youth, he remarked that he was like "un' macerone senza sale" ("a piece of spaghetti without any salt on it"), a humorous way of saying his childhood was bland and uneventful.

But all was not roses for Padre Pio; there were many thorns as well. If there were such exceptional blessings in his early life, one would have to assume exceptional trials as well. As the reader will see in this fine book, these trials—demonic attacks, severe illnesses and false accusations—were all to continue and intensify throughout his life. These sufferings were to culminate on September 20, 1918, in a mystical encounter with Jesus in which, after having offered his daily Mass he received the Stigmata. Our Lord had impressed His five great wounds visibly on Padre Pio. He was to bear these wounds for the next fifty years.

Now, if Padre Pio was a man of his time, he was also a saint for his time. Our times have been called a "post-Christian era" or a "neo-pagan era." It is characterized as an age of religious skepticism and disbelief, resulting in a secularism that has pushed God out of the picture of daily life. Padre Pio stands as a great challenge to the secularism of this time! This is because, as one writer put it, the measure of a person's holiness and effectiveness with others is the measure in which God becomes real in his or her life. God was very real for Padre Pio. This is why he exerted such a powerful influence on countless numbers of people.

Many who came to him were real skeptics, dismissing Padre Pio and all the amazing stories about him as mere nonsense or the work of a charlatan! This writer once met such a skeptic. Ironically, he was a Capuchin-Franciscan bishop named Bishop Louis Magliacanni.

The bishop told me the story of his encounter with Padre Pio. As a young priest he was sent from Italy to India as a missionary, where he was in charge of a little Catholic newspaper which the friars published for the people. Many of the articles were simply translations of articles he received from family and friends back in Italy. Quite a few dealt with Padre Pio. He told me he personally did not believe Padre Pio was genuine (he called Padre Pio "a fake"), but because the people enjoyed the articles on Padre Pio he put them into the newspaper.

In 1948, Father Louis was back in Italy for a family visit. When he was set to return to India, while waiting at Naples someone suggested that he go and visit Padre Pio. He objected. The friend finally prevailed on Father Louis saying, "At least go and see Padre Pio. If, after you see him you still think he is a fake, at least you can say, 'I did see him!'"

When Father Louis arrived at the friary at San Giovanni Rotondo, he met Padre Pio. At the end of the conversation Padre Pio told him, "Father Louis, I must tell you something. You will never go back to India. God has special work for you. You will go to Arabia!" At that, Father Louis said to Padre Pio: "You know, Padre Pio, before I came here I thought you were crazy. Now I know you are! I have my ticket, my passport and the permission of the Capuchin Superior General to return to India in two days! How can you say I will never go back?" Padre Pio just smiled at him and said, "You will never go back!" Father Louis decided to stay for lunch at the friary. The friary phone rang. It was a call from a Cardinal in Rome, a member of the Congregation for the Propagation of the Faith. He was looking for Father Louis. He told Father Louis not to get on the ship for India, but to return immediately to Rome.

There two days later, with the same Cardinal and the Capuchin Superior General, Father Louis had a private audience with Pope Pius XII.

The Pope told him, "Father Louis, you have been chosen to open a new mission in Arabia!" Father Louis responded excitedly, "Your Holiness, I knew that!" Pope Pius XII asked, "Father Louis, how could you possibly have known that? Only the Cardinal and your own Superior General knew what I am telling you." Father Louis answered, "Padre Pio told me. At the time I thought he was crazy. Now I realize, he is a saint!!!"

Among others who came to see Padre Pio were professed disbelievers. Some came out of curiosity, others to mock God and His holy servant, Padre Pio. One example: two men who were Freemasons and bitterly opposed to God and the Church plotted to make mock confessions to Padre Pio of sins they simply "made up" to desecrate the Sacrament of Penance. They went to him at separate times. As each began to

---

The Holy Spirit sanctifies us precisely by forming Jesus in us. The greater the likeness of Jesus, the greater the degree of holiness! In Padre Pio's case, the Holy Spirit formed a veritable living image of Jesus.

---

confess their made-up sins, he stopped them, told them he knew what they were up to, and then proceeded to tell each of them their real sins, as well as when, where and how they committed them! The two men were so overwhelmed that about three days later they repented of their sinful lives, returned to Padre Pio and made good confessions, and became part of his list of conversions.

Finally, the very sincere came to him in countless numbers. These included his many "devotees" from his prayer groups and other "spiritual children." Penitents came seeking his absolution, the troubled came seeking his counsel and consoling words, families sought his blessings, many sought his prayers for their needs, and some even sought miracles. I once received a letter from a woman who had been cured by Padre Pio. She had a life-threatening fever at about age six. She was brought to the "House for the Relief of Suffering." A doctor told the family there was no medical hope for the little girl. The doctor went to the friary to tell Padre Pio. He allowed the doctor to touch his hand to his wound on his side. The doctor ran back to the hospital and touched the little girl with his hand that had just touched Padre Pio's wound. The result: the fever immediately broke and the little girl was instantly cured!

One of the factors that delayed the cause for canonization of Padre Pio was the fact that whereas for most proposed saints about five cartons of documentation are submitted to the Vatican Congregation for the Causes of the Saints, in the case of Padre Pio over one hundred cartons of documentation were initially submitted! Padre Pio accomplished so much in his lifetime. Yet he said he would do even more once he got to heaven!

Padre Pio will have an increasingly profound influence on the lives of many Catholics and others as he becomes even more widely known. Pope Benedict XV once told a man who had been converted by Padre Pio: "Padre Pio is truly a man of God. You must assume the responsibility to make him known. He is not esteemed according to his merits." This present book, *Padre Pio: Wonder Worker*, is a valuable addition in the process of making Padre Pio better known and loved. It presents a valuable biography of Padre Pio's life (Part 1). This is followed by presentations of various aspects of his profound personal spirituality and the effects he had in so many ways on the lives of countless people.

Much of this material is presented by various writers who either knew Padre Pio personally or have done extensive research in compiling their own biographies of him over the years. As Padre Pio will no doubt become one of those saints who transcends his own time (like St. Francis, who is as popular today as he was in his own 13th century), so this book will always have a timeless value and appeal.

May the Blessed Virgin Mary, whom Padre Pio affectionately called "Madonnina" ("My Little Lady"), intercede to see that this book will enlighten, inspire and guide all who read it.

Table Of Contents

Part V

Part VI

Part VII

A St. Francis for Our Times

C. Bernard Ruffin

The *National Review* called him "the hottest thing in mysticism in the twentieth century" and "one of the chief religious forces in Italy." By the time Padre Pio of Pietrelcina died in 1968, he was receiving five thousand letters a month, and thousands of visitors were converging on him from all parts of the world, making their way through Italy's Gargano Mountains to the little sixteenth century friary of Our Lady of Grace. It was this humble friary just outside the town of San Giovanni Rotondo, which is near the city of Foggia, where the venerable Capuchin priest lived for more than a half century. There they would wait for days for a chance to make their confessions to him and would rise early in the morning to assist at Padre Pio's Mass.

Hundreds of books and articles have been written about him in his native Italy, and scores of stories have appeared in other countries as well. *Time, Newsweek,* and the *New York Times Magazine,* as well as other reputable American periodicals, from time to time have featured lengthy, serious articles about the man who was widely known as the second St. Francis. Padre Pio's visitors were predominantly Italian, but the devout, the troubled, and (to his annoyance) the merely curious poured in to see him from England, France, Ireland, Germany, Canada, America, Australia, and from various African and Asian nations. Although the vast majority of his visitors were Roman Catholic, the "Prophet of the People" was occasionally sought out by men and women of other Christian denominations, especially during the Second World War, when British and American troops were stationed nearby.

Although most of the pilgrims to the "Wise Man of the Gargano" were people of humble origin, Padre Pio also attracted large numbers of intellectuals and figures of international importance. During the Second Vatican Council (1962–1965), so many bishops consulted him that some observers wondered aloud whether the council was being held at Rome or at San Giovanni Rotondo. At least two popes said privately that Padre Pio was a saint. On March 9, 1952, Archbishop Giovanni Battista

Montini, later Pope Paul VI, told Giulio Antonacci, major general of the *carabinieri* (the Italian national police), "Padre Pio is a saint." A few minutes later, Pius XII, the reigning pontiff, having overheard the remark, saw fit to concur: "We all know that Padre Pio is a saint." Years before Pope Benedict XV did not hesitate to characterize Padre Pio as a "man of God."

It is not known whether Pope John Paul II has ever referred to him as a "saint" (indeed he could not after 1983, since Padre Pio's Cause for Canonization was pending), but he made his confession to Padre Pio in 1947, when he was a young priest; he visited San Giovanni Rotondo in 1974, when he was a cardinal; and he returned in 1987 as pope. It is known that on at least one occasion the Holy Father commended a sick friend to the Padre's prayers with startling results. It is he who had the distinction of beatifying him on May 2, 1999 and canonizing him on June 16, 2002.

The grizzled friar, described by *National Review* as having "the greatest moral prestige of any priest in Italy," was credited by several American news magazines with transforming the life of the region where he lived, bringing prosperity, jobs, education, and health care to a region that had for many centuries been cruelly impoverished. Because of him the ancient friary where he resided has become one of the great places of Catholic pilgrimage in the world. San Giovanni Rotondo, once a drab, out-of-the-way town, has increased in size by a third, as even to this day many settle there to "live near Padre Pio." An immense new church and conference center is being built to accommodate the swelling number of pilgrims.

Today in southern Italy many shops and homes prominently display pictures of Padre Pio. One sees occasionally graffiti bearing the legend: *"Viva Padre Pio!"* And for those who knew him in life, as for many who have come to know him only after his death, Padre Pio lives indeed! Even radicals and anticlericals regarded the venerable friar with respect and reverence. Even the modernist, Monika Hellwig, could testify that the stigmatized Capuchin did indeed lead people to "deep conversions." She stated, "What struck me most, is how much Padre Pio mediated the presence of the divine to all who came to him. People came away from him invariably inspired and assured of God's presence and care for them. In him they experienced a most immediate revelation of God's love and concern for them."

Padre Pio was almost an exact contemporary of Rudolf Bultmann (1884–1976), the German Lutheran theologian who, out of a regard for the difficulty modern men and women have in accommodating the traditional teachings of Christianity to their twentieth century perceptions, devised a theology that "demythologized" the Gospels, stripping away such uncomfortable baggage as miracles and other accoutrements of a "first-century worldview" in order to get at what he believed to be the essential kernel of truth underlying all the "mythological" paraphernalia. Bultmann's approach (or at least variations of it) has strongly colored much of the theological thinking of the last few decades. How different was Padre Pio in style and in results! Without publishing a book or delivering a single university lecture, he convinced thousands, even in the age of "historical criticism" of the Bible and the "Death of God" theologians, that miracles are not mythology but reality. Through his life and ministry, thousands came to accept the Bible and all the historical doctrines of Christianity.

Padre Pio was also a contemporary of Paul Tillich, Karl Barth, Pierre Teilhard de Chardin, Albert Schweitzer, and other famous professors, but he is attested to have communicated the existential presence of Christ more directly, more immediately, and to the satisfaction of many more people than did any of his immensely erudite contemporaries in their university chairs.

Bultmann wrote in *Kerygma and Myth:* "It is impossible to use electric light and the wireless and to avail ourselves of modern medical and surgical discoveries and at the same time to believe in the New Testament world of demons and spirits." Yet Padre Pio, Bultman's contemporary, convinced many a learned man that angels appeared to translate letters he received in foreign languages, that he cast out devils, and that he was, on many occasions, knocked bodily to the floor by irate demons.

Here was a man living in the time of air travel and astronauts, of moving pictures and mass communication, of computers and communications satellites, who lived the life of a biblical prophet or apostle and is reputed by rational people to have worked miracles similar to those performed by the prophets of the Old Testament and the apostles of the New. Here was a man in whom, if hundreds of testimonies can be believed, these words of Christ seem to have been fulfilled: "He that believeth in me, the works that I do shall he do also" (John 14:12). Hundreds of sane, well-educated, and unbiased men and women have said of Padre Pio, that, like Moses, "The Lord spoke unto him face to face, as a man speaketh unto his friend" (Exodus 33:11).

The archives of Our Lady of Grace Friary contain volumes of testimony that, through Padre Pio's prayers, more than a thousand people pronounced hopelessly ill by their doctors were delivered of incurable maladies and the effects of crippling injuries. Even more remarkable, thousands swear that when "The Holy Stigmatized Friar" celebrated Mass, he communicated to them the reality of Christ on Calvary, and that, during his Mass, Padre Pio's face and form underwent visible, physical changes.

One of the friars who assisted Padre Pio in the last years of his life declared that more people were deeply touched by Padre Pio through his Mass than through his healings, bilocations, ecstasies, and prophecies.

Perhaps more important, thousands testify that through Padre Pio's ministry, they learned to walk in holiness and to resign themselves to God's will, offering their suffering and heartache as a sacrifice to the Almighty for the conversion of sinners.

Would it not be best, then, to write off Padre Pio as a curious footnote to religious history, to dismiss him as a peculiar anachronism, a creation of the superstitious piety of a region, which, in his early years, had not yet become a part of the "industrialized world" or adopted a "scientific worldview"? Despite the reluctance of the modern materialistic sophisticate to accept Padre Pio and his ministry, one fact is incontrovertible: for thousands of people from all walks of life—physicians, scientists, intellectuals, as well as peasants and blue-collar types—Padre Pio made Christianity real. Through his ministry many were led to deep and permanent conversion experiences, and without any significant rate of recidivism. It cannot be denied that Padre Pio changed lives.

One must conclude that Padre Pio of Pietrelcina was one of the most significant figures in Christian history, a man of prophetic and apostolic stature, who, through great personal holiness and enlightened wisdom and through spiritual gifts inexplicable by science, tended to confirm the truth of the Gospels and the veracity of historical Christianity to an indifferent and unbelieving age; a man capable of conveying to an extraordinary extent a sense of God's love and care; an evangelist who never conducted a crusade, and yet who, without traveling more than a few miles from his friary in fifty years, was capable of transforming lives to a degree unimagined by the most successful evangelical preachers.

The life of Padre Pio is, to be sure, a life replete with events that seem strange, even incredible to the average reader, but it is also a life of a real human being with real emotions, real joys, real sorrows, and real defects, who strove to serve his fellow human beings in his day.

Although Padre Pio was a member of the Mother Church (and certainly one of the Roman Catholic Church's best "advertisements"), his life, his example, and his teaching are for all Christians, for they confirm the truth of the Scriptures and make faith real, impelling everyone—men, women, and children—to trust in Christ Jesus as their Lord and Savior.

A condensation by the editor of the Prologue of the book, Padre Pio: The True Story, *by C. Bernard Ruffin (See page 201). The last paragraph is from the concluding paragraph of Appendix 2 by the author.* (Printed with the permission of the author.)

PART I -- a biography

Above:
The young Padre Pio with a lamb which symbolizes He who is the Lamb of God and who went to His death like a submissive lamb for the slaughter. In imitation of Christ Padre Pio also bore his many sufferings with great patience and resignation for the salvation of souls.

Right: The house and the room where Padre Pio was born.

6

Early Life of the Warrior Friar

While bells were pealing to summon the faithful to church for Marian devotions during Our Lady's month, Francis Forgione, the future Padre Pio, was born at 9:00 a.m. on May 25, 1887. He was the second of five surviving children, two boys and three girls of Mamma Peppa, as Padre Pio's mother was popularly known. She gave birth to eight children, three of whom died at an early age. Throughout his life Padre Pio had a special preference and blessing for large families that lived according to the will of God.

His parents Grazio Forgione and Maria Giuseppa di Nunzio were married in 1881. The young couple, according to today's standards, would be considered poor. At that time in a very depressed area of Italy they were considered of modest means. They owned a small piece of land which was barely large enough for them to eke out a living. Both parents worked the land. Every morning before sunrise Grazio left for the little farm a half hour away from their home where he labored hard the year round. His work day ended toward sundown, when he nearly always brought home some fruit from the fields for the family table.

Maria Giuseppa, or Mamma Peppa, was a kindhearted, industrious housewife. She saw to it that her husband and her children were adequately provided for. She would rise at night to make bread and cheese. Though there was little of anything in their home, Maria Giuseppa knew how to manage it wisely. She prepared what was needed for each day and saved extra nice things for feast days. Every year Maria Giuseppa gave some of their farm products as an offering for the novena for the Poor Souls in Purgatory. She was generous in giving the first fruits of their harvest to the poorer families.

The small town of Pietrelcina where Padre Pio grew up is in south-central Italy. It is situated on the side of a hill. On one side a cluster of poor homes is situated around a small castle, which provided protection during the Middle Ages. The setting, even today, is rustic with its narrow, winding cobblestone streets, lined by humble stone houses built low to the ground to lessen the risk of their crumbling in the event of an earthquake. It has a unique charm in its littleness and poverty.

Like Assisi of St. Francis' fame it has changed little over the centuries. Like St. Francis of Assisi, Padre Pio had a deep love for his home town, Pietrelcina. Although it had a population of a mere three thousand in Padre Pio's youthful days, and today numbers few more, a future awaits it because of the glorious role played by its remarkable native son. One day Padre Pio uttered these prophetic words: "During my life I have cherished San Giovanni Rotondo. After my death I will cherish and favor Pietrelcina."

The inhabitants of Pietrelcina are hard-working country folks who jealously preserve long-standing traditions and customs. The people are warmhearted and hospitable. What they lack in the material goods of this world is amply repaid in a simple life-style from which our secularized society has much to learn. They like music and are fond of religious celebrations on days of special devotion and local interest, especially on the feast day of their patron, the lovely Madonna della Libera, whose shrine is linked with the miraculous.

Padre Pio was baptized the day after his birth in the old parish church of Pietrelcina, which was dedicated to St. Mary of the Angels. He was given the name Francis. Both his name and the church where he was baptized were providential as he will, no doubt, go down in history as one of the most famous sons of St. Francis. He is considered by many as the 20th century St. Francis. Both bore the stigmata. The favorite church of St. Francis, where he gathered his first friars around him and asked to be taken to die, was the little church of St. Mary of the Angels. No doubt both these coincidences reflect the Forgione boy's future vocation.

Though he was a handsome, healthy child, for some reason (explained later by Padre Pio) he tried his father's patience to the limit by his loud nocturnal crying and screaming. One evening after his father came home from a hard day's work, the child started wailing as if he were being strangled. Grazio tried his best to quiet the boy. He picked the boy up holding him in his arms but with no success. In exasperation he threw him on the bed, muttering angrily, "It is the devil who has been born in my home!" The boy slipped from the bed and fell to the floor. Maria Giuseppa was horrified and cried, "You've killed my child!" When Padre Pio would relate this story, with a twinkle in his eye, he always ended by saying, "From that day on I didn't cry any more."

Both parents attached great importance to the task of implanting in their children an appreciation of God and of religion. Every evening the family recited the Rosary together. This prayer held a place of honor. Other things might be sacrificed in that home, but not the Rosary.

In his own way little Francis began early to show an uncommon appreciation of religion. His mother has left us a meaningful detail about this. When Francis was about five years old he happened to hear a blas-

The parents of Padre Pio, Grazio Forgione and Maria Giuseppa di Nunzio who, according to our standards of living, were poor. But they were rich in all that matters—faith and in love for one another.

phemy. He then hid behind the door and wept. His innocent soul felt the wound of seeing God insulted.

One time when he was a little older he passed by the home of a shoemaker with whom he used to stop and talk; for they were on familiar terms. The day was Sunday, and he saw the man's daughter toiling away with her needlework, sewing a band on a dress.

"Andrianella, today we don't work. It's Sunday." Showing her annoyance, the girl answered, "Little boy, you are too small to talk like that."

Francis said no more, left her and a little later returned with a pair of scissors. He grabbed the band she had been sewing and cut it to pieces. The girl cried out in protest, but Francis was unmoved. Not that he would have necessarily behaved that way when older, but this illustrates Francis' uncompromising attitude toward the slightest sin. This was to mark his attitude for the fifty years of his apostolate in the confessional. God must come before all else. Even as a child he had in many ways the maturity of an adult.

From the age of five, he was not only very sensitive about matters pertaining to God, but began having visions of spirits, at times very beautiful ones, and at times very ugly ones. It was the horrible visions that scared him and caused him to cry as mentioned above. The child was in no position to appreciate the extraordinary character of these phenomena and diabolical interventions. He did not speak of them to anyone and considered such events to be ordinary occurrences in everyone's life. At that early age he was well aware that life has to do with two realms of opposing realities; which are, on the one hand, the reality of God and of heaven, and on the other hand, the reality of the devil and of things that are sinful leading to eternal separation from God. He committed himself entirely to God's side.

His sister Grazia tells us that one evening when the church bell was sounding, Francis went at once to his grandmother and said, "I want to go to church with you!" There were others present and one remarked, "But you have not had supper yet." Francis answered, "Who wants to think about supper? I must go to church with grandmother." Francis was assiduous and devout about attending church. He missed none of the parish functions. Each Sunday afternoon he attended catechism. He learned the hymns and attentively followed the pastor's religious instructions. He was allowed to remain in church after services when the doors were locked, to spend more time in contemplative prayer.

At the age of ten he made his first Holy Communion, and he was confirmed when he was twelve. He learned early how to serve Mass. He served with a devotion that drew attention from the mothers who used to watch him during the holy Sacrifice, using him as a model for their children. Although Francis was indeed a good, well-behaved boy and prayerful, it didn't keep him aloof during the games that children play. At the same time Francis never "let himself go" when it came to play. On one occasion he was wrestling with a friend and pinned the other boy down. The boy shouted some profanity, and Francis let him go immediately and ran away. He loved decency even in play; above all, he wanted in no way to be associated with sin, which made Jesus suffer.

One year his father, Grazio, took Francis to the shrine of St. Pellegrino, one of the Saints most loved by the people of Pietrelcina. The church was crowded with pilgrims from many different places. Francis went to a front pew to pray, where he was touched by the sight of a poor woman carrying a deformed baby. The mother kept her eyes fixed on the Saint's image, as she sighed and prayed, "Heal my son! Heal my son!" Francis was deeply moved and sympathetically added his own prayers to those of the unhappy mother.

After a while little Francis felt someone tugging his sleeve. "Francis, let us go," his father said.

"Let's wait a little longer, Papa." Meantime the woman kept on appealing with greater fervor for her son's cure. At a certain point, seeing she was not getting anywhere, she picked up her poor child and threw him onto the Saint's altar, crying, "If you don't want to cure him, take him! I don't want him!"

As soon as the child landed on the altar, he got up on his feet, standing quite erect, and cried, "Mamma! Mamma!" A miracle! The mother took her child and pressed him to her bosom. Meantime there was excitement all around her. Word quickly spread, even outside. A thick crowd gathered within the shrine. Another stronger tug from his father induced him to move. But it was too late. The dense throng compelled father and son to wait until it thinned out. After they had left, Francis' father rebuked him. But he would never forget the miracle that happened before his eyes, which convinced him of the power of prayer and of the intercession of the Saints.

Francis was given the responsibility to watch over the few sheep the family had. It gave him the opportunity to practice the little he knew about reading, which he learned in a little school house where the most elementary instruction was given. Francis was among the most attentive and diligent of this little group. He used to take his books with him to the pastures to study. At noon he used to eat his lunch. Unlike the others, he would do it with the manners of a gentleman. He ate his bread on a clean napkin spread like a tablecloth over his knees.

When Francis was ten he was stricken down with typhus, which was usually fatal at that time. He had a high fever and was more dead than alive. It was harvest time. The farmers on the Piana Romana were busy at work. In spite of her worry, Mamma Giuseppa had to prepare lunch for the harvesters. She made an ample platter of fried peppers, the kind that are hot and strong. But the harvesters only ate part of them. More than half were left over and she put them away in a cupboard. They gave off an appetizing scent. Although Francis didn't seem to have an appetite, he was very fond of fried peppers. As soon as he was left alone he got out of bed and crawled over to the cupboard, opened it, and ate all the peppers that were left over. When the mother returned, she found the platter with the peppers empty and could not understand how they had disappeared. Meantime Francis' feast was against all rules. It could have been fatal, but it produced a radical change for the better, curing Francis of the typhus and restoring his health.

When Francis was about ten years old two things happened that motivated him to join the Capuchin Franciscans. He heard a sermon on St. Michael the Archangel which made him aware of a clear strong call from God. The same year a Capuchin friar, Friar Camillo, came to Pietrelcina seeking alms. He was a likable person with a handsome black beard. Francis was impressed by his simplicity and humility. He told his parents he wanted to be a religious like Friar Camillo, with the long handsome beard. The good father responded, "Yes indeed! If you do your schoolwork well we will see to it that you become a monk." From that day onward the Forgione family began to talk more and more about

Francis' Franciscan vocation. Even during his later years Padre Pio would become deeply moved when he would recall, "My father crossed the ocean twice in order to give me the chance to become a friar."

It was necessary for Grazio to travel to America to earn enough money to send his son to a private tutor, Domenico Tizzani. His tutor thought that Francis wasn't a very promising student. When his father learned why Francis wasn't making progress in his studies he understood: Francis found it impossible to respect his teacher. Domenico was a former priest who attempted marriage and had not been inside a church for years. How could his son, who aspired to the priesthood, be comfortable in the presence of one who was unfaithful to that calling? Grazio, who was in America at the time, sent a telegram to his wife to change teachers. Peppa's choice for a teacher was a good one as the boy made rapid progress in his studies from then on and at the age of fourteen was ready to enter the Capuchin Franciscans.

Shortly before he was to leave for the monastery in Morcone he was praying over his vocation and wondering how he would be able to leave the world and his family whom he loved dearly for the penitential life of a friar, when he had an interior revelation similar to the "dream" that Don Bosco had concerning his life's work. Don Bosco was shown in a symbolic way what was to be his lifelong apostolate among youth. Padre Pio described, as a middle-aged friar, how at the age of fourteen he beheld a majestic man of rare beauty taking him by the hand saying, "Come with me, for you must fight a tough and aggressive warrior."

On one side of a great plain were many beautiful people standing by his guide, who was dressed in white, while on the opposite side there was a huge, black, hideous, evil looking man and in back of him were repulsive looking people. Francis' guide told him he would have to do battle with the powerful ugly man. Francis trembled, turned pale and stammered that he could not possibly prevail against such a formidable enemy. His guide reassured him. "You must fight with this man. Take heart. Enter the combat with confidence. Go forth courageously. I shall be with you. In reward for your victory over him I will give you a shining crown to adorn your brow." Francis with the help of his guide, defeated the evil one (the devil) as he did throughout his life, winning many souls for Christ, whom he realized later was the man in white. And so it turned out.

Preparation for Warfare

Even before he entered his vocation as a Capuchin Franciscan at their novitiate in Morcone the devil tried to sabotage his vocation on two separate occasions, by maligning him to his teacher and parish priest as not worthy of a religious vocation. In both instances he was accused of not showing modesty and proper decorum in regard to the opposite sex. His companions wanted to provoke a little scandal over Francis because they realized the great difference between his behavior and theirs, especially in associating with girls. It must have wounded him greatly to be thus falsely accused. But, when it was discovered that he was falsely accused he held no animosity to the boys involved or those who misjudged him.

Many years later his former female acquaintances testified that they had tried to provoke Francis' attention because they felt attracted by his good looks and seriousness. One went so far as to slip a note into his pocket expressing her affection. But Francis cared nothing about such things. He was unfamiliar with the ways of girls and wanted to stay unfamiliar. This explains how he kept his virginal purity throughout his life.

What hurt him most was to be deprived of even serving Mass for a while by the pastor who at first didn't trust him. This was to be a prelude of many false accusations and misunderstandings he was to suffer throughout his religious life by even the highest Church authorities. As his Master before him, Padre Pio was to be a sign of contradiction.

Meanwhile the day was approaching when Francis would become a Capuchin novice at the Morcone friary. Within his soul Francis was experiencing alternating light and painful darkness. "Two forces were tearing my heart," he was to admit later in life—his love for God and the love of creatures. The struggle was neither brief nor painless. The nature of the struggle was quite clear to him. It was between a religious vocation and the attractions of this world, though they were not sinful.

With the aid of prayer and earnest meditation, he was able to make a final break. After this struggle Francis experienced deep spiritual peace and the grace to break off definitely with the world. The date fixed for his entrance was January 6, 1903. On the eve of his departure Francis felt deep pangs of pain over the final separation from his family. How greatly he loved them! But during the night, instead of having the pangs of pain he feared, he had the comforting surprise of another heavenly vision. Jesus and Mary appeared to him and encouraged him. They reassured him of their special affection and that they were assigning him "a very great mission" known only to God and himself. Our Lord placed His hand upon Francis' head, bestowing on him the special strength of being detached from his family.

His mother deserves our admiration. When bidding him farewell she added something that reveals her noble faith: "Now you belong to me no more, but to St. Francis." Later, when Padre Pio would speak of his mother, he would always call her "my holy mother." This fitted her, for Mamma Giuseppa was a woman of uncommon faith, and was humble, wise, generous, and lovable, and enjoyed the favor and honor of having an extraordinary son.

The friary at Morcone was in an isolated place and ideal for a life of prayer. At last Francis was where he had longed to be. From that moment on he no longer belonged to himself or to his family. He belonged to Christ and to the Church. Fifteen days later, on January 22, 1903, he received the religious habit and Francis Forgione began a new life, with a new name—Fra Pio da Pietrelcina.

Religious life when strictly observed is a life for steadfast generous souls. It is not for the cowardly and the halfhearted. A religious vocation is a wonderful blessing, but it demands great courage. The virile, stern feature of Capuchin novitiate life in Morcone flourished then in an extraordinary way, at times reaching some excess, according to statements of some older friars. But it was precisely this rigor that drew good men to apply. Their novitiate was always full.

The friars' rooms were small and simple. There was a hard bed on which one slept clothed in his habit. The diet was frugal and the food plain. During winter the friary was as cold as ice (no central heating to be sure). At midnight the novices joined the friars in rising to pray the night office. They took the discipline three times a week; reflecting on how Our Lord was scourged in his bitter Passion. They fasted during the three Franciscan Lents as well as every Friday of the year. Every day at certain hours they assembled for common prayers. They kept perpetual silence, except during the short period of recreation in common. They received instructions on the holy Rule, on the Liturgy, and on good manners and read the lives of the Saints, whom they were to imitate, especially St. Francis. All this gave solid nourishment and support to a life of prayer and penance.

14

The Master of Novices, that is, the one having charge of the spiritual formation of the young novices, declared that Fra Pio was "a novice beyond reproach." If we reflect on the exceptional strictness of novitiate life and then realize that Fra Pio was a novice beyond reproach, we can gather that Fra Pio took his total commitment to God very seriously. When his mother first came to see him and brought him little gifts that her motherly heart had contrived, Fra Pio stood before her with eyes cast down and arms folded, with each hand buried in the opposite sleeve. His mother was grieved and departed with a sad heart. She could not understand why Francis acted that way. "If I had known he would act that way," she said, "I would never have come."

When she told everything to his father, Grazio, who had just returned from America, he decided to go at once to see Francis before the boy wrecked his health or perhaps became mentally unbalanced. When Grazio arrived at the Morcone friary, he was pleased to learn that Fra Pio had behaved as he did to faithfully follow the instructions given him and observe the discipline of the novitiate. Fra Pio was uncompromising and determined to be a saint. He allowed himself no halfway measures. Self-denial, mortification of the senses, patience and perseverance, sacrifices even in small things, expressed his great love of God and souls.

On Friday, January 22, 1904, before the image of Our Lady of Grace, Fra Pio consecrated himself to God by making his simple profession of the three vows of obedience, poverty, and chastity, as a follower of the Seraphic Father St. Francis. Now that his novitiate was finished, Fra Pio went back to his studies in preparation for the priesthood. Needless to say, he applied himself to his studies with great diligence. As he was making every effort to be a faithful religious, even to the point of scruples, it is easy to understand why Fra Pio's health began to fail him. Worried about his health, his superiors agreed to his taking a rest in his home town of Pietrelcina in the hope that the wholesome air would restore him. In spite of delicate health, Fra Pio went ahead with his studies.

After the period of temporary profession of three years, Fra Pio made his solemn profession at S. Elia a Pianissi on January 27, 1907. He was almost twenty years old. The periods he had to spend in his native Pietrelcina for reasons of health away from the usual Capuchin life created delicate problems that caused him further suffering. As best he could he was faithful to his Capuchin rule of life and was especially drawn into a deeper prayer life. To reach a solitary room where he loved to pray one had to mount a steep stone stairway up a rocky eminence, the Morgione. He liked the location for its solitude and silence. It reminds one of an eagle's nest.

With all, his health continually became worse. Some thought he suffered from consumption and that his condition was hopeless. People avoided him for fear of contagion. But in the midst of his many trials, the Lord granted him some extraordinary graces. He wrote his spiritual director: "Jesus began to favor his poor creature with heavenly visions not long after the year of novitiate ... " We know that Fra Pio's prayer life was fervent and intensified, especially his meditation on the Passion of Christ. This was often accompanied by tears which not only bathed his face, but trickled down on his kneeler and onto the floor.

One day his spiritual father asked the reason for this weeping. Fra Pio replied, "I am weeping for my sins and the sins of all men." He prayed a great deal. When living in a friary, his prayers extended beyond the hours of the community prayers. It was a common thing to find him in the choir when he was not in his room. He wanted to recite many Rosaries and one of the resolutions he made at that time was to pray fifteen Rosaries a day. He ventured to compete with another friar, Fra Anastasio.

One night he heard someone moving about in the next room. He woke up and thought Fra Anastasio made the noise and was still up reciting Rosaries. So Fra Pio got up, too, to say some more Rosaries, to keep up the competition. Eventually, from his window he called Fra Anastasio. Looking out to Fra Anastasio's window sill he saw there an enormous black dog with eyes glowing like embers. Fra Pio was petrified. The beast took a big leap to a nearby roof and disappeared. Fra Pio fell on his bed, feeling faint. The next day he learned that the adjoining room had been vacant. Fra Anastasio was occupying another room.

Fra Pio understood well that to become a priest one must also be a victim as well. As his health continued to decline he no longer hoped for a cure and he was resigned to die, if the Lord so willed. At the same time he ardently wished to celebrate holy Mass at least once, if God so willed. For serious reasons of health, priestly ordination could be given in advance to one who petitioned it. Since his superiors were very worried that death was approaching, they were favorably disposed to the idea.

Fra Pio received the diaconate on July 18, 1909, and submitted a petition at that time for an early ordination to the priesthood. He at once received a favorable response. He passed his examinations for ordination and was accepted for the priesthood. With intense prayer he prepared himself for the long-awaited day. At last, on August 10, 1910, Fra Pio was ordained a priest at the cathedral in Benevento. Among those present were his mother, whose heart was full, his sisters and brother, and the archpriest of Pietrelcina, Don Salvatore Pannullo. His father, unfortunately, could not be there; for he had gone to America the second time to alleviate the financial needs of his family.

16

Four days later, on the vigil of the Assumption, he sang his first high Mass in the church at Pietrelcina at the altar of the Madonna. Father Agostino, his theology professor, delivered the sermon. Addressing the new priest, "Your health is not good; so you cannot become a preacher. My hopes for you are that you will be a great and conscientious confessor." The utterance was prophetic and was fulfilled in an awesome way. On that day Padre Pio wrote a short prayer, which could be considered a program for priestly holiness: "Oh Jesus, my heart's desire and my life, as I raise you up in trembling hands in the mystery of love, may I be *with* you, the way, the truth and the life for the world, and *for* you a holy priest, a perfect victim." It wasn't long after that God took up the offer of the young generous priest of being a victim soul. On September 20, 1910, God gave him the invisible stigmata, which he bore for eight years.

After his ordination Padre Pio spent about six more years in Pietrelcina because of deteriorating health. Each attempt to restore him to religious life in a friary was unsuccessful. His priestly life at Pietrelcina followed a well-ordered plan. It included much prayer, with religious functions, theological studies, the teaching of catechism to children, and meetings he held with individuals and with families. He continually kept in contact with his spiritual director and his superior by letter while he was away from the monastery. These letters are a treasure that not only give an account of his spiritual journey, but are today the most valuable and extensive written spiritual legacy of Padre Pio.

Something truly providential happened during this last stay in his home town. One day he was passing by the home of his former schoolmaster, the unfortunate ex-priest Domenico Tizzani, and he found his daughter crying on the steps before the house. Her father was dying. It seems no one had the courage to approach him. Padre Pio, the student turned priest, at once asked to be allowed to visit the sick man. He entered, and he brought him reconciliation with God and eternal salvation for his soul. The dying man made his confession with earnest tears of repentance, and Padre Pio also wept with joy.

Padre Pio's whole day was divided between time spent in church, at home, in the tower room, and out on the countryside of Piana Romana seated beneath an elm, recollected as he prayed his breviary and many other prayers.

Throughout his long life Padre Pio not only suffered the usual temptations which is the lot of all men, but God allowed the devil to physically assault him.

The family farm house where Padre Pio as a young priest would often stay when he returned to his native town for health reasons. It was here that he experienced some of the assaults of the evil one.

The War Against Satan

It was beneath an elm tree (enclosed today within a chapel) that Padre Pio suffered many furious assaults from the devil, who used to appear to him in various guises. He later said, "Nobody knows what used to happen there at night," indicating graphically with his hands the blows he received. A phenomenon even more mysterious had its origin in 1910 near the elm tree. Padre Pio describes it in a letter to his spiritual director: "In the middle of my hands a red spot appeared, having the size and form of a nickel, accompanied by a sharp pain. This pain was more perceptible in the middle of the left hand, and it continues still. Also I feel a bit of pain on the bottoms of my feet." This suffering in his hands and feet is the first record of Padre Pio's stigmata, which were invisible until 1918. Eventually, they caused him "very sharp pain." One time when he was entering his home his hands felt as though they were on fire. His mother noticed it, and asked, "What is this? Do you imagine you are playing a guitar?" Padre Pio made no reply.

It was during this time that Padre Pio was drafted into the Italian Army in November of 1915, but he became so ill that they granted him a year's leave of absence in order to regain his health. He returned to Pietrelcina. One of the most painful and rather frequent phenomena in Padre Pio's life were assaults by devils, whom he called "ugly monsters" and "impure fiends." These were not only interior assaults, but exterior ones as well, accompanied by noises, tremors, howls, and flying objects. Padre Pio described one of these assaults as follows to his spiritual director: "It was late at night and they began their assault with devilish noise. Although I saw nothing at first, I understood who was producing the strange sound. Instead of getting terrified, I prepared for the battle by facing them with a sneering smile.

"Then they came before me under the most detestable appearances. Then to get me to abuse God's grace, they began to treat me with kid gloves. But thank heaven I told them off good, and dealt with them according to what they were worth. When they saw their efforts go up in smoke they hurled themselves on me, threw me to the floor, and gave me terrific blows, throwing into the air pillows, books, and chairs, at the same time letting out desperate cries and uttering extremely filthy words."

In visiting the places frequented by Padre Pio in Pietrelcina one can see the room where the furious assault took place. Sometimes the assaults would be renewed several nights in succession. At times the blows would be so hard and numerous that he would bleed at the mouth and they caused serious fears for his life. "They beat me so brutally," Padre Pio said later, "that I think it was a very great grace that I was able to stand it without dying."

His spiritual director summed up the different forms of diabolical harassment that Padre Pio suffered during his life: "The devil would appear in the form of an ugly black cat, or as a naked young woman performing an impure dance, or as a prison-guard who would whip him, or even in the guise of Christ Crucified, ... or of his spiritual father, ... of his Father Provincial, etc. At other times it was in the guise of his Guardian Angel, of St. Francis, of the Madonna." Padre Pio knew it was his task to live continually in a state of warfare. The vision he had as a boy of fighting the black giant, with the Lord at his side enlightened Padre Pio about his whole future of struggles against Satan. "He will always be making new assaults," his Guide had told him, adding, "Fight manfully and do not doubt that you have my help."

Although God allowed the devil to inflict terrible suffering and trials on Padre Pio, the holy Franciscan received many consolations, graces and remarkable gifts which God grants certain of His Saints to encourage them on in the battle for souls. On August 12, 1912, he received the mystical experience of a "wound of love." Padre Pio wrote his spiritual father: "I was in church making a thanksgiving after Mass when all of a sudden I felt my heart wounded by a dart of hot, blazing fire, so that I thought I was going to die ... " (more on page 146). Often after assaults from Satan he was comforted, sometimes "two or three times a day," by ecstasies and apparitions of Jesus, the Blessed Virgin, his Guardian Angel, St. Francis of Assisi, and other Saints. Some conversations during the ecstasies were recorded and they reveal Padre Pio's great charity in the interest of the salvation of souls, and his burning love for "sweet Jesus," his tender fondness for the Madonna, whom men "would call a goddess" if their faith did not teach otherwise.

Padre Pio received much help from his guardian Angel to whom he had great devotion. In a letter to his spiritual father: "Saturday it seemed that the devils wanted to finish me off with their blows and I did not know what Saint to turn to. Then I called on my guardian Angel, who after making me wait a while was right there at last to help me, and with his angelic voice he sang hymns to the Divine Majesty. I complained to him for making me wait so long, ... To punish him, so to speak, for being late, I tended to avoid looking him in the face and to move away from him. But he, poor thing, came up to me almost in tears, so that I lifted up my eyes, looking him in the face. Then he told me, 'I am always near you, dear friend. I always walk near you. ... This love I have for you will not end ... ' "

Padre Pio lived in intimate contact with his Guardian Angel, who enabled him to translate letters written in Greek and French. He used to keep Padre Pio up at night in order to chant God's praises with him and to ease the pain Padre Pio suffered from the beatings he took from the demons. Thus his Angel became his help-mate, and would carry messages from him to souls far away, bringing them comfort and blessings.

After nearly seven years in Pietrelcina, on February 17, 1916, Padre Pio departed for Foggia, where his superior assigned him to be the spiritual director of a chosen soul, Raffaelina Cerase, who was near death. She had "offered herself as a victim" to God "that Padre Pio might return permanently to the friary and by hearing confessions bring great benefit to many souls."

At Foggia, Padre Pio "very happily took his place as a religious among his fellow friars, with whom he was always cheerful and witty," according to his superior. At first, he spent his days in prayer and study. His holy Mass was very lengthy and devout, and he paid a daily visit to the shrine of the Madonna of the Seven Veils, where St. Alphonsus Liguori once had a famous ecstasy while delivering a sermon. It didn't take long before a "throng of souls" needing help and guidance began to gather around Padre Pio. This is what he wrote to his spiritual Father: "You need to know that I am not left free for one minute. A throng of souls thirsting for Jesus deeply concerns me. I run my hands through my hair wondering, "Whats next?"

Meantime he had painful and strange ailments, which caused a lack of appetite, spells of vomiting and perspiring. Most noteworthy were his periods of high fever that baffled all the physicians, who did not know how to treat him. His fevers were so high that the mercury shot out of the thermometer. Once using another type of thermometer, his temperature was recorded at 127.4 degrees Fahrenheit. Dr. Giorgio Festa observed these high fevers which broke all natural and scientific rules over a long period and attested to their authenticity. Several friars signed an affidavit also supporting the phenomena. And how did it affect Padre Pio? He made mention of it in a number of his letters to his spiritual director. Here is one: "I am all aflame, although there is no fire. A thousand flames consume me; I feel constantly dying yet I am still alive ... At certain moments the fire which devours me within is so intense that I make every effort to draw away from it, to go in search of water, icy water into which to plunge." The reason for this flame is summed up by the Padre as follows: "I am consumed by love for God and love for my neighbor."

Something even more strange began happening. It was mostly in the evening when Padre Pio was in his room. Loud thuds would be heard that frightened the friars. When they would rush to Padre Pio's room they would find him "drenched in perspiration, and his garments had to be changed from head to foot." Putting him under obedience to answer, the Father Superior asked the reason for the ungodly racket. Padre Pio replied that the devil was exerting all his powers to tempt him, and the two of them had a fierce battle. He concluded: "By God's grace, I always win. But as soon as Satan is defeated, in his rage he causes a racket."

Certain new arrivals at the friary would not believe the report of such strange goings–on, but laughed at it as a product of some friar's imagination. One such skeptic, a bishop, who was a guest of the friars, regarded their stories as fabulous medieval tales. But while he was having supper with the friars, a great rumbling noise in the ceiling startled him. He turned pale and trembled. He needed no more to convince him that the friars' accounts were true.

At the same time that Padre Pio was being tormented and assaulted by the devil, he had wonderful mystical experiences—visits from heaven and ecstasies. He seemed at times to be someone afflicted almost to the point of despair. At other times he seemed like another St. Francis of Assisi or St. Teresa of Avila, so overwhelmed with consolation of God that he "got spiritual indigestion," as he used to say. As he experienced these painful trials and unspeakable joys, he continued climbing the steep slope of Mount Calvary to transforming union with the Crucified.

Even towards the end of his life the devil was allowed by God to physically assault him. On one occasion he made such a loud racket that the friars rushed to his cell and there they found Padre Pio with a gash cross his face lying helpless on the floor. When they noticed a little pillow beneath his head, they asked him how that got there. He responded in a matter of fact way that his Madonnina* placed it there. If the devil was allowed by God to give Padre Pio opportunities throughout his long life to gain great merit and save souls through these torments, to be sure Our Blessed Mother was ever there as well to comfort and sustain him.

---

*The expression he used, "Madonnina," is a diminutive expression of endearment meaning "Little Mother." When Padre Pio made general reference to Our Lady he called her the "Madonna."

Regrouping His Forces

In February of 1916 his superiors sent Padre Pio from Pietrelcina to Foggia, and in July of the same year they assigned him to San Giovanni Rotondo for the first time. It was an out-of-the-way village on the Gargano peninsula, consisting of a few poor homes without plumbing, without electricity, and no sewer system. There were no paved roads nor modern means of communication. The place was isolated and unknown to the rest of the world. Village life was frugally austere and unexciting. The Capuchin friary was less than two miles outside the town, reached by a mule track used by shepherds with their flocks. Even more isolated than the town, the friary with its little church, Santa Maria delle Grazie (Holy Mary of Grace), reflected the poverty and ruggedness of the surrounding terrain which was rocky and craggy.

Padre Pio made his first trip there at the invitation of the Father Guardian of San Giovanni Rotondo, who had come to Foggia to preach. His visit to San Giovanni Rotondo was brief, from July 28 to August 5, 1916. Father Provincial hoped for some improvement in Padre Pio's health, which, in fact, did improve. On August 13, Padre Pio wrote his Father Provincial, suggesting "to spend a little more time at San Giovanni Rotondo," since the place had been so beneficial to his health. Under obedience, Padre Pio arrived there on September 4 "for a short time, for some relief and rest, to get a little mountain air." It was to be a temporary assignment, but the Lord's designs are wonderful. Padre Pio was to stay at San Giovanni Rotondo for the next fifty-two years, until his death in 1968.

His stay at San Giovanni Rotondo was interrupted, however, when he was drafted into the army during World War I (1914–1918). On December 18, 1916, he had to appear for duty at Naples. He was assigned to the Tenth Medical Corps. But since he was very ill he was given a sick leave. When he was called back a year later, he was given another six months' leave. He was then to wait for further orders. The summons to return to duty was delayed past the date he was to report for duty because the postman at San Giovanni Rotondo did not know that soldier Francis Forgione was none other than Padre Pio. He was accused of desertion but was easily cleared of the charge. Back to the barracks in Naples, on March 5, 1918, he was eventually given a permanent medical discharge. The medical officer brutally told him: "We are sending you home to die." His honorable discharge stated that "his conduct had been good and he had served with loyalty and honor."

Padre Pio appreciated the duty of a citizen to serve his country. He wrote these patriotic words to his spiritual director, "We ought to do our whole duty according to our ability. The order that comes from authorities we will accept with a peaceful mind and courage. If our country calls us, we ought to obey her ... At this serious hour we all have to cooperate for the common good and render the Lord's mercy favorable to us by praying humbly and fervently and by amending our lives." On the other hand his time spent in the army was a time of great trial. At times he could not always celebrate daily Mass. The bad language and blasphemies uttered among soldiers caused him much pain and affected his health. He had serious fears that he would die while in the army "departing from this world not in the cloister, but in the barracks."

Returning to San Giovanni Rotondo, Padre Pio served as spiritual director of the boys in the small seraphic seminary. Confessions, meditations, and spiritual direction of the boys occupied him day after day. "I love the boys tenderly for whom I do not spare myself personal hardship." Indeed, hardship and pains came his way from the devil who was provoked by the great spiritual profit the boys were gaining through Padre Pio. One night a boy was awakened by scornful laughs and the noise of iron pieces being twisted about and dropping to the floor, and of chains knocking against the floor, while Padre Pio was heard to continuously sigh, "O my Madonna!" The next morning the boys found the ironwork that supported the curtain around Padre Pio's bed all bent and twisted.

The boys besieged him with questions. He replied, explaining what had happened. "You want to know why the devil gave me a terrific beating? It is because I, as your spiritual Father, am willing to defend one of you." He continued, "The boy was suffering a strong temptation against purity, and when he called on the Madonna, he was calling on me as well. I rushed at once to assist him, and with the help of Our Lady's Rosary I was successful. The boy that had been tempted slept until morning, while I went through the battle, suffered the blows, but won the fight."

Another time, taking the boys on a walk he appeared very serious and sorrowful. The boys gathered around him and insisted that he tell them what was the matter. Padre Pio broke into tears as he said, "One of you has stabbed me in the heart." The boys were deeply shaken and ventured to ask for an explanation. Very sorrowfully, Padre Pio said, "Just this morning one of you made a sacrilegious Communion! And to think! I was the very one that give him Holy Communion during Mass." Immediately one of the boys fell on his knees in tears and said, "I was the one." Padre Pio had him get up on his feet and made the others go some distance away while he heard the boy's confession.

It was from August 1912 onward to September 20, 1918, that mystical experiences occurred which single him out as one of the great mystics of all times. The first experiences, called strokes and wounds of love, culminated in transverberation and stigmatization. The former is a phenomenon which the Spanish mystic, St. John of the Cross, calls, "the seraph's assault." St. Theresa of Avila and St. Thérèse of the Child Jesus are two of the most commonly known Saints marked by this special mystical experience. The heart of the mystic is pierced through by a mysterious fiery arrow or dart and is left with a wound of love which in an awesome way burns with love of God, while the soul is raised to the highest contemplation of love and of sorrow.

What did Padre Pio think of all this? It was a cause of alarm and confusion. His spiritual director wanted to give him some peace by assuring him that all that happened was only "the effect of love. It is a trial; it is a call to coredemption"—that is, a call to share in Christ's work of redemption. "Kiss the hand that pierced you," he added, "and sweetly press to yourself that wound, which is a seal of love."

However, it is the supernatural phenomenon of the stigmata that occurred on September 20, 1918, that has brought Padre Pio worldwide fame. The fact that he bore in his body the five wounds of the crucified Christ has drawn countless throngs to Padre Pio. Pope Paul VI magnificently described the reality of the stigmata when he called Padre Pio a representative of Christ on whom are imprinted "the wounds of Christ."

It happened when he was alone in the choir on Friday, September 20, 1918, while making his thanksgiving after a Mass. He had to tell everything "very exactly and out of obedience" to his spiritual director thirty-two days later in a letter dated October 22, 1918: " ... I saw a mysterious visitor before me, like the one I saw on the evening of August 5th; but he differed in that his hands, feet and side were dripping blood. The sight frightened me. I do not know how to express what I felt at that instant. I felt like I was dying, and I would have died if the Lord had not intervened to safeguard my heart, which I felt was bouncing out of my breast.

"Then the vision of the visitor passed away, and I saw that my hands, feet and side were pierced and dripping blood. You will imagine the pain I felt then and that I kept experiencing almost every day continually." Throughout the fifty years he bore the stigmata, in his deep humility Padre Pio begged God to take away the external signs of the wounds which drew too much attention to him while continuing the suffering and pain of the Crucified Savior. The Lord eventually heard his prayer, but only on his deathbed.

Padre Pio's stigmata were deep wounds at the center of his hands and feet and on his left side. They were literally pierced all the way through, and one could see light through the membrane that covered the wounds. Fresh blood emerged from both the upper and lower surfaces, especially during Mass. He wore half-gloves on his hands and dark stockings on his feet. The bandage on his side became soaked with blood during the night and had to be replaced the following morning (see chapters on pages 107 and 110). Doctors examined his stigmata on several occasions and the unbiased conclusion of a team of two was that Padre Pio's wounds are unexplainable. Their existence was beyond medical science's ability to explain.

Without the permission of his superiors no one was allowed to see the wounds. Some years later when he had to have an operation for a hernia, Padre Pio refused the anesthetic and had the doctor operate while he was fully conscious. He was afraid that someone might take the opportunity, while he was unconscious, to take a look at his stigmata. His suffering during the operation was great and towards the end he fainted. The doctor was then able to examine the stigmata and found them to be like freshly made wounds. When the priest regained consciousness, Padre Pio complained half-joking, half-serious, "Doctor, you betrayed me."

While he was still on the operating table in a room of his friary, someone came to the door and asked him how he was doing. Padre Pio answered, "I'm keeping this place ready for you." Some days later that same person unexpectedly needed surgery, and Padre Pio's prophecy came true. Padre Pio's gifts always served one purpose, namely to benefit others.

Through his gift of prophecy and other charismatic gifts he was able to attract thousands of souls separated from God, to convert them, to bring them to understand the ultimate purpose of life and to assist them in their physical as well as spiritual needs. He spread everywhere the fire of his charity, the smile of his kindness and understanding. He did all with simplicity, using both playful wit and a stern look as the situation warranted. His rustic sternness was often misunderstood, but led to the ultimate good—God and eternal salvation. "Mother could not make me sweeter, nor could she make me sterner," he once wisecracked. Through divine Grace both his sweetness and his sternness helped souls that approached him. One might say that everything was a grace from the hands of Padre Pio.

Charismatic Weapons

Padre Pio was the first priest to receive the stigmata and perhaps bore these wounds of Christ's passion and crucifixion longer than any other mystic. The stigmata were of such intensity and the loss of blood over the years so great that according to medical science he would not have survived long, let alone fifty years. The little food and drink that he took would not have sustained an infant. Most of his life he averaged less than a few hours sleep each night and frequently less than that because of the onslaughts of the devil. These extraordinary gifts, nonetheless, were but a few of the many charisms' that moved people first from Italy, then from other countries in Europe and finally throughout the world to come to San Giovanni Rotondo.

In the fifty years of his fruitful ministry the mule track leading from the town of San Giovanni Rotondo to the friary became a broad, paved highway, with hotels, restaurants, apartment dwellings, and gardens on either side. A huge 1,000 bed modern hospital built on a rocky hillside dominates what was once just a desolate landscape. Many individuals and families from Italy and other countries left their homes to live near Padre Pio. By virtue of his many supernatural gifts he was able to convert many souls who owe to Padre Pio the beginning of a new and virtuous life. These supernatural powers rank him among the most extraordinary Saints and wonder workers.

His gifts of bilocation, of perfume, of prophecy, of reading hearts, of healing, of interpreting languages, of abstaining beyond man's natural powers from both sleep and nourishment—these were charisms possessed by other saints, such as St. Francis of Assisi, St. Anthony of Padua, St. Teresa of Avila, St. Joseph of Cupertino, St. Alphonsus Liguori, and St. Gemma Galgani, but not it seems to the same degree.

Did not Jesus foretell that His disciples would "do greater works" than those which He did? (John 14:12) One can apply these words of Our Lord to Padre Pio, for it would be impossible to calculate the sum total of all the marvels that occurred in his lifetime, and even after his death to this day.

There are millions of persons who have been in Padre Pio's presence and received spiritual help by means of his gift of reading hearts, who have perceived the heavy fragrance that emerges from his person, whose hearts have been touched by the manner in which he celebrates Mass—and many others who have witnessed miracles worked through him and have felt themselves powerfully renewed and strengthened in faith. His powerful prayers and example have caused a renewal in Faith among many people the world over, inspiring them to live the fullness of the Christian life in imitation of Christ and the Saints.

When Pope Benedict XV learned of Padre Pio's wonderful gifts and the conversions that were taking place through his intercession, he remarked, "Padre Pio is indeed one of those extraordinary men whom God from time to time sends upon earth to convert hearts." Padre Pio's gifts have always had as their ultimate goal to attract souls separated from God in order to welcome them back to the Faith. He would spread everywhere a ray of light, of warmth, of charity, of kindness, all with the greatest naturalness and simplicity, at times using playful wit and at others a stern look. Who can forget Padre Pio's keen sense of humor and his rustic sternness which was, with the help of divine grace, capable of reaching the most hardened sinner?

To enumerate some of the more outstanding charisms' to win immortal souls for Christ:

The Aroma of Paradise

Frequently we read in the lives of the Saints that he/she died in the odor of sanctity, which can be interpreted both figuratively and literally. Many saints were gifted with pleasant scent that may be identified as the odor of sanctity. One day Dr. Romanelli, a good friend of Padre Pio, noticed a heavy fragrance as he came close to Padre Pio. He was scandalized—a friar with a reputation for holiness using perfume? He soon realized that the aroma was unidentifiable with any earthly scent. He was to learn that innumerable others experienced this fragrance either from Padre Pio's physical or his spiritual presence. Similar to St. Thérèse, who when she was going to prayers answer a petitioner's would send roses as a sign, Padre Pio indicated an answer to prayers by a heavenly aroma.

Dr. Giorgio Festa testified that the blood that coagulated around the stigmata of Padre Pio gave off a pleasant fragrance "like a mixture of violets and roses." The doctor adds, "One should consider that of all the parts of the human organism, blood is the quickest to decompose. In any case blood never gives off a pleasing odor." Furthermore, this scent could be attached to things belonging to Padre Pio and to things he had touched, and it would last a long time. Moreover, people used to perceive the fragrance at a distance coming in whiffs, to signify that Padre Pio was present in some manner at that moment. It often served as a hint—later to be substantiated—of some information, protection, a summons, or a reward.

Not all the scents are like perfume. Sometimes his presence is associated with a cigar smoke scent, though Padre Pio never smoked. Another scent is associated with a warning of danger ahead and has a strong medicinal odor, like disinfectant. An example of this occurred on a freeway in California when a couple of Padre Pio's spiritual children were returning home after giving a Padre Pio lecture. They experienced this scent. They looked at each other and around the car but kept driving. Just as they were approaching an offramp one of them screamed "Fire!" Close to the exit was a gas station where they parked the car and jumped out. An attendant came running to the car with a fire extinguisher. After the fire was put out, they cautiously continued on for another hour and a half to reach their destination. The next day when the car was towed to a nearby garage, the mechanic called and was amazed that they were able to drive so many miles after the fire was put out, as the car needed extensive repairs. Padre Pio was fulfilling his promise to continue watching over his spiritual children from heaven, for he had died just a few months before.

Bilocation

There aren't too many instances in the long history of the Church of a Saint having the gift of bilocation. However, Padre Pio had this gift on many occasions from the time he was a young seminarian (see page 97), up to the last years of his life. This miraculous phenomenon consists of being in two different places at the same time. In one place the person is present in body; while in the other, he is there in spirit clothed with what appears to be his physical body.

In 1916 a well authenticated instance of Padre Pio's bilocation occurred in the headquarters of an Italian General. At the same time that he appeared to the general he remained in the friary. General Cadorna had suffered a humiliating defeat in the battle at Caporetto where the Italian casualties were many and he was relieved of his command. He had picked up his revolver and was ready to commit suicide when Padre Pio appeared in his tent and persuaded him to lay aside his pistol. After the war ended the general, who had never met Padre Pio before, visited the friary at San Giovanni Rotondo, where he at once recognized Padre

Pio as the friar who had entered his tent on that night and dissuaded him from commiting suicide. Padre Pio's response was to remind him explicitly, "General, that was a rough night we had!"

Very noteworthy is a testimony of some English and American pilots who flew missions over Italy during World War II. On one mission they were ordered to bomb San Giovanni Rotondo. They didn't succeed. Why? Because they saw in the air before them a friar who stretched out his hands dissuading them from dropping their bombs. They recognized Padre Pio later as the friar that had appeared before their planes. Nor was this the only case at that time where such a sighting of the Padre in the sky occurred.

Reading Hearts

Reading hearts is a gift that Padre Pio made frequent use of in the confessional. He was able to read the minds and hearts of penitents like an open book. He could recall sins that the penitent had forgotten or withheld in shame. Almost always in the confessional, and sometimes outside the confessional, he gave evidence of knowing in advance what a person had to say and also details and facts somebody was trying to hide. There are many testimonies in this regard. The following are some instances attested to by Don Nello Castello, a diocesan priest from Padua, Italy:

"I went to confession to Padre Pio at least a hundred times. I recall the first time, his words both jolted and enlightened me. The counsels he gave me reflected exact knowledge of my whole life both past and future. At times he would surprise me with suggestions unconnected with the sins confessed. But later events made it clear that his counsels had been prophetic. In one confession during 1957 he spoke five times with insistence on the same question, using different words, and reminding me of an ugly fault of impatience. Furthermore, he enlightened me on the underlying causes that provoked the impatience. He described to me the behavior I should follow to avoid impatience in the future. This happened without my having said a word about the problem. Thus, he knew my problems better than I did and advised me how to correct them.

"A man from Padua, in order to get to confession to Padre Pio without the eight-day waiting period required between one confession and another, lied about the number of days since his last confession. Padre Pio sent him away, forcefully pointing out his lie. I went in search of the man and found him along the wall of the friary much dejected. In tears he repeated a number of times, 'I've told many lies during my lifetime, and I thought I could deceive Padre Pio too.'

"From that day on I found him frequently in church at Padua attending Perpetual Adoration. He confided to me that ever since that correction from Padre Pio, he went to holy Mass and Communion every day."

Cesare Festa, a lawyer and cousin of the physician George Festa, the personal physician of Padre Pio, went to visit the famous priest, whom his cousin had so often spoken of. As soon as they met, Padre Pio said, "You are a Mason." In a superior tone of expressing loyalty to the lodge and, "What are you going to do about it?" the lawyer answered, "Yes, Father."

"And what is your task as a Mason?"

"It is to carry on our fight against the Church in the political sphere."

There was a brief silence. Padre Pio fixed his eyes awhile on the lawyer, then took him by the hand and led him aside. He spoke to him privately with great gentleness about God's goodness, relating the parable of the Prodigal Son. In the end the Mason was on his knees before Padre Pio confessing his sins and begging God's forgiveness. The former Mason was convinced that Padre Pio could not have had such knowledge of him and his past by any natural means.

Prophecy

Prophecy, foretelling future events, is very much a part of the Bible. It is found frequently in the Old as well as the New Testament, where prophecies in the Old Testament pertaining to the coming Messiah were fulfilled many times in Jesus, the Savior of all men. In the history of the Church we find a number of privileged souls who had the gift of foretelling future events by a divine enlightenment. Padre Pio displayed this gift on a number of occasions. When he was a young seminarian during a walk in Pietrelcina he predicted that some day a Capuchin seminary would be built in his home town, pointing out its exact location. The following are two other examples from the many instances of his using this gift:

In 1944 Professor Settimio Manelli, the father of Fr. Stefano Manelli (see page 134) reported to Padre Pio that Hitler was alarming

---

Humility and charity are the master chords that all other virtues depend upon. The one is the lowest, the other the highest. The preservation of the entire edifice depends on the foundation and the roof. If the heart keeps itself directed in the exercise of these, no difficulty will be encountered in the others. These are the mothers of virtue, the others follow them as the chicks do their mother.

— *Padre Pio*

Besides the countless number of pilgrims who met the saintly mystic, Padre Pio received an enormous number of letters requesting prayers and spiritual direction. None were passed off in a general intention. Each individual received his personal intention and prayers.

the world by certain frightening sayings: "Come midnight, and there will be no more midnight."—"At midnight I have lost; and a minute after midnight I have conquered." Hitler was making clear references to the atomic bomb which he hoped to develop in time to level whole nations, massacring millions into submission. Though at the time he seemed to be losing the war, he expected to win suddenly by means of the atomic bomb. On hearing this report from the professor, Padre Pio's countenance became very serious. There were some moments of silence and reflection, then he spoke with assurance: "He will not act in time." And so it happened. Hitler did not succeed in having the atomic bomb ready for launching in time to win the war by means of a planned devastation never before seen on earth. His enemies won the war too soon for him to act.

A second instance happened a few years before Cardinal Montini was elected Pope. Alberto Galletti, who belonged to the nobility in Milan and was a spiritual son of Padre Pio, asked the holy friar's blessing for his Archbishop, who was known as Cardinal Montini. "Not a blessing, but something torrential," replied Padre Pio, "and my unworthy prayer! You tell the Archbishop that he will become Pope. Have you understood me? You must tell him that! For he must prepare himself." As we all know, Cardinal Montini became Pope Paul VI.

Battle for Souls Intensifies

Of all the charisms Padre Pio had, one without which he would have none of the others, though not recognized as such, was his charism or ability of praying at all times. Without his marvelous ability to communicate with God, his Mother Mary, his Guardian Angel and many Saints, the other charisms could not be considered genuine. This fact is verified by the Padre himself.

One day a journalist asked Padre Pio who he was. He answered meekly and kindly, "I am a poor friar who prays." Pope Paul VI likewise described Padre Pio as a "man of prayer and suffering." Certainly, prayer was Padre Pio's principal activity. He had the extraordinary gift of being able to pray always. It is significant that when his spiritual Father asked Padre Pio to redouble his prayers, Padre Pio replied that this was not possible because his time was "all spent in prayer."

His prayer was vocal and mental, affective and contemplative. Nothing was lacking in his prayer-life. He used to declare the excellence of prayer by quoting St. Gabriel of the Sorrowful Mother: "A thousand years of glory in palaces of men cannot be worth the sweetness of one hour spent before the tabernacle." Moreover, it was a matter of necessity for him to continuously intercede for his fellow-men before God. Therefore, he prayed not only in choir and in church, but in his room too, in the hallways, in the paths of the garden, by day, by night, in times of joy and times of dryness, when alone and when with others, with words and with a loving glance at a sacred image. A good witness of his intense prayer-life was the Bishop of Manfredonia, Msgr. Cesarano. He made an eight-day retreat at Padre Pio's friary. For eight nights in succession, rising at different hours to make a visit to the Blessed Sacrament, he always found Padre Pio tirelessly absorbed in prayer.

Prayer was ever the first priority with Padre Pio. He preferred to lengthen his hours of prayer rather than his hours in the confessional; for he said, "What mankind lacks today is prayer." Padre Pio devoted much of his later life to the work of "Prayer Groups" (see page 192), so that more people would be induced to pray and would receive help to pray well. The prayer Jesus taught us was the Our Father, the most divine and the most human of prayers. Just hours before his death, Padre Pio, aware of his imminent death, prayed the Our Father as a seal of his life of prayer, reciting it with unusual forcefulness and clarity, stressing every word.

His favorite private prayer was the Rosary. From the time he was a small boy he loved the Rosary. He prayed it so often that he could readily be called the "saint of the Rosary." His first visit to a Marian shrine was to the shrine of the Madonna of the Rosary of Pompeii. One rarely saw Padre Pio without the rosary in his hand. When he celebrated Mass, he obviously wasn't able to physically pray the Rosary, but during that most sacred action he lived the five sorrowful mysteries of the Rosary in his body and soul.

He repeatedly urged his spiritual children to pray the Rosary. He reasoned that if the Holy Virgin requested in her recent apparitions the recitation of the Rosary we have all the more reason for praying it. How true this is in the apparitions at Fatima where she repeatedly asked the children to recite it daily, identifying herself as the Lady of the Rosary (more on this on page 65). He reached the point of reciting an inconceivable number of Rosaries in the course of a day. So much so that one must conclude that Padre Pio had the mystical gift of praying at all times. All his projects and enlightened counsels and his victories over sin were linked with the power of the Rosary. Besides praying the Rosary at all times, he also upheld the truth that Mary is indeed the Mediatrix of all graces, of which St. Bernard said, "The Lord gives nothing but what passes through the hands of the Queen of Heaven." Once he was asked what legacy he would leave his spiritual children. He answered at once, "The Rosary." Shortly before his death, some of his spiritual children asked him for some words of wisdom. He answered, "Love the Madonna and make her loved by others. Always pray the Rosary."

When Padre Pio identified himself as a "poor friar who prays," he placed "poor friar" before that of "prayer," it underlined his vocation. In addressing a group of professional men in the field of medicine, Padre Pio spoke of every man's mission on earth, and said concerning himself: "What must I tell you? You, too have come into the world as I have, with a mission to accomplish ... I, a friar and a priest, have a mission. As a friar, as a Capuchin, it is the perfect and devoted observance of my Rule and vows." Winning spiritual battles depended first and foremost in being holy himself. "I hear a voice within me that persistently tells me, *Be holy and have a holy influence*." Padre Pio wrote those words in 1922, summing up the twofold mission of his life, namely, to develop holiness in himself and to make others holy.

Padre Pio understood well that to sanctify himself as a religious and a priest and to sanctify others demands heroism. He was responsible for reconciling thousands of souls with Christ and thus winning continual battles against the evil one with whom he was to do battle throughout his life as described in Chapter I. For sixty-five years he was a son of the Poverello of Assisi and lived "the perfect and devoted observance" of the Holy Rule. He died after renewing the profession of his vows a final time. He loved St. Francis with great veneration and devotion. Thus he strove to imitate St. Francis' devotion to Jesus Crucified, to the Divine Infancy of Jesus, and to Christ in the Eucharist (see page 167). He also endeavored to imitate St. Francis' efforts to be a "little" ("minor") friar. When his spiritual children extended warm congratulations to Padre Pio on his completion of sixty years of religious life, he broke into tears, saying, "Sixty years of unworthiness."

What shall we say of Padre Pio's love for the poverty of St. Francis? People said that Padre Pio was a saint who was both "beggar and multimillionaire." This is true. Many millions passed through his hands in the way of donations, especially when he was administering the building of the Home of the Relief of Suffering. But for himself there was the poverty of a humble friary and a small, simple room for fifty-two years. For him there was no time off for trips, no amusements, no ease and comfort. For many years his bedding was a straw mattress over a plank. During his last years when they put a sink, a radiator and an air-conditioner in his room, he protested that he absolutely did not want such things. He sorrowfully complained, "What would our Seraphic Father say?"

Concerning Padre Pio's obedience we can say that his whole life bore out his heroic submission to lawful authority out of love of God, through the many trials to which he was subjected. He loved the Church and his Order. One of the greatest pains he endured was when he was accused of being disobedient to an order from Rome (See more on obedience on page 70). And the sweet, powerful scent that came from Padre Pio's person—was it not a song pointing out his angelic chastity? He loved modesty in dress and did not hesitate to send women away from his confessional who he felt were not dressed modestly. Padre Pio had a special love and veneration for the Franciscan habit that he wore. He even thought himself unworthy to wear it. He always wore it, day and night. Only during his last years, to be obedient, he took it off at night in order to rest better. But he wanted to die clothed in the habit, which he did.

We are familiar with Padre Pio's special love for the Madonna (see pages 65 and 87). It was a tender, ardent, child-like love. We also know about Padre Pio's special devotion to St. Michael the Archangel and his guardian angel (see page 82). In these respects, too, he was an imitator of St. Francis. We also find in Padre Pio a warm, devoted zeal on behalf of the Franciscan Third Order. He was Director of a local Third Order group called the Brotherhood of Santa Maria delle Grazie. He remarked in a letter that he considered the Third Order a great means "to enable mankind to return to the light of the faith and to the sound principles of Christian morality."

How can one explain all that the innocent Padre Pio suffered if it were not for others? In mystical theology it is called mystical substitution. One who is guiltless pays the penalty for the guilty. Here we find unsullied heroism in love for neighbor. Such charity is immense. "Greater love than this no man has, than to lay down his life for his friends" (John 15:13). How many times did Padre Pio offer himself in "mystical substitution" to take away other people's sufferings? God alone can give the answer. We know that they flocked to him from all sides and that he never spared himself, allowed himself no respite, and never took a vacation. People saw him active in this role for fifty-two years, an untiring soldier doing battle against Satan's kingdom, a magnificent champion of God's love, totally sacrificing himself day after day for the sins of the people.

He followed to the letter God's word that "without the shedding of blood there is no remission" (Heb. 9:22). He offered himself totally, without holding back in any way, so that he might relieve the great needs of his fellow men who had sinned and who suffered. He wrote his spiritual director, "I have labored; I want to labor. I have prayed and I want to pray. I have kept watch; I want to keep watch. I have wept and I want always to weep for my brothers in exile ... " Padre Pio's life, as we have seen, was one painful passion, a succession of trials and sufferings in his body and soul. The most painful chapter of this passion was to suffer persecution from some of his brothers in the priesthood and in the religious life. The lament of the Prophets was verified in him: "If my enemies had reviled me, I would verily have borne with it ... but it was thou ... my friend and my familiar" (Ps. 54:13-14). Such things are necessary if one is to resemble the crucified Jesus. Jesus was a "sign of contradiction" and had forewarned his followers, "If they have persecuted Me, they will also persecute you" (John 15:20).

There were two long periods of persecution when his fellow men crucified Padre Pio. The first was from 1923 to 1933. The second was from 1959 until his death. During the first persecution attacks were chiefly made on his person and his ministry. During the second, the attack was on Padre Pio and his great work, that is, the Prayer Groups and the Home for the Relief of Suffering. During both persecutions there were serious calumnies and accusations against Padre Pio's doctrinal soundness, against his morals, his mental competence, and against his practical prudence.

Painful measures were taken. Several attempts were made to transfer Padre Pio from San Giovanni Rotondo to another friary far away. But it proved impossible; for it would have caused such travail and tumult among the local people, that it would have surely led to bloodshed. From 1923 to 1933 his spiritual director was taken from him, he was forbidden to write letters, and he was required to celebrate his holy Mass in the morning before dawn. During the last two years of this period (1931-1933), Padre Pio was kept secluded in his friary, suspended from hearing confessions and forbidden to have any contact with the faithful. He was a Christian without liberty to have a spiritual director. He was a father who could not communicate vocally or in letters to his spiritual children. He was a confessor par excellence who could no longer hear confessions. He could celebrate holy Mass only in the little private chapel of the friary with no one present but the server.

Things continued this way until July 16, 1933, when he was at last allowed to celebrate Mass again in the church and to resume hearing confessions. But in the meantime he was distrusted and eyed with suspicion. From 1959 on, he was subject to an even greater persecution. Newspapers and periodicals during those years carried articles on Padre Pio with derogatory headlines and shameful misrepresentations. In order to stop the stream of donations that supported the Home for the Relief of Suffering founded by him, his persecutors put together a dossier of absurd and ruinous charges, and took the sacrilegious step of putting microphones in his confessional in an attempt to find something blameworthy.

Hearing so much false accusation, certain offices of the Roman Curia conducted many investigations and inquiries, most of which were unfavorable to Padre Pio. The administration of the Home for the Relief of Suffering was taken out of Padre Pio's hands, and his Prayer Groups were left to languish. An iron railing and barrier was set up around his confessional to check the flow of penitents. Through it all he could say, "Sweet is the hand of the Church, even when she strikes, for it is the hand of One's mother." He was a crucified victim, forced into inaction, but through it all totally resigned and more effective than ever in saving souls even as Jesus was when nailed to the cross. One may get a concise idea of what Padre Pio was undergoing at the time from a statement made by a high ranking Church official: "They want to put a gravestone over San Giovanni Rotondo. But they have not been successful, because the finger of God is there."

This was true, because the holiness and the work of Padre Pio were truly built on the rock of truth and Grace. Therefore it could not collapse under the storm. His spiritual children, both clergy and laity, became an impressive force of loyalty and of defense for Padre Pio throughout the world. His "world-wide following" not only did not grow less, but increased uninterruptedly around Padre Pio, and was able to glory all the more in this victim whose life heroically fulfilled Christ's words, "Blessed are they that suffer persecution for justice' sake, for theirs is the kingdom of heaven" (Mt. 5:10).

In his later years, wherever Padre Pio went he was surrounded by devotees. He was always accompanied by a Friar to assist him in getting through the crowds. All this attention was but another cross to the humble Franciscan who bore it with resignation and love.

Old Soldiers Never Die

On August 10, 1960, Padre Pio celebrated his golden Jubilee of the priesthood. The bishop of Foggia at that time, Bishop Paola Carto, put things in focus regarding Padre Pio's priesthood when he wrote: "Padre Pio is a dispenser of graces not with a small "g" but Grace with a capital 'G.' He distributes sanctifying grace to countless souls through the Sacrament of Reconciliation ... The lapsed, the bewildered, those who have gone astray, the godless, regain God's grace through the ministry of this humble son of St. Francis. For fifty years this abundant distribution of divine grace has continued. Never a day's respite or rest, never a day spent elsewhere than San Giovanni Rotondo." Added to these fifty years mentioned by the bishop were another eight years of hearing confessions, right up to the day before he died.

Not indicated in this summary of the years Padre Pio ministered the Sacrament of Penance are the first two years of his priesthood. It is ironic that he who in later years was known as the "apostle of the Confessional," and the "martyr of the Confessional," was denied the faculty of hearing confession for two years after his ordination. Padre Pio wrote at least eighteen letters begging his superior permission to hear confessions. He was put off first because of his delicate health. His superior and spiritual director, Fr. Benedetto, felt that the sickly friar just was not up to what might demand long hours with long lines of penitents (would that such a "problem" existed in our day). The next reason: he was not thoroughly grounded in moral theology to adequately deal with the many moral problems he would encounter in hearing confessions.

It was true that his formal academic training in moral theology was at a minimum due to his continual ill-health, which prevented him from attending formal classes, but the Holy Spirit and the inscrutable designs of God would compensate for this many thousands times over. It is estimated that Padre Pio heard about five million confessions in his lifetime. He frequently heard confessions for fifteen hours a day and on occasion for as many as nineteen.

Once he was given the faculty to hear confessions he was in much demand as an enlightened confessor. People flocked to his confessional, first locally, then throughout Italy, and finally from Europe and all over the world. Penitents coming at a distance were shocked to find they might have to wait as long as a month before their turn in the long list of those waiting to go to confession came up. Although he wasted no time, reducing the confessions to essentials, he was unable to hear everybody's confession promptly, though at times he would pull a person out of line to expedite that person's reconciliation with God. On the average, a confession made to Padre Pio lasted only three minutes. He heard about twenty persons an hour. During a morning and an afternoon he would hear about sixty women and about sixty men. Thus, during his "good" years he heard over a hundred confessions a day.

Few confessors have the charism of reading souls and thus of administering this Sacrament in an extraordinary way. There are two other sainted confessors who had this gift in modern times, the Curé of Ars and St. Leoboldo Mandic, (the latter, like Padre Pio a Capuchin Franciscan). These extraordinary priests were raised up by God to meet a great need in this age of secular humanism. It was the great Pope Pius XII who said that the greatest moral problem in our day is not sin, but the fact that men have lost the sense of sin. Padre Pio was fully aware of what it cost Christ to redeem men from sin, and the devastation it has on the soul of the sinner. He freely paid the price for sin, and ransomed countless sinners, suffering in union with the redeeming passion of Jesus to make amends for the sins of his penitents.

From his earliest years (see chapter I) he had a horror and abhorrence for the least offence against a God so good. This holy man described himself as "the biggest sinner in the world," such was the awareness he had of what some might dismiss as insignificant imperfections. Contrary to his sensitivity to evil and sin, it is not uncommon today to find couples living together without the benefit of the Sacrament of Matrimony, ninety percent of young Catholic couples using some form of artificial contraceptives, contrary to the natural law and the ends of marriage—all living in sin, ignoring the natural law, the divine law and Church law, yet making sacrilegious communions, without the least hesitation or qualm of conscience.

Such laxity and hardening of conscience were readily exposed by Padre Pio in his confessional. He rightly demanded that every confession be a true conversion. He could not tolerate superficiality or lack of honesty in the use of the sacrament of forgiveness. His treatment hit hard those who made excuses, who showed themselves insincere, who sheltered themselves in compromises, who lacked determination. He required frankness and honesty in the account of one's sins, a sincere sorrow coming from the heart, and a firmness in a penitent's resolutions for the future. Above all he wanted penitents to sincerely acknowledge their sins.

If a penitent tried to excuse his sins by saying, "The temptation was stronger than I was. I did not have the power ... I could not resist." Padre Pio replied, "Here God must be the one to absolve. If you do not realize your guilt and would absolve and acquit yourself, then leave, and do not try my patience." How explain the fact that Padre Pio denied absolution to so many persons? And why did he often treat penitents with gruffness? Sometimes he would rebuke penitents with very severe words that he alone knew how to say. For example: "How irresponsible! Why did you sell your soul to the devil? ... How irresponsible! You are on the way to hell! ... O you irresponsible woman!" To immodestly dressed women, "Go away and get dressed! ... O you careless man, go first and get repentance, and then come here ... !"

These rebukes however, reveal Padre Pio's love for the welfare of souls. When someone asked him the reason for such strong language, he replied, "I do not give sweets to someone who needs a laxative." A soul in need of being shaken up should not be caressed. With Padre Pio's powerful gift of reading hearts, he perceived at once what was needed and did not hesitate in using the means that were both violent and saving, that of refusing absolution or giving a rebuke that sunk like a fiery blade into the center of the soul.

But he suffered, and he suffered a great deal when he was obliged to deny absolution or deal harshly with someone. He once said, in confidence to a priest: "If you knew how I suffer when I have to refuse absolution! ... But it is better to be blamed on earth by a man than in the next life by God." It is enough to add that the vast majority of those whom Padre Pio sent away unabsolved came back sooner or later to him. They could not remain without the absolution of the physician who stood for justice and salvation.

It is hard to find words to fully describe the extent of the martyrdom that Padre Pio endured every day between the three wooden walls of the confessional. He felt the full weight of this supernatural role. He once said to a priest, "If you but knew fully what a fearful thing it is to sit in the tribunal of the confessional! We are administering the Blood of Christ. We must be careful that we do not fling it about by being too easy-going or negligent."

He valued frequent confession as indispensable for progress in the spiritual life. He went to confession at least once a week himself, often several times a week. During the years when great throngs were coming to him for confession, he never wanted his spiritual children to stay away from confession more than ten days. Once a spiritual daughter had carelessly let a month pass without going to confession and mentioned it to Padre Pio. She was severely reprimanded "Oh, how neglectful! That you would not yet understand the value of confession and what you lost by neglecting this sacrament!" For Padre Pio was convinced that confession is a powerful means not only for removing sins, but also for increasing divine grace. He taught that an atom of grace is worth more than the whole created universe.

Pope Pius XII once asked the archbishop of Manfredonia, "What does Padre Pio do?"

"Your Holiness, he takes away the sins of the world," the archbishop promptly replied. A wonderful answer! He could not have summed up better Padre Pio's apostolic work and mission. He became a martyr—a victim of prayer, of sacrifice and of labor in order to deliver "his fellow men from Satan's clutches." And how much Padre Pio loved souls! For their sake he did not count the sacrifice, nor the prayers, nor the toil. He knew very well that souls cost blood. He said so himself: "Souls do not come as a gift. They are bought. You do not know what they cost Jesus. Today it is always with the same coin that they must be paid for."

Often he would say to his converts, "It was with love and pain that I begot you. How much you made me suffer! I bought you at the price of my blood." This pain was often evident on his face while he recited the sacramental formula of absolution. His lips writhed and he turned pale as he painfully stammered out every word. No one realizes God's goodness and holiness as the Saints do. Therefore no one appreciates as they do the ugliness and evil in every sin. Hence they react strongly and fight all kinds of battles, just to save God from being offended.

If we reflect that Padre Pio had before him and within him Jesus wounded and crucified by our sins, we are not so astonished at his tears and his indignation toward persons who "crucify Jesus anew in their hearts" (Hebrew 6:6). Once when he was hearing a confession he began to weep. When asked why, he answered, "I weep at men's ingratitude toward their supreme Benefactor. What more could we have expected Jesus, poor Jesus, to do than what He has already done?"

Almost all of Padre Pio's penitents bear witness that in his confessional they used to experience the awesome impression of standing before the judgment seat of God. A young man after receiving his doctorate admitted, "It is less frightening to take a difficult examination at the University than to go to confession to Padre Pio." Once Padre wrote his spiritual Father, "How is it possible to behold a God who grieves over sin and not grieve likewise? What do I do when I see God on the point of discharging His thunderbolts, and perceive that there is no other way to ward them off except to raise one hand to hold back God's arm, and to raise our other hand to urgently appeal to our brother to separate himself from evil and leave the way of sin promptly, for the Judge's Hand is about to be lowered upon him?"

It was a beautiful sight to see Padre Pio coming down to hear confessions, pausing before an image of the Madonna to pray fervently. He entrusted his ministry of mercy and pardon to the one who is "full of grace," the Mother of Mercy and the Refuge of Sinners. Padre Pio was painstakingly faithful to the ministry of confession to the very end of his life. On the morning of September 22, 1968, he was carried into the old sacristy where he heard his last seven confessions—that of seven men. During the following night, he passed into eternity.

His death coincided with a large gathering of the fourth international meeting of his prayer groups on September 22. Two days before they had joined him in celebrating the fiftieth anniversary of his stigmata. The 22nd of September was a taxing day for the feeble and weak priest. He said Mass for a large assembly of his spiritual children at the usual time, 5:00 a.m., assisted by a friar. All could perceive that he was worn out. He sang the Mass, but he seemed to sing it from upon the Cross. His deep voice was hoarse, labored, and painful to listen to. Finally at the end of the Mass Padre Pio collapsed. He would have fallen were it not for some nearby friars who grabbed him in time. Voices of alarm rose from the people as they saw him tottering. He still had the strength to repeat in a fatherly tone, "My children, my children." At 6:00 p.m. he blessed the first stone of the monumental stations of the cross to be erected on the mountain side. It was constructed through donations of his prayer groups. His spiritual sons and daughters could not think of a more agreeable gift to a man whose body bore "the brand marks of the Lord Jesus" for fifty years. Significantly, the sculpture had Padre Pio assisting Christ in carrying the cross in the fifth station, rather than Simon the Cyrenian. On the same day, the eve of his death, work on the crypt below the church was completed and blessed. Little did anyone realize then that within a week it would receive his remains. The marble tomb is now a place of continuous pilgrimage of people from all over the world.

He remained most of his last day on earth in his cell. That evening he gave his last blessing to the people assembled in the Church, and later waved to the crowd from his cell window before retiring. In the evening the prayer groups had a candlelight procession ending below his window, but he did not appear as expected. After midnight he asked the friar who was with him to celebrate Mass for him in the morning. Then he went to confession. He urged the friar to ask pardon from the friars for the disturbances he had caused them. From everyone he begged prayers for his soul, and he assured everyone of his blessing.

He renewed his religious profession as a Capuchin, and said the Our Father in a clear strong voice. Then he rose, dressed in his habit, went out on the terrace, and stood there a few minutes. When he was carried back indoors, he gazed at the wall where there was a picture of his mother, Maria Giuseppa, and said, "I see two mothers." The friar attending him told him he was not seeing well, because there was only the one picture of his mother. But Padre Pio responded, "Don't worry. I see very well. I see two mothers there."

Padre Pio began to turn pale. Perspiration formed on his forehead. His lips were livid as he repeated, "Jesus, Mary, Jesus, Mary!" At two a.m. the friar at his side realized that things were happening fast and was about to run for help. Padre Pio stopped him twice with, "Do not wake anybody up." The friar hastened off nevertheless. When, the Father Superior with some friars and a physician arrived, Padre Pio received the anointing of the sick. His lips barely moved as he kept repeating, "Jesus, Mary, Jesus, Mary!" It was the end. His head bowed over his breast and he breathed no more. He had passed into eternity.

Those present stood silent and recollected for a long while, almost petrified with grief. Then their feelings were released. They could not hold back their tears. The sad news spread rapidly; everywhere the evidence of grief was indescribable. All through the throng that filled the church and the square in front of it one saw faces stricken with sorrow, men weeping like babies. Most of the people were holding their Rosaries without seeming able to pray. There was a great void in everyone's heart, as if their own father or mother had passed away.

Immediately after Padre Pio's death something astonishing was discovered. The five wounds of the stigmata had totally disappeared. The flesh was once more intact, the skin appearing as uniform and smooth as that of an infant. Padre Pio's prayer to obtain the removal of these outward signs of the Savior's sufferings was finally heard. Who knows what scientific studies men might have wanted to make on the mystery of those wounds? But the "secret of the King" (Tobias 12:7) remained with God, to our confusion. The total disappearance of every sign of his suffering the Passion of the Master evokes the conclusion that in his flesh he now prefigured the Resurrection of Christ.

Padre Pio's funeral took place four days after his death. The funeral procession seemed endless. People had come from all parts of the world to honor the remarkable Capuchin. According to estimates, about a hundred thousand persons had come for the funeral. In the blue sky overhead aircraft in formation paid a last tribute, as the procession which extended nearly five miles made its way to the square in front of the shrine and the celebration of the holy sacrifice of the Mass and the blessing of the remains. The whole ceremony was marked with majestic solemnity and devotion. It was as if he was being publicly acclaimed a saint by popular demand. But that had to wait another twenty-five years until his beatification on May 2, 1999.

With his holy death there were those who were quite sure that the shrine would greatly decline, that the flow of pilgrims would dwindle and all related projects of the Padre would have a difficult time. Just the opposite occurred. Padre Pio had said some years before, "I will make more noise when I am dead than when I was alive." Also, "In paradise I will work with both hands." In fact from the time of his death onwards, the development of San Giovanni Rotondo has been a spectacle. Pilgrims continue to flock to the shrine; the *Casa Sollievo* has been enlarged; the hotels and restaurants thrive. Newly completed are the impressive Via Crucis, the Rosary Park and now the huge pilgrim church, which will seat 10,000 with chapels, a large confessional chapel, an extensive service center, and offices. The Padre Pio Prayer Groups continue to flourish worldwide and new ones are established daily. In the United States a large Padre Pio Shrine is being built in Barto, Pennsylvania (see page 197). And so as long as the battle for souls goes on there will be Padre Pio in the forefront working with both hands, for "old soldiers never die."

Pope Pius XII once asked the archbishop of Manfredonia, "What does Padre Pio do?" "Your Holiness, he takes away the sins of the world," the archbishop promptly replied. A wonderful answer! He could not have summed up better Padre Pio's apostolic work and mission. He became a martyr—a victim of prayer, of sacrifice and of labor in order to deliver "his fellow men from Satan's clutches."

Part II

Padre Pio received the stigmata on Sept. 20, 1918. This picture was taken two years later by one of his confreres. The visible stigmata were a source of embarrassment to the Padre, as they drew too much attention to himself. He would prefer to have the pain without the visible evidence. (See the chapter on "The Bleeding Stigmata," pg. 107).

Above: After it became known that he had the stigmata, pilgrims began to arrive in ever increasing numbers.

The Capuchin chapel and friary of Our Lady of Grace on the rocky slope of the Gargano on the outskirts of the small town of San Giovanni Rotondo, as Padre found it in 1916.

The Secret, Mystery and Message of Padre Pio

by His Eminence Corrado Cardinal Ursi

One of the most startling phenomena to occur in the Catholic Church in modern times has been the stigmatization of the Capuchin Franciscan priest, Padre Pio da Pietrelcina. The only priest in the history of the Church to receive the mystical gift of the wounds of Christ, Padre Pio for over 50 years lived a life of extraordinary and stunning witness of Christ Crucified and the Gospel. The spiritual meaning of Padre Pio's life is explained here by the late Archbishop of Naples, Italy, his Eminence Corrado Cardinal Ursi. This chapter is excerpted from an address the Cardinal gave at San Giovanni Rotondo in 1971 where Padre Pio spent most of his religious life, dying at the age of 81 in 1968.

Throughout the centuries God sends forth certain men to stand like powerful summonses to the People of God. Such men incarnate in themselves the social appearance of Christ, the redeemer and renovator of the world. In our times God has sent forth Padre Pio. In Padre Pio he has molded another image of Christ for our day, and indeed the quiet but explosive witness of the priest has been shaking the world for fifty years; his testimony has echoed irresistibly in every country on earth, and now, after his death, it pours itself out and reaches ever more deeply into our souls.

What is it that Padre Pio is telling us? First of all, Padre Pio wishes us to contemplate in him, and to feel in ourselves, the mystery of the death and resurrection of Christ. He wants us to see how this mystery glorifies God and works out God's plan of salvation. Throughout his life Padre Pio lived the mystery of the cross. He was a man who, like Christ, suffered, shed tears, and was crucified. Like Jesus he put up with, in peace and serenity, many sufferings, humiliations, misunderstandings and betrayals, all in obedience to God "even unto death." Not only men but also the demons made him suffer morally and physically.

Every day at evening time there came to him from every part of the world the products of sin—moral disorders, suffering, despair and cries for help—as innumerable penitents crowded his confessional. The stigmata, which produced physical pain in his hands, feet, side, and right shoulder, were external signs given by God and not arising from natural causes—of his interior crucifixions.

Padre Pio has also given us a sign of the resurrection, and this not only by his moral life, which appeared angelic! The Father Guardian of Padre Pio's friary only yesterday evening told me of how, after he "had passed from this world to the Father," his lifeless body shone, the stigmata disappeared, the tissues rapidly renewed themselves and the skin appeared fresh and tender. Is not this a sign of the resurrection? According to Paul, all of us, when we rise from the dead, will be "new creatures," and, according to Christ himself (Mt. 22: 30), we will be always young, immortal, incapable of suffering and without any deformation.

Padre Pio, like Christ, was made to suffer in his body in order to destroy the evils and sufferings of the modern world, but, suddenly after his death, his flesh, in the parts injured by his mysterious wounds, was regenerated in order to show the certainty of the final resurrection and the renewal of humanity. It also showed the credentials of the special mission, given him by God, for the good of his brothers and their recall to salvation.

Secondly, Padre Pio has in a special and efficacious manner taught us about personal conversion through the sacrament of penance. I believe I am right, and in line with the opinion of the Bishops, priests, and laity—for we are all called to decipher the challenge which God has hurled at us through Padre Pio—to say that this Capuchin has made conversion, along the lines described by Jesus in his prayer at the Last Supper and St. Paul in his epistle to the Ephesians, more intelligible, cogent and attractive. For the sake of this conversion, Padre Pio was throughout his life literally nailed to the confessional. More than prayer, penance and prodigies, the most important ministry of the confessional was peculiar to him.

Almost all the people who came to him from all parts of the world wished to confess to him rather than to seek grace and miracles. Solely for this, they faced the discomfort of long journeys and long waits at San Giovanni Rotondo as they waited their turn at the confessional of Padre Pio. Further, the confessions of Padre Pio were not easy and accommodating. These were not the pious caresses which we all make light of, but rather, they brought about great inconvenience—especially when someone was insincere or would not open his heart to penance and a change in his mode of living.

At this confessional of his, the mercy of God reached only the man who accepted God's light, was willing to bear the penalty for sin, and who disposed himself to die and rise again. For if the sacrament of the confessional is, as it were, the renewal of Baptism, which cannot itself be repeated, like Baptism it conforms the sinner to the death and resurrection of Christ. Of what use is confession to the sinner who does not intend to die to sin and rise again to the life of God in the fullness of love for the Heavenly Father and his brethren on earth? It is this that the Holy Spirit re-enkindles in the sinner, in order to lead him to a more conscious, more vital and more responsible life in the community of the Church.

Were the confessions heard by Padre Pio different from those heard by other confessors? Essentially they were in no way different. But he had a special grace for his ministry, a grace which enabled him to penetrate consciences with greater ease, to stimulate and aid his penitents, to raise them up into God's grace so that they humbly accused themselves with sincere repentance and hope of being set free. He could bring them— sometimes roughly and by refusing absolution in such a manner as to shake even the most hardened of hearts—to die and rise again, to change their lives. Many such remarkable conversions are known.

Did he really perform miracles? Had he the gift of bilocation? Could he discern spirits and foretell the future? And, if he did, what did these gifts mean? It is not for us to pronounce on the authenticity of all we hear, though facts are facts and can hardly be denied. Nevertheless, if he did these wonderful things as an instrument of Divine Love they were providential means to guarantee that ministry of reconciliation with God which he fulfilled with absolute self-surrender.

These things were witnesses to God's reconciling love for many sinners, particularly hardened habitual sinners who could not be touched by any other ray of Divine Grace and brought to spiritual cleansing, to rebirth and repossession of the greatest liberty, the liberty of the sons of God.

The voluntary mortifications of Padre Pio were means of growth and purification in his own Christian and religious perfection. But they also enabled him to act as a channel of the grace and mercy of God towards sinners and to see clearly into God's plans and indeed into the hearts of sinners whose consciences were sluggish, twisted or even completely closed up. The words of Jesus are, "Blessed are the pure of heart, for they shall see God" (Mt. 5: 8).

His lengthy prayers, especially at night, were for him a means of remaining in constant contact and living colloquy with God, like a flower which springs up under the influence of the sun and feeds on it. At this time too he spoke with God about the salvation of his penitents and prepared himself for a successful encounter with sinners and with Satan. All that he was, all that he had received from God, and all that he did, was referred to the confessional. One could say that earthquakes of conversion to God and to one's fellow men were caused by him there, thus opening the way to Christian renewal in so many families and in society.

I believe that through this marvellous attraction to the confessional of Padre Pio, God wanted to warn many priests and laymen who misinterpret the *aggiornamento* called for by Vatican Council II in regard to Confession and violently attacking this sacrament in a way which contradicts Catholic teaching about sin and justification. In fact, so many souls are being led astray, and the confessional is being so frequently abandoned by confessors and penitents that the outlook in this matter gives cause for real anxiety.

Will God hear the voice of Padre Pio, who now in heaven is praying above all for priests who are called to the ministry of the confessional? It is up to us, to whom the mission of the Church is entrusted, to penetrate deeply into the mystery of Padre Pio and to reveal its message. For this mission is to save sinners and to bring about the final victory over evil both in the individual and in society.

Thirdly, Padre Pio's life tells us about the Eucharist. The celebration of the Eucharist was for Padre Pio the source of light, of strength, and of nourishment in his laborious slavery for the salvation of sinners. We can say that he lived through and from the Mass. In spite of the length of time Padre Pio took to say Mass, people came in crowds to his Mass even before sunrise. They did not grow tired, for there they drank to the full from a mysterious reality. They drank in the mystery of Christ as they gazed at the suffering and transfigured face of this minister who seemed to be crucified with Christ at the altar.

But the whole life of Padre Pio was a continuous sacrifice. For long years he lived shut up in a little friary—no journeying, no preaching, no sacred functions except Holy Mass, and no relief, no consolation, as well. Variety in the ministry is a relief and certain sacred ministries are a consolation. But for him all was monotony, heaviness, bitterness. Through endless hours and endless days he sat in the confessional among constantly demanding crowds who easily fell into uncontrolled fanaticism, a fanaticism that hurt and offended him in a manner he could not always hide. Yet no one has ever exercised a more fruitful apostolate. He brought thousands upon thousands of people to God, he raised up all over Italy, indeed all over the world, centers of prayer and voluntary suffering; he re-established families and rectories and religious communities which had been eaten away by evil; he led to Christ scientists, artists and politicians; he gave a new outlook and a new spirit to hospitals by constructing one which he called, "the house where suffering is relieved."

That silence of his, so full of God and surrender of himself in the confessional, was his preaching and his apostolate. His was a silent witness, yet it was an immense influence. It is a powerful corrective to those who consider the apostolate to consist almost entirely in activities, in organizations, in material means, while they treat as of little value the interior life, prayer, humility, obedience and sacrifice. It is true that words, organizations, technical means, etc., are useful, but the essential element of every apostolate is the "bearing witness" which consists in possessing and radiating the Spirit of God. Jesus has said, "You will be witnesses to me unto the uttermost parts of the earth" (Act. 1: 8), as he bears witness to the Father (Tim. 1: 6-13), as the Holy Spirit was sent to bear witness to Christ (Jn. 15: 26). The apostolate today is too activist and this exposes the apostle to the danger of human vanity by withdrawing him from intimate and hidden communication with God. We must say with Charles de Foucauld what Padre Pio felt and showed: "We must proclaim the Gospel with our whole life."

Padre Pio lived the passion of Jesus Christ in his life, he expressed it in Holy Mass and poured it out on souls, renewing hearts and families and society. This is the secret, the mystery and the message of Padre Pio. Shall we answer his call? Shall we allow ourselves to be inspired and guided by him on the road to a profound Christian renewal? (Edited from *The Voice of Padre Pio*).

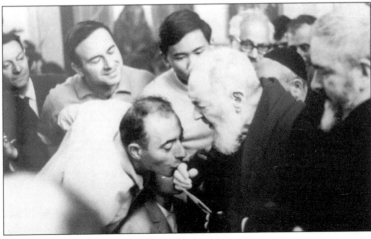

Pilgrims ever sought to kiss his gloved hands that hid the wounds of Christ in Padre Pio's stigmatized hands.

The portrait of the saintly face of Padre Pio was seen wherever one turned on the day of his beatification. It displays a gentleness and compassion that drew many souls back to God. At the same time there is strength and depth of character that inspires the trust of a child who is assured of this spiritual father's love.

Love of God

You must speak to Jesus also with the heart, besides the lips; indeed, in certain cases you must speak to him only with the heart.

Do not worry over things that generate preoccupation, derangement and anxiety. One thing only is necessary: to lift up your spirit and love God.

The heart of our Divine Master has no more amiable law than that of sweetness, humility, charity. Often place your confidence in Divine Providence and be assured that sooner heaven and earth shall pass away than that the Lord neglect to protect you.

Thank and sweetly kiss the hand of God that strikes you, because it is always the hand of a Father who strikes you because he loves you.

My past, O Lord, to your Mercy; my present, to your Love; my future, to your Providence!

God loves man with an infinite love and when he punishes he does so with reverence, almost fearing to hurt.

God can reject everything in a creature conceived in sin and which bears the indelible impression inherited from Adam. But he absolutely cannot reject the sincere desire to love him.

Have you not for some time loved the Lord? Do you not love him now? Do you not long to love him forever? Therefore, do not fear! Even conceded that you had committed all the sins of this world, Jesus repeats to you, "Many sins are forgiven thee because thou hast loved much!"   — *Padre Pio*

The Three Loves of Padre Pio

Padre Bernardino of Siena

Christ, the Church, and the Blessed Mother—these are Padre Pio's three great loves. Indeed, they are the three great loves of all the saints. These loves are intimately connected; they constitute one love reciprocally strengthening each other. Love for Christ, the source of life, spills over into the Church, His mystical body, and the Blessed Mother, the Mother of Jesus and the Mother of the Church.

To understand the power of these loves well, it is necessary to know their theological bases. Christ came into this world to carry out the divine plan, which is: God wants to call all men to salvation and unite them into a single family, the family of God. He wants to give his life to each one personally. "The Eternal Father," as the Apostolic Constitution *Lumen Gentium* of Vatican Council II states, "by a free and hidden plan of His own wisdom and goodness, created the whole world. His plan was to raise men to a participation in the divine life. Fallen in Adam, God the Father did not leave men to themselves, but ceaselessly offered helps to salvation, in view of Christ, the Redeemer, 'who is the image of the invisible God, the firstborn of every creature' ... The Son, therefore, came sent by the Father. It was in Him, before the foundation of the world, that the Father chose us and predestined us to become adopted sons, for in Him it pleased the Father to re-establish all things. To carry out the will of the Father, Christ inaugurated the Kingdom of heaven on earth and revealed to us the mystery of that kingdom. By His obedience He brought about redemption."

Christ's mission, therefore, is for men, for others. It is to establish God's family, the Church, to which he gives himself and the treasures of his love. But it is necessary for every man to have a personal encounter with Christ in order for this divine plan to be carried out, for divine life to be transmitted. During His earthly life Christ was able to come in contact with but a few thousand people in His homeland. But the divine plan is universal. Therefore, the encounter with Christ must come to all men for all times. This lengthening of Christ's life for all times is the Church which makes it possible for Christ to communicate personally with all men. Each member of that Church brings his particular gifts for the good of the whole Church. Padre Pio inserted himself in this divine plan of God in a most extraordinary way.

However, there was one human being who was given a preeminent role in God's divine plan, and that is the Blessed Virgin, Mother of God and Mother of the Church. She is the Mother of Christ the head of the Church and thus its members as well, as one can not separate head from body; they are one. As the Mother of the Son she is also the beloved daughter of the Father and the Spouse of the Holy Spirit. Because of this Triune relationship she far surpasses all creatures, both angels and men. We find in her, moreover, all the perfections the Church will have at the end of time. This is why she is justly honored by the Church with a special cult. With what strength and power of life and love Padre Pio inserted himself in this mystery of salvation! With his ardent love for the three we will better understand Padre Pio's various attitudes if we keep these truths in mind.

Padre Pio's intimate union with Christ is found in his giving of his entire life to Him, the ardent desire to re-enact not only a part of Christ's life but all of His life. For this Padre Pio bore sufferings of every kind: humiliations, calumnies of the worst type, terrible interior desolation, loss of blood, and his cruel crucifixion. The Holy Father Paul VI called him "Christ's representative, stamped with his stigmata."

Padre Pio's love for the Church and his brothers, to whom he gave everything—mind, heart, energy, time, prayers, and sufferings—was a burning anxiety to bring all to salvation and holiness, fulfilling the Divine Plan. Hence Padre Pio's love for the Pope, the bishops, and the priests who are given the threefold responsibility of teaching, governing and sanctifying. From this flowed his complete submission to lawful authority in the Church, his total, unquestioning obedience towards the hierarchy, even when its hand weighed heavily upon him.

The Blessed Mother, who is bound to Christ in the most intimate way as His mother, is present in the Church as its mother. Hence Padre Pio's attitude towards the Blessed Mother, his unconditional love for her who is his guide and help for his own sanctification and a sure way to bring men back to God. Others have spoken and will speak of Padre Pio's love for Christ, but this love is inseparable from the other two loves. Love of Christ is the measure of one's love for the Church and the Blessed Mother. Padre Pio is a man who believes in the mystery of the Church and who abandons himself to the love of the Blessed Mother, Mother of the Church. Indeed there is one light that envelops these two realities—it is motherhood. Padre Pio stretches out his two hands to the Church, his mother, and that of Our Lady, the Mother of the Church. Hanging on to their hands, he walks toward the mount of perfection. In this infallible way he cooperates in the building up of Christ's mystical body.

His Love of the Church

Padre Pio loved the Church because it contains the fullness of the mystery of salvation. When he heard the arrogant protests that have spread within and outside the Church causing a decline in the salvation of souls, he was bitterly afflicted. "Who makes them do it?" ... he asked. And he adds, almost in tears, "Thank heaven I am old, that I am near death." His last letter was one of loyal and filial devotion to the Apostolic See. Then he passed away in silence. Padre Pio loved the Church as the people of God. The individual members of the Church cannot remain closed in on themselves. They cannot be wrapped up in themselves. Each member must work for the salvation of others. He existed for the service of others. He felt responsible for the salvation of others to the extent that they would not be saved without him. The measure of his giving is Christ Himself, who gave everything for our salvation and sanctification.

Padre Pio imitated Him marvelously in this. His whole life was an ardent desire to save others. His life was a total gift for the salvation of his brothers. He gave his time, his prayers, his sufferings, all of his blood for this intention. His heart was like a volcano of love for God and neighbor. He wrote the following to Father Benedetto, his spiritual director: "I must confess first of all that for me it is a great misfortune not to be able to express and explain this great volcano in me which is always burning. Everything can be summed up in this way: I am devoured by the love of God and the love of my neighbor. God is always fixed in my mind and engraved on my heart. I never lose sight of him ... and then for my brothers ... Oh my! How many times, not to say always, I must say to God the judge like Moses: Either pardon this people or strike me out of the book of life." The fear of not being able to gain all his brothers for God threw him into great anguish. He writes:

"Poor me! I cannot find rest. I'm tired and I'm immersed in extreme bitterness, in the most desperate desolation, in the greatest anguish. This is not because I cannot find my God. It is because I cannot gain all my brothers for God. What should I do? I don't know. I suffer. I ask God to save them, but I don't know at all if God accepts my moans. Indeed I must add that sometimes I doubt that I am even in God's grace. And this very painful doubt is strengthened by the fear that I am in darkness as to whether the Lord accepts what I do to make up for others' miseries. It is also strengthened by my observing that my heart is always arid, disquieted, made anxious by seeing so many suffering souls without being able to help them.

"My God! My father, this state is truly unbearable, painful, desolating, and almost insupportable. At certain times, if the grace of God did not help me, I would be on the point of dying from a heart attack ... I am the most unhappy creature. Who will free me from this living death, from these two opposite extremes that tyrannize me and devour me?" He would like to die, but he wants to keep on living for the good of his brothers. "If I could only find a little relief, as I used to, in the one ardent desire to leave this exile and be united with Jesus. Today this relief has not been given to me. I am dizzily led to live for my brothers, and as a consequence to be inebriated and satiated by these sufferings which, at the same time, I lament irresistibly."

And again: "What can I tell you about my spirit? I am in extreme desolation. I am alone in bearing the weight of everyone. And the thought of not being able to give some spiritual relief to those that Jesus sends to me, the thought of seeing so many souls who want to justify their sins and thus spite the highest good, afflicts me, tortures me, makes me a martyr. It wears me out, wracks my brain and breaks my heart." Indeed, he would have given his life a thousand times for them. He wrote again: "I have worked. I want to work. I have prayed. I want to pray. I have stayed awake. I want to stay awake. I have cried. And I want to cry always for my brothers in exile. I know and I understand that this is very little, but I know how to do it. I am able to do this, and this is all that I am able to do."

On the fiftieth anniversary of his priesthood he said, "The only thing I desire is to love, to suffer another fifty years for my brothers, to burn for everyone with you, Lord, with you on the Cross!" He asked for help and prayers for souls, not for himself. He said, "Help me to suffer. Help me to save souls. Don't ask anything for me. But ask everything for souls so that they can be saved." This ardent desire to save souls was not merely a pious one, but it was a powerful force that pushed him to action. First of all, he consecrated himself as a victim for his brothers. He wrote to his spiritual father: "I come, my father, to ask you for permission. For a long time I have felt in myself the need to offer myself as a victim for poor sinners."

He considers such an offering a real mission from the Lord. He writes: "He chooses some souls, and among these, in spite of the fact that I do not deserve it, he has chosen my soul to help in the great negotiations for the salvation of many. And the more these victim souls suffer without receiving any comfort, the lighter become the sufferings of the good Jesus. This is the real reason why I want to suffer more and more without receiving any comfort and this is my whole joy."

And Jesus revealed to him again: "My son, I need victims to calm my Father's divine and just anger. Renew the sacrifice of your whole self to me and do it without reserve." And Padre Pio answers: "I have renewed the sacrifice of my life to Him, and if I feel in myself some sense of sadness, it is because I contemplate the God of sufferings ... If you can, my father, try to find souls who will offer themselves as victims for sinners. Jesus will help you." For Padre Pio, being a victim was not to be taken lightly. He wrote: "Jesus, his beloved Mother, and my angel together with others are encouraging me. They don't fail to repeat to me that a victim, to call himself such, must lose all of his blood. If I have at my side such a tender father, the battle is sweet and consoling" *(Epist., p. 315)*.

And again he writes to Father Agostino: "Didn't I tell you that Jesus wants me to suffer without receiving any comfort? Hasn't he perhaps requested me and elected me to be one of his victims? And the most sweet Jesus has unfortunately made me understand the full meaning of the word victim. It is necessary, my father, to reach the *consummatum est* of Calvary." And so his terrible sufferings of every kind—physical and moral, the interior torments, the macerations, the incessant prayers, the apostolate of the confessional, daily and fatiguing, poured and diffused an immense good into Christ's mystical body.

How many souls Padre Pio led to the path of sanctity! How many sinners and sheep he brought back to the fold of the Good Shepherd! An entire world of misery gravitated on Padre Pio, and it was an uninterrupted procession of thousands and thousands of people that he received. They besieged him in Church, in the confessional, and in the friary. They wanted to meet him in order to speak to him, to hear words of light and of comfort. And Padre Pio welcomed all of them paternally and fraternally. He listened, enlightened and spurred them on. He made everyone realize the merciful goodness of the Lord. If he was sometimes brusque, it was to shake souls out of their torpor and their sins.

And how much charity he showed to the poor, the sick! It is sufficient to think of the *Casa Sollievo della Sofferenza* (the House for the Relief of Suffering) that he wanted not so much for the relief of bodily suffering as for the spirit. Truly, Padre Pio's soul was a volcano of love and reparation for the salvation of the entire world. Padre Pio's love for the Church was authentic and efficacious. He was not selfish about grace. He knew how to share it, like leaven. He knew how to give it to others, to transplant it in others. Thus he participated in the building up of the mystical body of Christ in a wonderful way.

Love Expressed in Total Obedience

Padre Pio held firmly to the traditional hierarchical structure of the Church. For him the Pope was the gentle Christ on earth. Consequently he had the same attitude towards the Pope as towards Christ— a sincere love, with full and unconditional submission. He said, "For me, after Christ there is no one but the Pope!" It was a love that was a participation in the sufferings and anxieties of the Holy Father. In one letter, among others, to the Pope he writes: "I know that your heart is suffering very much these days ... I offer you my daily prayers and sufferings as a little, but sincere thought from the least of your children, so that God will comfort you with his grace. In this way you will be able to continue on the straight and fatiguing path. This way you will be able to keep on defending eternal truth, which does not change with the changing times."

Many times he was heard to repeat, "I would give my life a thousand times for the Pope and for the Church." One time, when professor Enrico Medi asked Padre Pio what he should say to the Pope (Paul VI), he answered, "That I immolate myself for him and that I always pray that the Lord will preserve him for his Church for a long time." One time when a preacher mentioned the souls that offer themselves as victims for the Pope, Padre Pio covered his eyes and wept for joy. His first prayer in the morning was for the Pope. In his cell he had three little holy pictures illuminated by a lamp: St. Michael the Archangel was on one side, the Blessed Mother in the middle, and on the other side Pope Paul VI. When he adjusted the lamp he wanted a ray of light to shine on the Pope's picture.

One day the chamberlain of his Holiness, Msgr. Paganuzzi, said to Carlo Campanini: "Carlo, when you see Padre Pio, tell him that His Holiness loves him very much." It was as if Padre Pio had been struck by lightning when he heard this, and two tears came out of his eyes. Then he said to Campanini, who had told him this: "You could not have given me a greater joy." His fidelity and obedience to the Pope were without reserve.

One day a friar was joking about the antipope, Clement Colin. He said, "So, Padre, we have two popes." And with this he showed Padre Pio a card with the portrait of the antipope. Padre Pio raised his eyes, and with a brusque movement tore up the card, spat on it, and threw it on the ground. He would not admit even the smallest joke about the Pope's authority, or about superiors in general. If sometimes he expressed doubts and fears about the present condition of the Church, these were about the danger of a progressive weakening of the principle of authority and a comfortable and elastic interpretation of obedience. He firmly believed in these two values.

The most sincere proof of his fidelity and of his love for the hierarchy stands out above all when obedience cost him much, in moments of sorrow caused by those whom he loved so much. To recall three events in Padre Pio's life which caused him great anguish: First, when he was told that it was decided that he must leave San Giovanni Rotondo. This is what Father Luigi of Avellino tells us about his behavior when he learned of this order:

"I showed Padre Pio the order and read it to him. I ordered him to be ready to carry out my wishes and that he would be sent to the Father Provincial of the Marches. Padre Pio bowed his head, and with his arms folded said to me, 'I am at your disposal. Let us leave at once, because when I am with my superior, I am with God.' Then I added, 'But would you come immediately with me? It is late at night. Where would we go?' Padre Pio answered, 'I don't know. I will come with you whenever and wherever you wish.' It was midnight."

A little later he wrote to the same superior: "I don't believe it is necessary to tell you how much I thank God that I am disposed to obey any order whatever that is given to me by my superior. Their voice is the voice of God for me. I wish to remain faithful to this voice until my death, and with the help of God, I will obey any command, no matter how painful it may be for me." Mayor Morcaldi, deeply moved, asked him, "And will you leave your people forever?" The mayor tells us, "Padre Pio opened his arms, and embracing each other we wept together. I said, 'And are you going tonight, with the police?' And Padre Pio answered me, serenely and with conviction, 'If I have the order to do so, I can do nothing but carry out the will of my superiors. I am a son of obedience.'"

His fidelity was shown for a second time when his priestly duties were curtailed. At first he was forbidden to say Mass at a set hour, with a preference to very early Mass in the morning and in private. He was forbidden to give his blessing to the people. He was forbidden to show the stigmata to anyone, to speak of it or let anyone kiss his hands. He was forbidden to have any further contact with his spiritual director, Father Benedetto of San Marco in Lamis. He was ordered not to answer the letters that were sent to him by devoted people asking for advice, graces, or other things. And as if this were not enough, his superior advised him that even more severe prohibitions and restrictions would be made by the Roman congregations. His superior said to him, "Prepare yourself to drink the bitter cup." Padre Pio, with perfect calm, said, "I hope that they don't make us wait too long, that they tell us soon what we must do." And then other restrictions followed immediately.

And Padre Pio? He bowed his head and obeyed, without saying a word in his own defense, without criticizing the orders he had received in any way. Thus he stopped communicating with his spiritual director, who had had such a great part in guiding the life of his soul. In the twenty years following, until Father Benedetto's death, Padre Pio never saw him, spoke to him or wrote to him. This separation threw him into the most absolute spiritual solitude. But he obeyed in silence. Contacts with other people also ceased. He thus remained a recluse for a long time, in his little cell and poor friary.

But the most important restriction was when he was suspended from every priestly duty for a period of two whole years (1931–1933). Truly we are profoundly moved and full of admiration when we learn how Padre Pio accepted this prohibition, the hardest and cruelest of his whole life. Let us listen to the same superior who was charged with telling him this. "I took courage, and after vespers, when Padre Pio had stayed as usual to pray in the choir, I called him to the parlor. He came immediately and I told him about the decree of the Holy Office. It forbade him to say Mass in public and to hear the confessions of religious and laity alike. He raised his eyes to heaven and said, 'May God's will be done!' Then he covered his eyes with his hands, bowed his head and said nothing more. I tried to comfort him, but he found comfort only in Jesus hanging on the Cross, because a little later he returned to the choir and stayed there until after midnight."

If we think only of how great Padre Pio's zeal was for the salvation of souls, we can measure the immense pain that this prohibition must have caused him. Some days later, the same Father Agostino, his spiritual director, came to San Giovanni Rotondo. He writes in his diary: "I found Padre Pio very low. As soon as we were in his cell together, he started to cry. I was deeply moved, but I was able to check my emotion, and I let him cry for a few minutes. Then we talked. The beloved Padre Pio told me that he felt this unexpected trial very deeply. I consoled him as best I could. I told him that he must obey completely ... 'You must continue to stay on the Cross. Men will keep on driving in the nails ... and everything will work for God's glory and the good of souls.' 'But it is precisely for souls that I feel the pain of this trial,' he told me. I answered: 'You will keep on praying and suffering for souls and Jesus will be able to save very many of them, even without your ministry, by accepting your sufferings.'"

During the two years of his trial Padre Pio didn't make the slightest complaint. He was always docile, humble, obedient, and patient with everyone. Those who tried to comfort him in some way never heard a complaint or the slightest criticism of authority. For him this was God's will. He would say, "The hand of the Church is gentle even when it strikes us because it is our mother's hand." And he bore his imprisonment, as he called it, with strength and faith. He recognized the will of God in it more and more. And he wanted to fulfill His Will and he did so willingly. Father Agostino tells us again: "Certainly, he suffers very much, because of his great love of souls. But he offers up his sufferings to Jesus. And he prays in his exile." And yet Padre Pio was accused of being disobedient!

When he was informed that his faculties had been restored to him, he accepted it with humility and gratitude towards the Holy Father. The Father Provincial had come to San Giovanni Rotondo to give him the good news. He made the announcement in the refectory in the presence of the religious community. "Padre Pio can say Mass in church and hear the confessions of religious." Padre Pio got up, went to kneel at the feet of the Provincial. He kissed his hand and thanked the Holy Father for his fatherly goodness.

Padre Pio was very severe with those who attacked authority because they felt unjust restrictions had been placed on him. Doctor Festa, in his book, *Mysteries of Science and the Light of Faith*, had written irreverent words about the Father General and accused him of not having taken Padre Pio's defense. Padre Pio wrote Dr. Festa a letter in which he begged him to leave out these words and even threatening him with divine punishments. The mayor of San Giovanni Rotondo also learned something about this persecution and had prepared a white paper which he intended to have printed in defense of Padre Pio. But when Padre Pio read it, he took the author by his neck and shouted at him in one of his outbursts of sacred fury: "Satan, go and throw yourself at the feet of the Church instead of writing this foolishness. Don't oppose your mother."

Padre Pio did not protest or dissent, which is so much in fashion today. He did not judge his superiors' actions. He bowed his head and obeyed. Prohibitions might rain down on him, but Padre Pio went on with life as usual. He was calm and obedient at the slightest hint of a superior's will. He did not criticize the innovation forced on his usual way of living. His usual smile was always on his lips. He was cordial to everyone, as always. Only when they told him to celebrate Mass in the space of a half hour did he answer, "God knows how much I would like to be able to say Mass like the other priests, but I can't do it."

Padre Pio had special charisms for the salvation of souls but he wanted these to be always subject to the control of ecclesiastical authority, leaving every decision to God. Who knows how many graces his obedience bore, in other ways, for the good of souls? He had a special veneration for his superiors for he saw Christ in them. If he had his hood up or even a scarf over his head and he met a superior, he always took it off. If a superior came into his cell, he would stand up. Later in life when he could no longer stand up because of his poor health, he made humble excuses.

He wrote to his superior: "I work only to obey you because God let me know that this is the one thing most pleasing to Him. And for me it is a means of hoping for salvation and singing victory ... Obedience is everything for me ... God forbid that I should knowingly go against him who has been designated as my interior and exterior judge even in the slightest way."

Up until a couple of years before his death, every evening before going to bed he went to his superior, uncovered his head, and with his hands joined, bowed and asked for his blessing. He kissed his hand, then embraced him and went to his cell. One of his superiors tells us: "The first evening he wanted to kiss my hand, I refused and said that someone my age could not let someone his age do that. Padre Pio said, 'But no, you are my superior.' I didn't want to give in, so he said, 'Then let us embrace each other.' And it was the same every evening." Another of his superiors tells us: "It was enough for him to have guessed the superior's intention and he immediately came to him and put himself at his disposition."

When the superior was unwilling to give an order, Padre Pio would say, "Father, let me know what I should do; I am ready for anything." He asked permission even for the littlest thing. One day his superior said to Padre Pio jokingly: "You, who are obedient, must not die without permission from your superior." And Padre Pio said, "All right." And at the times when he yearned for heaven most, when he met his superior he reminded him, "Father Superior, when will you give me this permission to go to heaven?"

This was Padre Pio's heroic obedience toward God's representatives in the Church.

Padre Pio and the Blessed Mother

Padre Pio's attitude toward the Blessed Mother was not only devotional; he saw in the Blessed Mother the way that led to Christ and the surest way to bring Christ to his brothers. He saw the Blessed Mother in the light of God's saving plan. He felt himself intimately united with Christ in this vision. He wrote to Father Agostino: "This most tender Mother, in her great knowledge, mercy, and goodness, has desired to punish me by pouring into my heart so many graces that when I find myself in her presence and that of Jesus, I am obliged to exclaim, 'Where am I, where am I? Who is near me?' I feel myself burning all over, but there is no fire. I feel close to Jesus and bound to him by means of this Mother. But I don't even see the chains that hold me so tightly. A thousand flames consume me. I feel as if I am continually dying, and yet I am still alive. ... "

The Blessed Mother introduced him to the mystery of the Cross. He wrote to Father Agostino: "May the Sorrowful Virgin obtain for us from her most holy Son the grace to penetrate the mystery of the Cross more and more and to inebriate ourselves with her on Jesus' sufferings. ... May she obtain for us love for the Cross, suffering, and sorrow for sin. And may she who was the first to practice the Gospel teachings in all its perfection, in all its severity, even before it was made known, obtain for us also the desire to go to her immediately. ... Let us always stay close to such a dear Mother. Let us go outside Jerusalem with her, beside Jesus to Calvary."

She helped him enter ever more deeply into the mystery of the Eucharist. Padre Pio wrote: "My poor little mother. How much she loves me. I realized it again at the beginning of this beautiful month of May. With how much care she accompanied me to the altar this morning! It seemed to me that she didn't have anything else to think about but me alone." By following this way Padre Pio yearns for transformation into Christ. "May the Mother of Jesus and our Mother obtain for us from her Son the grace to live a life entirely after God's heart, a totally interior life and one that is entirely hidden in Him. May this dear mother unite us to Jesus so closely that we will never let ourselves be taken up or fascinated by anything in this world. May she keep us always close to that infi-

What can we say about the many Rosaries said by Padre Pio? They called him the living rosary. He always kept it in his hand. For him the Rosary represented the continual meditation on the profound mysteries of God's plans for eternal salvation.

nite loveableness which is Jesus. And only then will we be able to say with St. Paul that we are sons of God amidst a depraved and corrupt nation."

It is just because of this that he puts his eternal salvation into Mary's hands. Through her motherly protection he is able to repulse all the devil's attacks. "The strength of Satan, who is fighting me, is terrible, but God be praised, because He has put the problem of my health and a victorious outcome into the hands of our heavenly Mother. Protected and guided by such a tender mother, I will keep on fighting as long as God wishes. I am safe and so full of confidence in this mother that I will never succumb. How distant the hope of victory is when seen from earth, our land of exile. Instead, how close and sure it is when seen from the house of God, under the protection of the most holy Mother."

And how grateful Padre Pio was for this protection! He wrote to Father Benedetto: "My Father, I am sorry only because I don't have sufficient means to be able to thank our beautiful Virgin Mary, through whose intercession I don't doubt at all to have received such strength from the Lord. Thus I can bear, with sincere resignation, the many mortifications to which I am subjected day after day." He is convinced that he can bring souls to Jesus more certainly through Mary. He invites everyone to love the Blessed Mother. He writes to Father Agostino: "I would like to have such a strong voice as to incite the sinners of the entire world to love the Blessed Mother. But since this is not in my power, I have prayed and I will keep on praying to my little guardian angel to do this favor for me."

The day before his death some people asked him, "Say something to us, Father." He replied, "Love the Blessed Mother and make her loved. Always say the Rosary." How much Padre Pio loved the Blessed Mother! One of his followers described it like this: "I always have engraved on my heart his figure as it appeared to me in my boyhood years. How beautiful it was to see him in the silence of his cell when we young seminarians went to confession to him! A dim light gave a mystical tone to his emaciated but radiant face. He had in front of him a photograph of his mother, who had died a short time before, and a little statue of the Blessed Mother. He talked to us about her and taught us to love her. Walking along the central path of the friary garden he was absorbed in prayer, as he ran the beads through his wounded hands. How warm his voice was, when he recited the Angelus together with the others in the garden, in the choir and at his window! Who is there who did not feel his heart melt when he saw him walk shakily to the altar for the evening service and in a voice broken by tears, recite the prayer on the, 'Visit to the most holy Mary.'

When he spoke about his heavenly mother, as he called her, he could hardly ever contain his emotion. When he recited the "Visit to the most holy Mary," he often could not keep back the tears and the emotion in the tone of his voice. And sometimes he was seized by such violent sobbing that he could not continue the recitation of the prayer. Every time he passed in front of the picture of the Virgin which was at the foot of the stairs that led to the sacristy, Padre Pio would stop there for several minutes, in contemplation and prayer.

In the evening, before falling asleep, he wanted the superior or one of those present to begin the Ave Maria. He and the others responded to it. Then followed the invocation, "Mother of Divine Grace, pray for us." He stared at the large picture of the Blessed Mother that hung on the wall at the foot of his bed. And only then would he close his eyes and go to sleep. When he was forced to go to bed because of peripheral circulatory disturbances in the brain, he confided to his superior, "What made me suffer more than anything was not being able to say even only one Ave Maria."

What can we say about the many Rosaries said by Padre Pio? They called him the living rosary. He always kept it in his hand. One day his superior asked him how many Rosaries he had said that day. And Padre Pio answered, "Well, I must tell the truth to my superior. I said thirty-four." For him the Rosary represented the continual meditation on the profound mysteries of God's plans for eternal salvation. This had been carried out by Jesus on Calvary in the presence of his sorrowing Mother.

Padre Pio felt a fascination for the Ave Maria! One witness says: "We always saw him with his rosary in his hand, in the friary, in the halls, on the stairs, in the sacristy, in Church, even in the brief interval when going to and coming from the confessional. A follower asked him, 'Teach me a prayer that is most pleasing to the Blessed Mother.' And Padre Pio without hesitation answered him, 'And is there one more beautiful or more pleasing than the one she taught us herself? More beautiful than the Rosary? Always say the Rosary.' He would say, 'The Rosary is a weapon in our hands.' One evening before going to bed, he realized he had forgotten his rosary. He asked one of his brothers, 'Go get my weapon.' The brother did not understand, so he added, 'The rosary, that is my weapon.'" Another witness adds, "Near the end of his life he didn't talk much. We told him our thoughts, we asked him for help but all he did was to show us the rosary, always the rosary."

Padre Pio never allowed Mary's privileges to be questioned. One day he heard certain errors being talked about—errors that were rearing their ugly heads in theological schools and reviews in regard to the Blessed Mother's perpetual virginity and the correct interpretation of the Annunciation. Padre Pio asked the Father Superior to excuse him, as he said: "I'm going away because it upsets me very much to hear such things."

Editor's note: The author relates here the touching story of the Fatima Pilgrim Virgin's visit to San Giovanni Rotondo and how the priest, who was extremely sick at the time managed to venerate the statue. After the visit when the helicopter took off, he complained to his mother, "My mother, you came to Italy and I was ill. Now you are going away and leaving me sick!" No sooner had he made his complaint known, than he felt a shudder throughout his body and was immediately cured (for a more detailed account see pages 90-91). When he was asked later on why the blessed Mother came to San Giovanni Rotondo rather than the larger, more prestigious nearby city of Foggia, he answered in all simplicity, "The Madonna came here because she wanted to cure Padre Pio." Padre Bernardino concludes his talk:

Christ, the Church, the Blessed Mother—Padre Pio loved them immensely, totally. He gave them everything, without reserve. And when he came to die he would say, "I can't stand it anymore." He fell at the foot of the altar after his last Mass. Oh Padre Pio's Mass! It made us feel and relive Jesus' Passion. Padre Pio died tightly hanging on to the rosary, murmuring the names of Jesus and Mary.

The message that Padre Pio gives today's world, which is in a crisis of faith, is very much alive. He indicates the obligatory way of rebirth—the Church as Mother and the Mother of the Church. He reveals to us the drama of the Church and exhorts everyone to pray for its mission of salvation. He wrote: "I will not hide from you the pain that my heart feels at seeing so many souls that are leaving Jesus, ... that these souls are going away from God, the source of the living water. The harvest is great, but the laborers are few. Who will gather the harvest in the field of the Church? Will it perhaps be dispersed on the ground because there are so few laborers? Will it be gathered by the messengers of Satan? There are unfortunately very many of these, and they are very active. Oh! May God never permit this! ... Let us pray for the cause of the Holy Church, our most tender Mother."

He encourages all men to walk behind the Mother of the Church. He writes, "May the most Holy Virgin ... who was the first to practice the Gospel teaching in all its perfection give us the impetus from herself to go to her immediately ... Let us make an effort ... to always follow behind the Blessed Mother, to always walk close to her, because there is no other road that leads to life."

The chapters from pages 55 to 70 are an edited and slightly condensed version of a talk by Fr. Bernardino of Siena who was the Postulator General of Capuchin Friars Minor. It was given at the First Congress of Studies on Padre Pio's Spirituality at San Giovanni Rotondo, May 1 to 6, 1972.

A panoramic view of the small town of Pietrelcina where Padre Pio was born and spent his early childhood and some years on sick leave from the monastery. Like Assisi made famous by St. Francis so too this picturesque town has been made famous by its native son. Padre Pio. He uttered these prophetic words: "During my life I have cherished San Giovanni Rotondo. After my death I will cherish and favor Pietrelcina."

His Heroic Practice of the Virtue of Obedience

A striking example of the heroic degree to which he practised this virtue has come to us from the pen of Dr. Giorgio Festa. The event to which this doctor refers took place in 1925 when he returned to San Giovanni Rotondo for a friendly visit. On this occasion Padre Pio told him that he had been suffering from severe abdominal pains for some time and asked the doctor to examine him. Dr. Festa discovered a serious inguinal hernia on the right side and told Padre Pio that an operation was necessary. The patient agreed, but as he was not allowed to leave the friary it was decided to equip a room there, while the doctor sent at once to Rome for everything required for the operation, which took place on October 5, 1925. It was only when he entered the improvised operating theatre that Padre Pio told the doctors they were to use no anesthetic, while he assured them that he would remain perfectly still under their instruments.

It must be remembered that the Holy Office, for prudential reasons, had placed him under obedience not to allow anyone to see the stigmata, while he himself was aware how anxious Dr. Festa was to see them again after a lapse of five years. Padre Pio had continued to obey this injunction to the letter, and in the present circumstances, rather than disregard an order from Rome, he preferred to endure agonizing pain for more than an hour on the operating table. As the ordeal continued he uttered no complaint, but was heard to murmur: "Oh Jesus, forgive me if I don't know how to suffer as I ought." Just as the doctors ended their work, he lapsed into unconsciousness and Dr. Festa was unable to resist the temptation to look at the five wounds. He reports that he found them just as they were five years before, although this time the heart wound appeared quite fresh. On this occasion Padre Pio had practiced obedience at the cost of atrocious suffering.

AGAINST TEMPTATION

Do not fear. Jesus is more powerful than all hell. At the invocation of his name every knee in heaven, on earth and in hell must bend before Jesus; this is a consolation for the good and terror for evil.

Remember that it is not the feeling of guilt that constitutes sin but the consent to sin. Only the free will is capable of good or evil. But when the will sighs under the trial of the tempter and does not will what is presented to it, there is not only no fault but there is virtue.

Let the world turn topsy turvy, everything be in darkness and Mount Sinai all aflame, covered with lightning, thunder—God is with you. But if God lives in the darkness and Mount Sinai is all aflame, covered with lightning, thunder, and noise, will we not be safe near him? — *Padre Pio*

A Model Friar

Mary Ingoldsby

Padre Pio has received wide publicity throughout the world by reason of the extraordinary aspects of his long life: bleeding stigmata, bilocation, ability to discern the exact state of conscience of those who sought his counsel even for the first time. However, if it is God's will to propose him to the world as a model of Christian life, it will not be for these exceptional charisms' which in themselves do not prove a man's virtue. Rather will it be for his perfect observance of the Capuchin rule, for the high degree of virtue he showed at all stages of his religious life, his unequalled charity towards his confreres, his outstanding spirit of humility, his prompt obedience to authority at all levels.

Francis Forgione entered religion a full sixty years before the Second Vatican Council opened its doors, but it is interesting to observe how fully his life corresponded to what the council Fathers laid down in the Decree on the Renewal of Religious Life, *Perfectae Caritati* (P.C.). During these post-conciliar years most religious congregations have endeavored to apply this decree to their community life. In most cases the emphasis has been placed on aggiornamento and efforts have been made to update the pattern of religious life by introducing what are sometimes drastic changes. An attentive reading of the decree itself shows how carefully its authors seek to safeguard the fundamental values of religious life. Before speaking of "appropriate changes and renewal" they point out that "all those who are called by God to the practice of the evangelical counsels ... bind themselves to the Lord in a special way" (P.C. 1) and that "since the final norm of religious life is the following of Christ as it is put before us in the Gospel" (P.C. 2), religious "should follow him, regarding this as the one thing necessary" and "be solicitous for all that is his" (P.C. 3).

Nobody can deny that Padre Pio regarded this as "the one thing necessary"; his solicitude "for all that is his" was so thorough that it led him quite soon to deep union with Christ and to a spiritual state which places him on a par with the greatest mystics the Church has known. His vocation was evident while he was still very young, when he distinguished himself among his companions by attendance at daily Mass and his devout demeanor as a Mass server. Admitted to the Capuchin novitiate at fifteen, he soon became an exemplary novice. His superiors and companions are unanimous in testifying to his holy life at this stage, although there were no external signs to presage the remarkable future in store for him. Endless examples might be quoted to illustrate his exact observance of his rule during novitiate and student days.

The conciliar decree already quoted attaches great importance to obedience, which is the acid test of a good religious. "Moved by the Holy Spirit, they (religious) subject themselves in faith to those who hold God's place, their superiors" (P.C. 14). All those who lived in community with Padre Pio express their admiration for his constant and exemplary obedience which was sometimes tried to an extreme degree. Padre Pellegrino, who lived close to him during the last decade of his life and assisted him in his final hours, has many anecdotes to relate in this regard. He points out that obedience was not easy for one of Padre Pio's temperament, to one so strong-willed and of such keen intelligence. His conception of obedience was profound and completely supernatural. "The more useless the order I receive, the more willingly I obey," he confided to Padre Pellegrino on one occasion.

His letters to his superiors during the period of enforced absence from his community bear eloquent witness to his spirit of obedience. "I am acting out of pure obedience to you, for the good God has shown me clearly that this is the only thing acceptable to him and the one hope of salvation for me ... Obedience is everything to me ... God forbid that I should deliberately disobey even to the slightest degree the one who has been appointed to judge my exterior and interior acts" (August 26, 1916). During his whole life Padre Pio did everything under the banner of obedience. Misunderstandings arose and he sometimes received a sharp letter of rebuke. Although he was distressed by what was undeserved reproof, his spirit of obedience never wavered and his immediate reply to his superior revealed unconditional and humble submission.

His observance of poverty was no less remarkable. While living outside his community he was most attentive to his vow and his superiors had to question him continually to discover his material needs. When his doctors prescribed expensive injections he wanted to do without them. In March 1916 he wrote to his superior:

"You already know that according to the doctor's prescription I have to have an injection every day. I want you to know that if these injections are to be continued they will prove very expensive. My heart bleeds to have so much money spent on me by our poor communities. Would it not be lawful to do without these things? Is a poor man to be blamed when for lack of means, obliged by his poverty, he refuses such treatment? And if this is lawful, why should it not be lawful for me when, after all, I am by chosen profession poorer than anyone who is poor by necessity?"

In later life when his fame as a director of souls was drawing immense crowds to his friary, when money and gifts poured in for his charitable works, he showed utter detachment from such things. A poor old woman who wanted to donate something and had nothing but a box of matches, pressed this into Padre Pio's hands. He was more profuse in his thanks for this gift than for a substantial check received the same day from a rich benefactor. When the project for the large hospital near the friary was on the way to realization, Pope Pius XII dispensed Padre Pio from his vow of poverty so that he might receive and manage the funds which were flowing in from all parts. In the late fifties, when the hospital opened its doors, it would have been lawful for him to live there, availing himself of the papal dispensation. But while he followed carefully the work and development of the hospital, he continued to live in strictest poverty in his austere Capuchin friary close by.

Later in life, one benefactor seeing how he suffered from the heat, which can sometimes be oppressive even in San Giovanni Rotondo at nearly 2000 feet above sea level, a man who had benefited by his spiritual counsel sent an air conditioner to be installed in his cell. The Superior got the workmen going on it at once while Padre Pio was busy elsewhere. When he returned to his cell and discovered what they were doing he begged them not to go on. "What will our Seraphic Father say?" he groaned. To him that air conditioner was an offense against the poverty so greatly esteemed by St. Francis.

He held the vow of chastity in such high esteem that as well as being strictly observant himself in this respect, he frequently recommended this vow to people who were seeking perfection in the world. A number of men and women still living in San Giovanni Rotondo pronounced the vow of chastity under his direction and continue to observe it. His spirit of mortification distinguished him even as a student. All those who lived with him in the friary at San Giovanni Rotondo where he spent the greater part of his life can testify to the manner in which he mortified his body at all times. The bleeding stigmata were a source of continual and often excruciating pain, but he hungered for further suffering. When Dr. Festa first examined him in 1919 he also reported on his way of life:

"He takes very little nourishment. A small plate of green vegetables between 1 p.m. and 2 p.m. and three or four sardines at suppertime are usually all the food he takes. Even then, his stomach often refuses to retain what he has eaten. He drinks neither milk nor wine but just a little weak coffee. When possible he willingly takes a small drink of beer along with his meal. Although his physical strength is greatly reduced on this account, the same cannot be said of his spiritual energy and strength of will, which are just wonderful. He is capable of devoting long hours to confessions and conversations with his visitors and, as he told me himself on several occasions, he hears confessions for eighteen hours at a time."

As regards his frugal nourishment, Padre Giovanni (whom we quote in the following chapter) reports: "After community prayers we went to supper, but Padre Pio remained in the church to pray. He never took breakfast or supper. Only at the midday meal did he eat anything, perhaps a fifth of the amount eaten by a normal man." This was prior to 1946. A young American friar who entered the community in the sixties and assisted him daily for the last three years of his life had occasion to observe his virtue. One of "Brother Bill's" duties was to carry a tray to him in his cell. At that time a Milanese doctor named Milillo used to come over frequently from the hospital to the friary to see Padre Pio. On one occasion as the Brother carried away the tray of food almost untouched, Dr. Milillo remarked that "a one-year-old couldn't live on what he eats." The American friar himself tells us that he never saw Padre Pio finish any food brought to him.

(© *Padre Pio: His Life and Mission,* by Mary Ingoldsby, first published by Veritas Publications).

RESIGNATION TO GOD'S WILL

Walk in the way of the Lord with simplicity and do not torment your spirit. You must hate your defects but with a quiet hate, not troublesome and restless.

Lean on the Cross of Jesus as the Virgin did and you will not be deprived of comfort. Mary was as if paralyzed before her crucified Son, but one cannot say that she was abandoned by him. Rather how much more did she not love him when she suffered and could not even weep?

You should rather humble yourself before God than be distressed if he reserves for you the sufferings of his Son, and makes you experience your weakness. You should offer up to him the prayer of resignation and hope, even when you fall through frailty, and thank him for all the benefits with which he continually enriches you.

When you are exposed to any trial, be it physical or moral, bodily or spiritual, the best remedy is the thought of him who is our life, and not think of the one without joining to it the thought of the other. — *Padre Pio*

Part III

Padre Pio's Encounters with Devils

At a time when modern man is becoming more and more obsessed with, and at times possessed by the devil and those dark arts that lead to devil worship, Padre Pio comes on the scene to show men by his own personal encounters with the devil just how impotent the devil really is. He compares the devil to a fierce dog tied to a chain. "Beyond the length of the chain he cannot seize anyone. But, if you approach within the radius of the chain, you let yourself be caught. Remember that the devil has only one door by which to enter—the will. There are no secret or hidden doors."

Though the devil found it impossible to enter the heavily barricaded door of Padre Pio's soul, he tried just the same to intimidate the saintly priest in frightening ways. God occasionally allows this in certain saintly souls for the greater merit they will acquire, and to humiliate the devil who is invariably defeated. When he was but five years old, Francis (his baptismal name) began to experience diabolic apparitions which assumed obscenely human, or more frequently beast-like forms. Don Nicola Caruso, the young priest who taught him mathematics at this time, recalled how the young boy once told him of frightening experiences he had had occasionally on returning home from school. "He would find blocking his doorway a man dressed like a priest," Don Nicola relates, "who would not let him enter. As Francesco would pause, not knowing what to do, a barefoot child would approach and make the sign of the cross. Immediately the 'priest' would disappear, thus enabling Francesco to enter his house."

This incident shows that though God may allow the devil to tempt or frighten his chosen souls in extraordinary ways, he is ever at their side with divine assistance. Our Lord gave the devil crushing defeats at the hands of Padre Pio. In this battle between Satan and the humble Franciscan friar the stakes were high. As time went on the struggle would become more and more intense, the temptations stronger and more subtle. God would even allow the devil to physically manhandle him. But in his role as victim for the salvation of souls, the more he suffered the more effective he was in snatching souls away from the domination of Satan and opening them up to the saving grace of Christ.

Fr. Augustine McGregor, O.C.S.O., in the *Voice of Padre Pio* magazine in his masterful article, "The Adversary," describes the many onslaughts the devil used against the young religious:

"Now with his entry into Religious life there is an intensification of diabolical fury. Hell unleashes the whole of its malice on the young friar, venting its rage in any number of different ways: terrifying visions, assaults camouflaged under bodily appearances. The enemy comes in many guises, even under the appearance of an 'angel of light.' In one period he plays on the still unpurified senses by lewd, obscene and impure visions and suggestions and in general acts externally; later, in another period when the soul is more purified, while the first diabolical manifestations do not entirely disappear Satan now directs his assaults to the superior part of the soul—the intellect and will—striving with all his might to impede the young friar in the exercise of the theological virtues and his growth in divine love ... .

"By the time Padre Pio was ordained Satan obviously was fully aware of the work which Divine Providence intended to effect through him, and by particularly malicious solicitations sought by every means the young priest's downfall. Padre Agostino records how the devil employed his superior faculties to tempt Padre Pio. Using the triple concupiscence (1 Jn. 2: 16; 5: 19) and man's own corrupt nature the devil came at Padre Pio in the first place by a series of attacks on the senses: animals, black and filthy; naked females dancing lasciviously; sometimes without any apparitions, there would be such tricks as filthy spitting into his face or he would be tormented with deafening noises; at other times, he received beatings from a "cruel man" (carnefice). Under the guise of good the devil appeared even as the Crucified and often came in the form of his Spiritual Father or Father Provincial. He also appeared to him in the form of saints such as St. Pius X and St. Francis and even as our Lady and in the form of his Guardian Angel."

On one occasion the devil appeared in the likeness of his spiritual director Father Agostino, a Capuchin priest who lived some distance from the friary where he was stationed. The false friar advised him to give up his penitential life, for God did not approve of it. Surprised at such advice, Padre Pio had the presence of mind to ask the "friar" to repeat after him, "Blessed Be Jesus!" The devil left at once in a cloud of smoke, leaving behind a sulphurous smell.

His intense struggle to overcome the devil in those early years can be understood better from his own words:

"The struggle with hell," wrote Padre Pio in 1915, "has reached the point in which it is no longer possible to go on. The ship of my soul is about to be overwhelmed by the ocean waves ... I feel crushed by the infernal forces and I am afraid of being reduced to nothing from one minute to the next." Or again: "Many times the darkness which assails me is such as to make me doubt, or else, I find it difficult to discern that which is good from that which is not good." Often in Padre Pio's letters there is the recurring confession of "anguish" caused by repeated diabolical assaults: " ... also in the hours of rest the devil does not refrain from afflicting my soul in different ways."

" ... the enemy of our health is so irate that he does not leave me one peaceful moment, waging war in various ways. ... In these days the devil is really at me in every possible way and keeps at it as much as he can. The 'miserable one' will redouble his efforts to harm me." In another period when Satan was trying to gain entry to the superior part of his soul the very effort to make an act of faith he found almost impossible: "The devil roars and shouts continuously around my poor will, which does and says nothing else with firm resolution than: 'Long live Jesus ... I believe.' But who could tell you how I pronounce these words? With timidity, without strength and without courage, and I must do myself violence."

In the monthly bulletin, *I Fratini* of the Capuchins in Foggia, a former seminary student who had Padre Pio as his Spiritual director and confessor, writes about how the devil manhandled the sickly friar. One night he and his fellow students heard the frightening noise of iron bars banging together in Padre Pio's room, as well as a sound like a train traveling at high speed through a tunnel. In the morning they found their director worn out from his ordeal with the devil. The iron bars that held his curtain were twisted by hands of enormous strength. Padre Pio was in no condition to talk about what happened at the moment, but a few days later he related how the devil had beaten him because he could not bring about a sin of impurity in one of the fratini due to the prayers of Padre Pio.

Numerous were the cases of physical assault by the devil on Padre Pio throughout his long life. Even as late as 1964 Padre Pio was so bruised from an attack of the devil that he could not say Mass. On occasion the visible black and blue marks remained for weeks. Such cases of physical assault by the devil are nothing new in the lives of the saints. St. Catherine of Siena, St. Teresa of Avila, St. Nicholas of Tolentino and in more recent times the holy Curé of Ars, all experienced the same fury of the evil one.

To our very scientific age where everything has to be proven in a controlled laboratory setting in order to be considered credible, these constant direct interventions of the devil in the life of Padre Pio may seem simply impossible to take seriously. For who of us has seen or who knows of anyone who has seen the devil? Yet, we have the above evidence in a man who practiced the Christian virtues in a heroic degree, was very human, had a keen sense of humor and displayed none of the tell-tale signs of a neurotic. Then too, we have the evidence of the many miracles he performed. With eyes of faith, we need but open the Bible and especially the New Testament to understand the reality of the devil in our Lord's time.

There are some today who deny a personal devil, and who look upon the great evil we see on all sides as a result of ignorance and defective educational and political structures. But this view does not square with the Gospel accounts. One of the most noticeable features of the Gospels is the continuous conflict between Christ and the "adversary," as the devil is called in the Scriptures. We have the account of Christ's temptation in the desert, the many accounts of Christ's power over the devil in driving him out of possessed souls, and the numerous times he speaks of the battle between the "Prince of this world," or the "powers of darkness," and how Satan and his followers will eventually be totally defeated and cast into hell forever.

While modernist theologians reinterpret Scripture to fit their own fancy, that Satan is just a poetic symbol for the current concept of evil, the Church is ever ready to reaffirm his existence. The existence of pure spirits has ever been taught by the Church, in her Council decrees and by many Popes in the long history of the Church. Pope Paul VI attributed the confusion and hostilities that arose after Vatican II to the work of "something preternatural that has come into the world for the very purpose of destroying the fruits of the Council ... ." In November 1972 he dealt at some length with the subject of the devil at a general audience, and again affirmed the devil's real existence as he had done implicitly five years before, in his famous "Credo of the People of God."

The Church does not base its doctrine on the devil upon such awesome instances as we find in the life of Padre Pio. On the contrary, Padre Pio's experiences are explained and rendered intelligible by the Church's doctrine. The ordinary Christian would be foolish indeed to ignore the testimony of Padre Pio's experience with the evil one. It is a powerful and existential dramatization of the traditional Catholic teaching that the devil is indeed working through our imagination and senses to bring about our downfall. Though he is clever and a master of deceit, he can never directly move a person's intellect or will. He is relentless in his attempts to destroy the Church and human souls, but our victory is sure if we follow the example of the stigmatic Franciscan of Pietrelcina.

Padre Pio speaks to us today by his life and his words. "Temptations, discouragement and unrest are the wares offered by the enemy. Remember this: if the devil makes noise it is a sign that he is still outside and not yet within. That which must terrify us is his peace and concord with the human soul." And again, "The field of battle between God and Satan is the human soul. ... The soul must give free access to the Lord so that it be fortified by him in every respect and with all kinds of weapons: that his light may enlighten it to combat the darkness of error; that it be clothed with Jesus Christ, with his justice, truth, the shield of faith, the word of God, in order to conquer such powerful enemies. To be clothed with Jesus Christ it is necessary to die to oneself. ... The Cross is the standard of the elect. Let us always keep close to it and we will succeed in conquering in everything and over everyone."

Padre Pio never saw this beautiful "Way of the Cross" which was dedicated on May 25, 1971. Sculptured in bronze by the renowned artist Francesco Messina, he has Padre Pio in the fifth station helping Jesus carry the cross, which indeed he did throughout his life.

His Guardian Angel to the Rescue

"Angels are out, devils are in," seems to be the norm in our contemporary society's assessment of the spirit world. As inordinate interest in occultism increases, the devotion to the good angels and their possible influence in our lives decreases. Even those who are hesitant in accepting the existence of spiritual beings, without bodies, admit the possibility of the existence of devils more readily than good angels. The preternatural havoc caused by evil spirits is all around us, while the ministering of the good angels is less apparent. Why is this so? They have been forgotten and left unsolicited. It was not always so, and certainly not with Padre Pio.

If it is true that he experienced the full fury of Satan and his accomplices, he also had the consolation of being on intimate terms with St. Michael the Archangel, the good angels and in particular his Guardian Angel. Towards the end of his life he frequently spoke with affection of his Guardian Angel as "the companion of my infancy." This was no exaggeration, but the truth. His Guardian Angel was a very real person in whom he confided and whose help he sought in time of need.

There are countless recorded incidents in which angels took an active part in his life. When he was still a boy, his Guardian Angel appeared to him in the semblance of another child. This Guardian Angel was not only the companion of his childhood, but helped him in the year of his novitiate, with his studies and in preparation for the priesthood. He led him on the way of extraordinary holiness, and was near him during the assaults of the devils. One of the most interesting tasks that Padre Pio gave his angel was to help him read languages he had not studied. Padre Agostino, his confessor, tested Padre Pio in this regard by writing to him in Greek and French. Padre Pio did not understand either language and upon being questioned on how he was able to read the letters so well he candidly replied: "You know, my Guardian Angel explains everything to me."

Both inside and outside the confessional, he was ever encouraging people to have devotion to the angels. In bidding farewell to pilgrims he would use such phrases as, "May the angels of God accompany you."

"May the angel of God open closed doors for you."

"May the angel of God be for you light, help, strength, comfort, and guidance."

To some of his penitents in great need he would tell them to send their Guardian Angels to him. One friend lamented the great distance which would separate him from the Padre when he had to make a very difficult decision. Padre Pio's simple solution was to have the gentleman send his Guardian Angel to him. "But Padre," he asked, "do you listen to him?" Padre's short reply to one who questioned the possibility of communicating with the angels, "And do you think 1 am deaf?" No doubt anyone of us could have made the same innocent query and wonder at Padre Pio's rather curt rebuke.

Padre Pio could readily see the angels at work in the lives of others too. There is the case of the lawyer, Attilio De Sanctis of Fano, Italy. He had the mystifying experience of falling fast asleep at the wheel of his car and had traveled twenty-seven miles without running off the road or hitting any oncoming cars. He visited Padre Pio soon after and inquired to what he could attribute his good fortune. Padre Pio without a bit of hesitation answered: "You fell asleep and your Guardian Angel drove your car." Fantastic? Not at all, if we are to take the Gospels seriously. It is filled with many incidents of their direct intervention in the affairs of men. Remember how St. Joseph was told by an angel in a dream to flee with the Infant Jesus and his Mother to Egypt and later was told by an angel to return when it was safe?

There are many instances in the history of the Church of certain privileged souls seeing their Guardian Angels in visible form. St. Gemma Galgani, who lived at the turn of this century, frequently conversed with her angel. When she was not faithful to the inspiration of grace he showed his displeasure by not looking at her and giving her the "silent treatment." St. Francis of Assisi had great devotion to St. Michael. It was customary for St. Francis to fast 40 days before the feast of St. Michael, and it was during this forty day fast that he received the stigmata on Sept. 17, 1224. Padre Pio also received the stigmata in September, the month in which we honor the angels. He also visited the famous shrine of St. Michael on the Gargano mountain as Francis did many centuries before.

The shrine of St. Michael the Archangel on Mt. Gargano has been recognized as a sacred place since the days of Pope Gelasius (492–496). At that time St. Michael appeared in visible form in a cave in the mountainside and revealed to the local bishop that the mountain was under his special protection for the honor of God and of the Holy Angels. It was indeed providential that this shrine, which is practically the only notable one dedicated to the Holy Angels, is situated but a short distance from Our Lady of Grace Friary in San Giovanni Rotondo.

The angels figured strongly in Padre Pio's devotional life, in particular his guardian angel and St. Michael. The famous St. Michael shrine in the Gargano mountains is not far from San Giovanni Rotondo. Both St. Francis and Bl. Padre Pio made pilgrimages there seeking his protection and intercession.

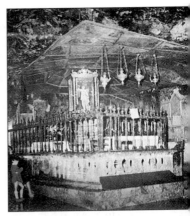

When Padre Pio came to live in this friary situated on the slopes of Mount Gargano he seemed to have an agreement with St. Michael, the Prince of the heavenly hosts. He petitioned St. Michael to assist him in defeating Satan and his followers on the battleground for human souls. Padre Pio in turn would direct and encourage people to go to St. Michael for help in warding off the attacks of the evil one.

Clarice Bruno in her book, "Roads to Padre Pio," has a number of chapters devoted to Padre Pio and the angels. She recounts how one pilgrim to the shrine of St. Michael, an Italian air force officer, related in San Giovanni Rotondo a most unusual story. While the pilgrims he was with were praying before the statue of St. Michael in the grotto, he was occupied, with his back to the altar, looking at various souvenir medals, statues, etc., at the entrance of the church. We can gather from this that the young airman was not greatly interested in the grotto or in making his petitions known to the Archangel. Suddenly he heard a terrifying scream, more of a howl, coming from his group near the shrine. Before he had a chance to turn around to see what had happened, he saw a horrible looking creature, part monster and part human, run past him with the speed of lightning to the choir balcony and then disappear from sight in the valley below.

The young man later learned that some members of the pilgrimage had brought a friend with them whom they considered possessed by the devil. Their faith was not in vain. St. Michael, who is credited with defeating Satan and the rebellious angels under the banner entitled, "Who is like God?" had won another battle and liberated another soul from the tyranny of the devil. So impressed was the officer by the experience he had at the grotto of St. Michael that he went tirelessly from group to group at San Giovanni Rotondo bearing witness to what he saw with his own eyes.

There are a number of well-authenticated cases in which Padre Pio personally freed persons from the domination of the devil. In September of 1947 an Italian woman was brought forcibly to San Giovanni Rotondo by her sons to see Padre Pio. As soon as she was brought into the church she began to scream. At the Communion of the Mass she burst out with a whole litany of curses and blasphemies.

Padre Pio ordered her out of the church. She shouted back: "I'd rather die than go out." As he raised the Sacred Host above the ciborium, Padre Pio fixed his piercing eyes upon her and said, "It is time now to put an end to this." At these words the woman fell over as if she were struck dead; shortly after she rose to her feet and walked to the corner of the church where she sat quietly. She was free from the devil's possession and returned frequently to San Giovanni Rotondo telling many people of how Padre Pio had freed her from the devil's domination. She would say with a good deal of enthusiasm, "He is more powerful than St. Michael."

This excusable exaggeration might have received a rebuke from the holy friar had he heard it. For Padre Pio recognized, as the Church does, the power the Archangel Michael has in keeping the devil in check. The Church calls upon his help numerous times in the official prayer of exorcism. He is invoked as God's standard-bearer in the liturgy of the Church and is often represented bearing the scales of divine justice in which the lives of souls are weighed. He also presides over the worship of Christians, for he is the angel whom St. John saw in heaven near God's altar, a golden censer in his hand, offering the fragrant incense of the prayers of the saints.

All this, Padre Pio was aware of and much more, for it would take a book to relate all the experiences he had with the angels. It has been said that Padre Pio has been and is a modern "Gospel" on the angels. However, in spite of Padre Pio's living testimony, and in spite of the numerous passages in the Bible dealing with angels, both good and bad, there is a conspiracy of silence, hatched in hell, to prevent the angels from becoming known and appreciated in our day.

One day when Padre Pio's penitents were talking with him about the diabolical influence in the world, he emphatically stated: "My hand will crush the devil!" This could very well be a prophetic utterance; for does not his life and writings on the devil and the good angels give us reason to hope that the conspiracy of silence will be eventually broken? Padre Pio counselled many of his spiritual children to engage their guardian angel in some way, to entrust tasks to him, to have him go to Jesus and to the Madonna, to this or that person. With utter confidence in their friendship and power for good, he encouraged them to get their guardian angel to "fly" so as not to let "his wings get rusty."

The Queen of all Virtues

Charity which has not truth and justice for its foundation is faulty. He who offends against charity, offends the pupil of the eye of God.

To fail in charity is like wounding God in the pupil of his eye. What is more delicate than the pupil of the eye? To fail in charity is like failing against nature.

Charity is the queen of virtues. As the pearls are held together by a thread, thus the virtues by charity; and as the pearls fall when the thread breaks, so too the virtues are lost if charity diminishes.— *Padre Pio*

Padre Pio praying under the gaze of St. Mary of Graces, the patroness of the monastery where he spent over fifty years of his religious life. He often stopped in the gallery of the new church in order to pray in front of the image of Our Lady of Grace. Father Alessio Parente, beside him in the photograph, assisted him lovingly in the last years of his life.

(Photo by Michele)

The Madonna in Padre Pio's Life

Bro. Francis Mary F.I.

Every canonized Saint bears witness to an important fact: holiness is intimately connected with devotion to Mary, the Spouse of the Holy Ghost who is the Sanctifier. How could it be otherwise considering all graces come to us through the Mother of God and the Mother of the Church. According to St. Louis Mary De Montfort in his classic Marian work, *True Devotion to Mary,* assaults by Satan will be most fierce and intense in the latter times.

In speaking of the great saints and apostles of the latter times who will eventually triumph over Satan and his followers he gives what seems to be a pen sketch of Padre Pio, "They shall be true disciples of Jesus Christ, walking in the footsteps of His poverty, humility, and contempt of the world. ... They shall carry on their shoulders the bloody standard of the cross, the crucifix in their right hand and the rosary in their left and the sacred names of Jesus and Mary in their hearts ... " (these were the last words on the lips of the dying Padre Pio).

Padre Pio's Marian devotion was a profound part of him from infancy to old age. He related later in life how as a boy he went to the shrine of Our Lady of the Rosary in Pompeii, near Naples, without permission, knowing that his mother would not give him the permission. He visited her shrine frequently when he was stationed in Naples as a soldier. Nothing could stand in his way when inspired to give Mary his love. The particular area of Italy where Padre Pio was born, Pietrelcina, had as a special patroness, Our Lady of Liberty. However, his devotion to her was expressed more in action than in words.

Though he wrote a brief meditation on her Immaculate Conception, and there are scattered references to her in his early letters (later on he was forbidden to write letters by the Holy See and as a result his written testimonies on Mary are few), yet, throughout his priestly life the most beautiful and effective "sermon" in her honor, was the Rosary which he prayed constantly. It was this chain of hope that linked him with heaven and the supernatural, that world which is unexplainable to the rationalist, and materialist.

Similar to another great Franciscan Marian Saint of our times, St. Maximilian Kolbe, Our Lady appeared to Padre Pio as well. Upon being asked twenty years later why he had kept this and other supernatural visits a secret he replied in all sincerity that he thought everyone saw our Lady. His spiritual director, Padre Agostino of San Marco, relates: "One day he ingenuously asked me, 'Don't you see our Lady?' At my negative reply he answered, 'You are just saying that out of holy humility!'"

When Francesco chose to join the Franciscans he undoubtedly was largely motivated by the long Marian tradition of the friars going back to St. Francis. It was they who were the great champions of her Immaculate Conception and her Assumption into heaven. Today, they will be found among those championing her role as Mediatrix of All Graces. His devotion to Mary was centered in identification with Mary at the foot of the cross of her crucified Son—the Man of Sorrows. From the Queen of Martyrs Padre Pio learned how to bear the painful stigmata and so many other sufferings heroically. In spiritual direction to others he said: "Lean on the Cross like the Virgin Mary and you will not be without comfort. Mary was petrified before the Crucified Christ, but you cannot say that she was abandoned. She was loved better then, when she could not even cry.

The frequent use Padre Pio made of the Rosary, this simple prayer of both the learned and illiterate, rich and poor, young and old, gives us an indication of his awareness of Mary's presence and protection over her spiritual children through the Rosary. Towards the end of his life it was ever in his hands. It was as if he were telling his devotees: "Here is peace of heart, the victory over evil, the strength to overcome every obstacle on the way to heaven." It was through the Rosary that the whole array of gifts and miracles he received for souls came. His power to draw sinners to an amendment of life and to encourage his sons and daughters to seek personal holiness were the fruit of his prayer life, in particular the Rosary.

When he was asked one day what inheritance he wished to leave his spiritual children, he answered at once, "The Rosary." He pointed out to his followers that if the Holy Virgin has urged the recitation of the Rosary wherever she appeared in recent times, isn't that an indication that we should pray it every day. How many Rosaries did he recite each day? He responded as many as thirty-five complete Rosaries. Amazed at this seemingly impossible number, he was asked how could he say that many in one day. He responded, "How can you not pray that much?" It is evident from his reply that he was able to do several things at the same time.

Regardless of the number, his example contradicts those who have discarded this devotion as not being Christ-centered enough. Here is a holy person who bore the visible wounds of our Lord's passion for fifty years who continually prayed the Rosary, holding it up to all men as a perfect means of reviewing the central acts in the great drama of our redemption, through the meditating on the joyful, sorrowful and glorious mysteries in the lives of Christ and his Mother. He spoke of the Rosary as that prayer in which "She triumphs over everything and everyone." Two days before he died he repeated: "Love Our Lady and make her loved. Recite the Rosary and recite it always and as much as you can."

Was this great devotion he had to the Rosary tied in with Our Lady's apparitions at Fatima in 1917, where she identified herself as our "Lady of the Rosary" and requested its recitation daily? It doesn't seem likely. Yet when acquainted with Fatima, Padre Pio lived its message and Mary's formula for world peace, through prayer, penance and consecration to her Immaculate Heart, throughout his whole life. These words of Our Lady to the three seers in 1917 were perfectly understood and lived by Padre Pio: "Many souls go to hell because they have no one to pray and make sacrifices for them ... I have come to warn the faithful to amend their lives and ask pardon for their sins. ... They [sinners] must not continue to offend Our Lord who is already deeply offended. ... Say the Rosary every day, to obtain peace for the world. ... If people do what I tell you, many souls will be saved and there will be peace. ... In the end my Immaculate Heart will triumph, Russia will be converted, and there will be peace."

Padre Pio understood the vitally important role and responsibility of all men as coredemptors, "Filling up that which is wanting in the sufferings of Christ." (Col.1: 24). He said once, "Souls are not given as gifts; they are bought. You do not know what they cost Jesus. Now they still have to be bought always with the same coin." How many souls he purchased through his heroic patience in a life of suffering, endured out of love of God and united to Christ's suffering, will be a surprise to all when revealed on the day of judgement!

Pope Pius XII, the Fatima pope, in 1952, heeding her urgent request for prayer, urged his spiritual children to form prayer groups. When Padre Pio heard about this appeal he immediately encouraged his spiritual children to heed the admonition of the Holy Father. These prayer groups soon came to be known as Padre Pio Prayer Groups and have spread throughout the world.

The Blue Army of Our Lady of Fatima sought his approval and help in furthering the message of Fatima. The founder of the Blue Army, the late Msgr. Harold Colgan, asked Padre Pio if he would be the spiritual director of the Blue Army and accept its members as his spiritual children. In accepting the charge, Padre Pio smiled and added gently: "May they only behave well!" He is known to have said on one occasion that Russia would be converted when there are as many members of the Blue Army as there are Communists.

In 1959 the Fatima Pilgrim Virgin statue was touring the major cities in Italy aboard a helicopter. We know from his confreres how much he looked forward to her visit at San Giovanni Rotundo. The day it arrived in Italy, May 5, Padre Pio was struck down with a bad attack of pleurisy. An exceptional change in the schedule was made so that the statue could visit Padre Pio and the large crowd that had gathered there to celebrate the forty years he bore the stigmata. Padre Pio spoke from his sick bed over the loudspeaker, exhorting the people to prepare for its visit with Christian renewal. On the day it arrived in San Giovanni Rotundo, August 5, he announced with deep emotion, "In a few minutes Our Mother will be in our house. ... Open your hearts." He urged them to give thanks, to commit themselves "enthusiastically ... permanently, just as Our Mother's eye is permanently on us."

During the morning of August 6 he was able to go down to the church where they lowered the statue before his face so he could kiss her. What follows is best described by the mayor of San Giovanni who was a good friend of Padre Pio.

"It would seem that everyone ... not only from San Giovanni but from the whole region ... was gathered here to receive her. And poor Padre Pio, whose devotion to our Blessed Mother is one of his most outstanding characteristics, longed in his sick bed to at least pay homage to her in some way. And when the statue was lifted from the helicopter in order to be taken into the Chapel of the hospital, he insisted on getting up to render her homage. In vain all tried to dissuade him. Since the superior did not forbid it and with two of the friars supporting him by the armpits, he went to honor our Lady.

"Despite his great will power, three times he had to stop. But finally, dissolved in tears, he knelt in prayer before the famous image of Our Lady of Fatima ... who had predicted the present suffering of the world and had promised to convert Russia and bring peace to mankind if her requests were heard. ... Father Pio was back in his sick bed when the helicopter soared above the great crowds to bear the statue to other waiting throngs, in other parts of the country. As he heard the roar of the motors and crowd, Father Pio exclaimed aloud to our Lady: 'On May 5th, the day you arrived in Italy, I fell ill. Now you are going to leave me. ... ' The pilot of the helicopter later reported that for some reason he could not explain, as he was heading away, he suddenly decided to turn around and brought the aircraft back to the monastery, circled a few times, and finally flew away.

"A few moments later Padre Pio said to those around him: 'I felt myself tremble violently, and now I feel as strong and healthy as never before in my life.' Later Padre Pio made a formal declaration of his instantaneous cure by Our Lady of Fatima and in gratitude sent a crucifix to Fatima. A few months later a Blue Army delegation presented him with a hand-carved statue of Our Lady of Fatima which was placed above the vesting table of the sacristy, where he prepared for Mass each morning.

"When people asked him how it was that San Giovanni Rotundo was chosen over the nearby city of Foggia, which was much larger, and the most important city in that part of Italy, with childlike candor he replied, 'She wanted to come and cure Padre Pio.'"

Like another great Marian saint, St. Louis De Montfort, Padre Pio would cry out to all men, "Of Mary there is never enough!" When pressed to speak about her he showed the depths of his tender love for Mary by shedding tears of joy and emotion. The saying above his door was from the great Marian saint, St. Bernard of Clairvaux, "Mary is the reason of all my hope." One of his confreres wrote down some of the beautiful epithets spoken by Padre Pio on our Lady: "Abyss of grace and purity; Incomparable Masterpiece of the Creator; Tabernacle of the Most High; Receptacle of divine secrets; Woman bathed in light; Exquisite Dove."

As a true son of St. Francis, and in the Franciscan tradition, he was ever conscious of Mary's first great prerogative and its importance. "The Immaculate Conception," he said, "is the first step on the path of salvation." He did not hesitate to affirm her universal mediation. "All things revert to her, all grace passes through her hands." In the last years of his life he said only the Mass of the Immaculate Conception. And lest anyone would ge the impression that he stopped at Mary and did not have her Son as his final goal he might consider these words he directed

To the Immaculata:
"Oh, gentle Mother, make me love him. Fill my heart with the
     love that burned in thine ...
Purify my heart that I may know how to love my God and thy God!
Purify my spirit that I may adore him in spirit and in truth!
Purify my body that it may become for him a living tabernacle!"

Even as Jesus frequently appeared in person to Padre Pio, so too did Mary. On one occasion he describes her physical presence as she accompanied him to the altar: "With what care she accompanied me to the altar this morning! It seemed to me as though she had nothing to think about other than me filling my heart completely with saintly affections. I felt a mysterious fire from my heart which I couldn't understand.

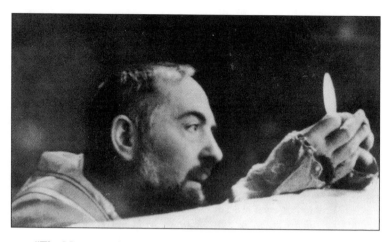

"The Mass was the center of the spirituality of Padre Pio. His day was a continuous preparation and a continuous thanksgiving for it; the stigmata recalled to him that on the altar he really represented the crucified Christ. ... His voice was broken with emotion, from the Consecration on. His eyes were glued on the Host and on the chalice; his person was totally taken up by the Divine Presence and as if it were annihilated by it. A profound peace, which shone from his transfigured face, invaded him. Celebrated in this manner, the Mass imprinted itself on the mind and on the heart of those present so that it never effaced itself from them again. They carried with them the suffering and the joy mixed with the tears of Calvary."

— *P. Ricardo Fabiano*

I felt the need to put ice on it to extinguish this fire which was consuming me! I should like to have a voice strong enough to invite the sinners of the whole world to love our Lady!"

It is said that at the moment of death one sees in an instant a "flash back" of his whole life. At such a time the dominant direction of one's life stands out, whether it be toward evil or good ends. As Padre Pio lay dying on the morning of September 23, the dominant direction of his life was vocalized in two words, "Gesu ... Maria," "Gesu ... Maria," "Jesus ... Mary," "Jesus ... Mary." These were his last words.

The crucified Jesus who had shared his cross with his faithful servant Padre Pio, and Mary who stood at the foot of her Son's cross, are the spiritual legacy this Franciscan stigmatic would leave to all mankind. If we share in their sufferings, after the example of Our Lady and her Son, and Padre Pio, we are sure to share in their glory.

The Mass of Padre Pio

Malachy Gerard Carroll

There have been many accounts written about the Mass of Padre Pio, but few have captured as well as Malachy Gerard Carroll, the essence of his mass: the hidden meaning behind this great drama which makes Calvary present again. He personally witnessed Padre Pio's Masses in the early fifties. The following is excerpted from the chapter, "The Mass of Padre Pio," from his book, Padre Pio.

Calvary is a place, and the crucifixion of Christ took place at a definite time; but by his mighty words: "Do this in commemoration of me"—Christ instituted the Sacrifice of the Mass as the real renewal of that death, in an unbloody manner, "from the rising of the sun to the going-down thereof," as the prophet Malachias had foretold. After that, every moment became a mystical Calvary, for at every moment of the day and night, somewhere in the world, Christ is brought on the altar by the words of a consecrated man whose priesthood gives him the power to command Divinity, which is immolated anew in a bloodless manner.

When that priest bears in his own body the mystic marks of that reality, we kneel down in wonder. This is the secret of that intensity we feel palpably around us when we assisted at the Mass of Padre Pio. ... The Mass of Padre Pio jolts us to the realization that the world is too much with us; that we must take steps to remove the dust of neglect from those spiritual wonders that are ours to command.

The first distinguishing feature of the Mass of Padre Pio is its length, varying between an hour and a quarter and an hour and a half. The audible parts of the Mass, are, however, said just as any other priest would say them; there is no hint of dramatic resonance in his voice or any slow emphasis. The length of his Mass is due to the long pauses of contemplative silence into which he enters at various parts of the Holy Sacrifice.

When he first ascends the altar, before reading the Introit, he makes a considerable pause before the tabernacle as though in contemplation of the mighty work he is about to perform. The celebration of the

Mass always meant pain and suffering for Padre Pio, and sometimes a little trickle of blood would be seen flowing from the wounds in his hands. He always puts a handkerchief on the altar for such moments. Is it fanciful to see an analogy here between that first moment of Padre Pio's Mass and the moment when Christ first faced his passion? Is there something of the shadow of Gethsemane on the soul of Padre Pio in that silence before the tabernacle?

After the Orate Fratres he again stands silently as he savors, perhaps, the deep significance of that *meum ac vestrum sacrificium.* This is followed by a long pause at the memento of the living, for Padre Pio has many to remember. The sorrows of the world all come to him, and he accepts them as his own. In that deep silence, the congregation crowded behind him really feel that he is taking their lives, their worries, their ambitions, their sins and their sorrow for sins all the spotted reality that is their human nature, with its heroisms, its groping, its cowardices, and is lifting them up to Christ in hands that are shadowed with Christ's wounds. It is a mighty moment for any man whose name is in the heart or on the lips of Padre Pio.

For example, there was the lady who approached him after Mass with a request that he should pray for a matter that was vital to her. Before she could do so, he greeted her with the news that he had already prayed during the Mass at which she had assisted, told her what her intention was, and assured her that all would be well. Other examples of this can be found in the books published on Padre Pio. A similar pause comes at the memento of the dead, when Padre Pio's hands of prayer reach mercifully and longingly towards Purgatory. I have been told that, on one occasion, a peasant whose son had just died, came running towards San Giovanni Rotondo, and shouted as she passed to some workers in the fields: "My poor Francesco is dead! But Padre Pio will put his hands into the flames and he will be safe!" This is the feeling of every person who has the good fortune to commend some dear deceased one to Padre Pio: he will reach hands of prayer towards Purgatory for him, and everything will be all right. The greatest silence of all descends on Padre Pio at the priest's communion; for it is now a silence that seems to deepen itself in the breath of the Holy Spirit, until it becomes one with the abysmal silence of the Eucharist.

The great things in life are paid for with pain. Turn to the story of any of the great Founders or Foundresses who have given splendid religious Congregations to the Church, and you will find that the debt was paid by them. When Christ calls a soul to a special vocation, he marks that soul with the seal of his elect—with the seal of pain. Padre Pio has been privileged to be a living witness to the wounds of Christ, and he has a mighty vocation of mercy to his fellow men in the wasteland of the twentieth century. Kneeling at his Mass, we get glimpses of the pain at the heart of his ecstasy—the price he too is called upon to pay.

Perhaps it is safe to say that nowhere in our world is there another priest who celebrates Mass as though he were bearing Christ's cross through every moment of it. He indeed bears witness to the Passion of Christ in his body. There is an expression of suffering on his face at the supreme moments of the Mass, and his body sometimes is seen to twitch with pain. His fingers tremble and hesitate about breaking the Host, as though the veil has been rent for him and the reality of what he is doing has become too intense. His lips shiver as he raises the Chalice. When he genuflects, it is as though an invisible cross has crushed him down, for he rises painfully and with the utmost difficulty. There are moments when he seems lost in colloquy with God, when he moves his head as though nodding assent and he speaks some abrupt words. Sometimes he weeps, as though a shadow of the world's sin has come between him and the Eucharistic Jesus. His compassion for the Christ he sees mocked again is great. And there are those hands exposed during the Mass, and otherwise hidden by the brown woolen mittens he constantly wears. Those hands can be seen, with the stigmata on them, the mystic shadow of the nails. And sometimes they bleed. ...

When the Mass is ended, every man sees a hand raised in blessing over him—a hand marked with a bloody wound. Calvary becomes a reality, and the Mass appears in all its shattering wonder for each and all. It is impossible to have any more than a vague, groping questioning about the silence of Padre Pio as he stands transfixed on the altar. That silence keeps its secret. But of one thing we can be certain—this silence reaches out to the silence in the heart of each one kneeling there, and according to the depth of spiritual silence within each heart will the real message of Padre Pio be felt. The great, radiating meaning in the life of Padre Pio is his Mass. ...

... Behind the wonder that is Padre Pio, there is a Divine purpose, and that purpose may well find its supreme expression in the Mass of Padre Pio. We need a cosmic recall to the things of the spirit—and above all to the Mass, the pulsating heart of Christianity. May it not well be that Christ struck down Padre Pio and marked him with his Five Wounds, in order that he might stand at the altar as the living image of the Crucified, and that through him the Mass might become vital for us? For it is the Mass that matters, and until its power is again felt in the heart of our civilization, all will not be well.

Crucified at the altar

Fr. Stefano Manelli, F.I.

Jesus Crucified and Padre Pio stigmatized made an impressive combination during his holy Mass. The renewal of the Sacrifice of Calvary took place without disunity. The same Jesus was sacrificed upon the Cross and in Padre Pio. This was especially evidenced at the moment of Consecration when Padre Pio stammered out painfully the words of consecration, "Hoc est enim Corpus Meum ... Hic est enim Calix Sanguinis Mei." These words sounded like blows of a hammer upon the nails that pierced the hands and feet of Jesus and Padre Pio.

A remark of Padre Pio discloses his active share in Jesus' crucifixion, which he re-lived at the altar during Mass. When a spiritual daughter asked him how he could manage to stand up throughout the Mass when the wounds on his feet were paining him, Padre Pio replied, "My daughter, during Mass I am not standing on my feet. I am hanging." Being with Jesus suspended on the Cross—this was Padre Pio's Mass. His penetrating glances, the unique gestures of his hands, the almost imperceptible movements of his body, his serious and earnest tone, his slow, painful genuflections, the forceful blows he gave his breast at the "mea culpa" and at the "Domine non sum dignus," the mystifying expressions in his face, and his many, many tears—how can one forget these things that were all a part of Padre Pio's Mass?

The writer remembers' the times that, while serving the Mass, he witnessed Padre Pio's ecstasies, during which his body was as motionless as a statue and his face was transfigured. With another movement or jerk, likewise almost unnoticeable, he used to come out of it and carry on with the holy Mass. His Mass was something that lived Christ's sorrows and Christ's love, wrapped in mystery; yet it reached the heart, so that Padre Pio gave you a glimpse into the depths of the mystery of his bleeding, of his tears, of his prayer—all ordained to remind you of the suffering Jesus. (see pg. 134 for further information about Fr. Manelli and Padre Pio).

Padre Pio First Met Her at St. Peter's, Rome

The first recorded case of bilocation of Padre Pio occurred when he was a young seminarian. It was the beginning of a most fascinating account as narrated by Padre Alberto.

One day in February, 1905, while Padre Pio was still a seminarian studying philosophy at the Capuchin Convent of St. Elia a Pianisi, he described in writing one of his bilocations to a palace in the city of Udine. "Several days ago I had an extraordinary experience. About eleven o'clock in the evening (January 18, 1905) Brother Anastasio and I were in the choir. Suddenly I found myself at the same time in the palace of an extremely wealthy family. The master of the house was dying just as his daughter was about to be born.

"Then the Blessed Mother appeared and, turning to me, said, 'I am entrusting this unborn child to your care and protection. Although she will become a precious jewel, right now she has no form. Shape and polish her. Make her as brilliant as you can, because one day I would like to adorn myself with her.'

"I replied, 'How can this be possible? I am only a poor seminarian and don't even know whether I will have the joy and good fortune to become a priest. Even if I do, how will I ever be able to take care of this girl since I will be so far away from here?' The Blessed Mother admonished me, 'Don't doubt me. She will come to you, but first you will find her in the Basilica of St. Peter in Rome.' ... and after that I found myself back in the choir," finished the young Capuchin.

Many years passed following this conversation between the Blessed Mother and the young seminarian, during which time the baby matured into a lovely lady whom we shall call by her initials, G.R. Meanwhile, Padre Pio's written documentation of the incident had been carefully preserved by Padre Agostino da St. Marco in Lamis, his spiritual director and the former Father Superior of the Capuchin Monastery in San Giovanni Rotondo, who presented it to G.R. when she was a young lady. After reading it, she spoke to Padre Pio and received from him a confirmation of its authenticity. After he died, she returned the document to the Capuchin Fathers so that they could use it as part of the Cause for his Beatification. Since that time she has also testified about this before the ecclesiastical authorities. She also presented me with a photocopy of the document.

The father of G.R. had been a registered and practicing member of a Masonic Order in Udine. As his death became imminent, his fellow Masons surrounded the palace day and night to keep any priests from entering to confess him. A few hours before he died, while his pious wife was tearfully praying beside his bed, she saw the figure of a Capuchin friar leave the room and disappear down one of the corridors of the palace. Immediately she went after him, but he had vanished.

At that moment, sensing the approach of death within the palace, the watchdog that was tied outside began to howl. Unable to bear the mournful sound, the lady went downstairs toward the door with the intention of letting him loose. Suddenly and unexpectedly, without any pain or complications, she gave birth to a baby girl. Only the steward was present to assist her. Afterwards, she even had the strength to carry her prematurely born daughter upstairs to her bed.

The steward knew that outside of the palace a priest was trying to pass through the line of Masons in order to hear his master's confession. Therefore, using the birth of the premature baby as an excuse, he went outside and told them, "You have the right to keep a priest from going to the bedside of my master because he is one of you, but you cannot prevent him from entering to baptize the premature baby that has just been born inside."

As a result, the Masons permitted the priest to enter the palace, and he proceeded directly to the dying man's room, where he helped him straighten his affairs with our Lord and confess. A few moments later he died, begging God to have mercy on his soul. After her husband's death, the widow went with her infant daughter to Rome to live with her parents. The little girl grew up without ever hearing of Padre Pio or learning of the divine plan that was to guide her life. Although she received a good religious education, when she was in high school her faith was tested by a number of her teachers who did not believe in God. To make matters even worse, she knew no priests who were well enough versed in theology to answer her questions. Then late one summer afternoon in 1922 she went to St. Peter's to confess. Unfortunately, at that time no priests were hearing confessions. The custodian suggested that she return the following day since the church was about to close. Besides, many priests would be available then to hear confessions. He did suggest, however, that she look around and if she did find a priest to ask him to hear her confession. No sooner had the custodian walked away when she saw a young Capuchin friar coming toward her.

"Father, please let me go to confess," she pleaded. The priest assented and entered the second confessional from the door on the left side of the Basilica. After making her confession, G.R. asked him to clarify a question she had about the mystery of the Holy Trinity. Using language that was simple enough to be readily understandable to the young girl, he proceeded with great intelligence to give her an explanation. "My daughter, when a housewife makes bread, what does she use? Three different ingredients: baking powder, flour, and water. She rolls the dough, which has been mixed and formed into one single substance. The dough is one substance. She uses this dough to make three loaves of bread. Each loaf is of the very same substance yet separate in form from the other two. From this example we can proceed to God, who is one Being. At the same time he is Three Persons, each one equal yet distinct from the other two. God the Father is neither the Son nor the Holy Spirit. The Son is neither the Father nor the Holy Spirit, nor is the Holy Spirit either the Father or the Son. God the Father begets the Son; the Son proceeds from the Father; and the Holy Spirit comes from the Father and the Son. They are three real persons, equal and at the same time distinct. Nevertheless, they are one God only, because the Divine Nature is unique and identical."

Elaborating upon this mystery of faith, the confessor, who had been inspired by the grace of God, was easily able to dissipate the doubts that had troubled the girl. G.R. happily left the confessional and waited to thank him, but he did not come out. Soon the custodian approached and told her that since the church was about to close she would have to leave but could return the next day if she wished to go to confession. She replied that she had just finished making her confession and was only waiting for the priest in order to thank him. Pointing to the confessional, she indicated that the Capuchin father who had confessed her was inside. When the custodian went to see for himself who the priest was he opened the door ... and found the confessional empty.

"Young lady, there is no one here." Bewildered, she exclaimed, "But where can he be? I have not moved from this spot and have not seen him come out." Perturbed by this strange incident, she went home.

During her summer vacation in 1923 G.R. went with a friend and her aunt to San Giovanni Rotondo for the first time to see Padre Pio. When they arrived in the afternoon, the corridor that connects the sacristy with the interior of the convent was thronged with many people who had come long distances to see him. Despite the crowd, G.R. found herself directly in his path as he passed down the corridor. Padre Pio stopped and looked closely at her.

"I know you!" he said. "You were born the same day that your father died." He then gave her his hand to kiss (an Italian custom) and blessed her. The following morning her aunt, who had by this time confessed with Padre Pio, suggested that she do likewise. As a result, G.R. soon found herself in line waiting to go to confession. Finally her turn came. After giving her his blessing, Padre Pio welcomed her.

"My daughter, finally you have come! I have been waiting for you for so many years!"

Surprised, G.R. immediately replied, "Father, you don't even know me. This is the first time I have ever been in San Giovanni Rotondo. Undoubtedly you have mistaken me for someone else."

"No," Padre Pio assured her, "I have not taken you for someone else. You already know me. Last year at the Basilica of St. Peter in Rome you came up to me. Don't you remember? You were looking for a confessor. Then a Capuchin priest came along and confessed you. I was that Capuchin friar."

G.R. was completely taken aback and confused by this explanation of the mysterious appearance and disappearance of the Capuchin confessor at the Basilica. Padre Pio had gone there by bilocation just as the Blessed Mother had predicted so many years before when she told him his spiritual daughter would come to him in St. Peter's. Padre Pio explained, "Listen my daughter. Just before you were born the Blessed Mother took me to your home, and I witnessed the death of your father. She indicated that through her intercession and the merits of his wife's tears and prayers her father had obtained salvation. After telling me to pray for him, our Lady informed me that his wife was about to give birth to a baby girl and that she was placing this child under my care."

"My daughter," concluded Padre Pio, "you are my responsibility." Filled with emotion, the girl began to cry. "Father, since I have become your responsibility, please tell me how I should direct my life. Should I become a nun?" "No," replied Padre Pio, "you should not. Come to San Giovanni Rotondo frequently. I will guide your soul, and you will live according to the will of God." After receiving Padre Pio's blessing, G.R. left the confessional with tears in her eyes. Although her aunt inquired about why she had taken so long to confess and why she was crying, the girl said nothing and kept her new knowledge to herself.

Sometime later, as Padre Pio invested her in the Third Order of St. Francis, he suggested that she take the name of "Sister Jacopa." Because

"This will be the last time you will confess with me ... " "But," she asked, "why can't you confess me any more, Father?" Padre Pio answered, "I have already told you that I cannot because I am going away."

the name did not have a pleasant ring to her ears, she asked if she could not instead be called "Sister Clare." Padre Pio was insistent, "No, you shall be called Sister Jacopa!" "Have you read the life of St. Francis of Assisi?" he asked. "In one chapter a noble Roman lady appeared named Jacopa de' Settesoli, whom St. Francis called 'the beloved mother of our order' because of her generosity and protection to the Franciscans. Just as she received the grace of witnessing the death of St. Francis, you will be present when I die."

Under the spiritual guidance of Padre Pio G.R. continued along the path of virtue and developed into a pious and lovely lady. She married and brought up a beautiful Christian family.

Frequently she went to San Giovanni Rotondo to visit her spiritual father. However, for some months during the last year of his life she was unable to do so. One day she heard his voice sweetly advising her, "Come soon to San Giovanni Rotondo because I am going away. If you take too long, you will miss me."

By now G.R. was an elderly lady. Nevertheless, she hurried to San Giovanni Rotondo with a friend and registered at a hotel there. Four days before Padre Pio's death she had the good fortune of confessing to him for the last time. When Padre Pio saw her, he said, "This will be the last time you will go to my confessional. I absolve you now of all the sins you have ever committed." She asked, "But why can't you confess me anymore, Father?" He replied, "I have already told you that I cannot because I am going away." Finally she realized that Padre Pio was going to die and left the confessional in tears.

On the evening of September 22, 1968, Padre Pio gave his last blessing to the thousands of spiritual children who had come from all over the world to visit him on the fiftieth anniversary of his stigmata. He then retired to his cell to prepare for his meeting with Sister Death. At this time G.R. found herself present in spirit in Padre Pio's cell to witness in detail the last hours of her spiritual father, as he had predicted many years before when she took the name "Sister Jacopa." The pious lady saw him suffer and pray. She watched as he confessed with Padre Pellegrino and renewed his religious vows. She saw him taken from his bed to the veranda. Then she saw three doctors dressed in white minister to him. Later she watched as Padre Pio received the Last Rites of the Church.

As she saw him die, she cried "Padre Pio is dead! Padre Pio is dead!" Her cries awakened the lady who had accompanied her and many of the people in the hotel as well. Although her friend tried to calm her, telling her that she had only had a bad dream, G.R. immediately dressed and hurried to the convent. Already a small crowd had gathered in the square in front of the church, where a Capuchin friar was officially announcing the death of Padre Pio. Several days later G.R. came and told me that she had witnessed the death of Padre Pio. I didn't want to believe her. Wishing to give credence to her words, G.R. told me, "Padre Alberto, I will describe Padre Pio's cell as I saw it when he was dying."

At that point I would like to stress the fact that before December, 1969, Padre Pio's cell had never been photographed, nor had any woman been permitted to enter it. Imagine my wonder when she proceeded to describe his cell to the smallest detail. I could not keep from exclaiming, "Enough! I believe that you were present in his cell when he died." G.R. herself narrated the above account to me with the understanding that her name would not be made public. She is a very pious, charitable lady and is loved by all who know her. She has testified before the ecclesiastical authorities on everything that I have narrated. Her testimony was used in the Process for the beatification of Padre Pio.

Reprinted, with permission, from The Voice of Padre Pio.

Left: Padre Pio was born in this house in Pietrelcina, Italy. Above: The old part of San Giovanni Rotondo where he spent most of his life in the friary of Our Lady of Grace. Note the poverty of both locations.

It was during the Holy Sacrifice of the Mass that Padre Pio's wounds bled the most and were extremely painful.

The more Jesus intends to raise a soul to perfection, the more He tries it by suffering. So rejoice, I say to you, in seeing yourself so privileged, in spite of your unworthiness. The more you are afflicted, the more you ought to rejoice, because in the fire of tribulation the soul will become pure gold, worthy to be placed and shine in the heavenly palace.

—*Padre Pio*

The crucifix before which Padre Pio was praying when he received the stigmata.

PART IV

The Visible Stigmata by Koda

The Bleeding Stigmata

Mary F. Ingoldsby

Padre Pio's mystical ascent was to culminate in the grace of the bleeding stigmata. His letters during the period leading up to that memorable date can be compared to the finest pages in the annals of Christian mysticism. He is on fire with love, wounded by love, consumed by the desire to be united with his divine Lover, but at the same time his soul is plunged in the depths of the "dark night." He undergoes unspeakable torments, spiritual and physical. Satan seems to him to be getting the upper hand and on June 4, 1918, he fears he has lost his God for ever. "Tears are my daily bread. I have gone astray and have lost you, but shall I find you again? Or have I lost you for ever? Have you condemned me to live for all eternity far from your countenance? My supreme Good, where are you? I no longer know you or find you. My God, my God, why have you forsaken me?"

He appeals desperately to Padre Benedetto to come to the rescue. He is "lost in the unknown." He no longer understands anything and fears he has been abandoned by God for ever. "I clutch or try to clutch at obedience, but even this seems to elude me." Then he asks his director's blessing and concludes with the most touching phrase in all his letters: "I never cease to offer myself for you to the God whom I have lost."

On June 19 we find him writing: "The animal in me shows up in all its abominable reality. All the beauty of grace has been torn out of my soul, and when one is left completely to oneself one comes close to the level of the brute beast. ... I approach the altar with disgust and repugnance for the monstrousness and foulness that accompanies me." Moreover, he is tortured by the thought that he may be deceived and may be "manifesting as true what might not be true." He refers continually to his state as "confinement in a harsh dark prison from which there is no escape." He believes he is being punished by God's justice for his infidelities. On July 27 he feels he is "contemptible in God's eyes and deserves to be cast off, rejected and abandoned by him." Yet it is in the midst of these torments that he experiences the "divine touch" which he describes in the same letter. He is continually beset by grievous temptations.

"Satan is constantly at my side with his tireless promptings. I make every effort to fight him, but I realize that I am powerless to free myself by a strong act of my will. I am afraid he is gaining some advantage, because he is always around me and returns continually to the attack. The opposing forces are advancing, dear Father, and they strike at the very center of my defense. Holy obedience, which was the last prop left to keep the tottering fortress from falling, seems to be yielding like the rest before the Satanic invasion" (September 5).

Then, significantly, he is silent for over a month, and it is during this period, on September 20, 1918, that his sufferings and his mystical journey culminate in the stigmata, the inflicting on his frail and tortured body of the bleeding wounds of Christ's passion. In Padre Pio's case, transverberation was the prelude to stigmatization. The former is considered as a grace which sanctifies the soul on which it is bestowed, while the gift of the stigmata is of a charismatic nature granted by God for the benefit of others, although it is the complement, the outward sign and projection of the wound within the soul. Padre Pio had experienced the first symptoms of stigmatization as early as 1910, very soon after his ordination to the priesthood. As he told his spiritual director, the pain of the wounds continued although the outward signs soon disappeared. In 1912 he wrote to Padre Agostino, his confessor at that time:

"From Thursday evening until Saturday and also on Tuesday there is a painful tragedy for me. My heart, hands and feet seem to be pierced through by a sword. I experience great pain on this account." The prodigy was completed on September 20, 1918, and from that time until the last year of his life the bleeding wounds were always visible. He was most reluctant to speak about such an extraordinary favor, but after repeated requests from his spiritual director he overcame his enormous repugnance and sent him, on October 22, 1918, a sincere account of the event which marked a decisive stage in his earthly existence and set the seal on his extraordinary priestly ministry:

"What can I tell you in answer to your questions concerning my crucifixion? Dear God! What embarrassment and humiliation I suffer by being obliged to explain what you have done to this wretched creature! On the morning of the 20th of last month, after I had celebrated Mass I yielded to a peacefulness similar to a sweet sleep. All the internal and external senses and the very faculties of my soul were immersed in an indescribable stillness. Absolute silence surrounded and invaded me. I was suddenly filled with great peace and abandonment which effaced everything else and caused a lull in the turmoil. All this happened in a flash.

"Meanwhile I saw before me a mysterious person similar to the one I had seen on the evening of August 5, but this time his hands and feet and side were dripping blood. The sight frightened me and what I felt at that moment cannot be described. I thought I should die and indeed I should have died if the Lord had not intervened and strengthened my heart which was about to burst out of my chest.

"The vision disappeared and I became aware that my own hands and feet and side were dripping blood. Imagine the agony I experienced and continue to experience almost every day! The heart wound bleeds continually, especially from Thursday evening until Saturday. Dear Father, I am dying of pain because of the wound and the resulting embarrassment. I am afraid I shall bleed to death if the Lord does not hear my heartfelt supplication to relieve me of this condition. ... I will raise my voice and will not stop imploring him until in his mercy he takes away, not the wound or the pain, which is impossible because I wish to be inebriated with pain, but these outward signs which cause me such embarrassment and unbearable humiliation."

Excerpt taken from the book, Padre Pio: His Life and Mission, *First published by Veritas publications. Used with permission.*

Padre Pio giving a boy his first communion at the last Mass he was to celebrate on Sept. 22, the day before he died.

Medical Science Examines the Stigmata

Malachy Gerard Carroll

The central wonder in the life of Padre Pio, and his life was full of wonders, was the stigmata. The first priest to be marked with the visible and painful marks of the crucified Savior, he was subjected to painful and extensive examination by medical men. A condensation of their report follows.

The medical profession first examined the stigmata of Padre Pio in 1919 in the person of Doctor Luigi Romanelli, who had been invited by the Father Provincial to make an examination. His conclusions were: "that the wounds are not superficial, the blood is arterial in character; the lesions on the hands are covered with a thin membrane, reddish brown in color, with no bleeding points, no swelling, no inflammation of the tissue; the tissues around the lesions ... are painful even to a light touch." Romanelli sums up: "I saw Padre Pio five times in the course of fifteen months. I found some modifications, but I have nothing which enables me to make an authoritative classification of these wounds." He describes his experiment on the stigmatic as *seemingly barbarous.* "I repeated this seeming barbarous experiment several times in the evening ... and in the morning."

When we realize that it consisted of pressing his fingers to the front and back of the wound, and exploring for a gap such as would suggest complete transfixion; and when we remember that we have the doctor's own word for the hypersensitivity of these regions, we begin to have some idea of just what this gift of stigmatization meant to Padre Pio in regard to suffering. He must have suffered intensely from this examination; and we must emphasize that he submitted to it all cheerfully and without the least complaint.

Romanelli was followed in July, 1919 by Professor A. Bignami, an agnostic of the Roman University who was sent by ecclesiastical authorities to make an examination. He stayed two days at the friary and though he was thorough in describing the stigmatic wounds, Bignami never entertained the thought that they were of a supernatural origin. He seems to have come to Padre Pio with the same attitude which Zola brought to Lourdes, ruling out anything that science could not explain. There could be no denying the wounds, but he minimized their significance to the utmost by pronouncing them "superficial," a matter on which Romanelli was later to challenge him.

He could not conclude that they were deliberately self-inflicted, unless he wished to be convicted of inferring that this holy man, Padre Pio, was a fraud. He therefore concludes that the lesions were due "to a necrosis of the epidermis of neurotic origin, artificially maintained by the use of chemicals," and were "probably attributable to unconscious suggestion." Yet he admitted there was nothing that he saw in Padre Pio that would classify him as a typical neurotic. The chemical used in this instance was iodine. Padre Pio had been advised to use iodine "to cauterize, if possible, the wounds, and to protect them against infection." But when they stopped using iodine and used soap and water there was, of course, no difference in the wounds that persisted for fifty years and miraculously disappeared shortly after his death, not leaving even a scar. The stigmata, in Dr. Bignami's opinion, must be attributed to natural causes no matter how forced and unscientific his conclusions might be.

The next doctor to examine him was Doctor G. Festa of Rome, in October, 1919. He believed the stigmata were genuine and had come down heavily against a natural explanation. His meticulous examination and descriptions of the wounds was substantially in agreement with Dr. Bignami's examination but their conclusions were miles apart. He had discovered no trace of the neurotic in Padre Pio, in any shape or form. There were, however, what Festa called "many inaccuracies" in Bugnami's report, and Dr. Festa decided to return in 1920, accompanied by Dr. Romanelli. They established fully that "the scabs or pellicules on the lesions are crusts of dried blood, which when removed show the actual wounds, continually bleeding."

This time one is relieved for the good Padre Pio's sake, to read that no attempt was made to determine the depth of the wound, "owing to the hypersensitivity of the surrounding tissue." The conclusion of the doctors was that the wounds were "true and proper lesion of the *continuum,* deep as if made by a pointed instrument." So deep were the wounds that light could be seen though the stigmatic hands.

Dr. Festa examined Padre Pio five years later and at that time the Franciscan confided in him that he had a hernia which was causing him considerable pain. In an improvised operating room of the friary he performed a successful operation. The operation wound went through the perfectly normal process of healing, without the least sign of infection, leaving a scar as is common with any operation, contrary to the stigmatic open wounds that persisted to bleed for fifty years. Hysteria was suggested, but Padre Pio was a perfectly normal man "genial, humorous and apparently most unimpressionable," therefore not subject to neuroses.

We owe to Dr. Sala, who was the personal physician of Padre Pio, a detailed report on how the wounds gradually disappeared in the last months of his life. Some months before his death, his feet became dry, but his hands showed the same symptoms up to the day before his death. On this day there was an accentuation of the pallor of the skin, a diminishing of the formations of the crust, and the disappearance of the wounds on the back of the hands.

"During the very short agony the palm of the left hand still had a crust. Ten minutes after his death, Padre Pio's hands, thorax, and feet were held up by me ... and were photographed by a friar in the presence of four other friars. His hands, his feet and his thorax and every other part of his body did not show any trace of injury, nor were scars present on his hands and feet, neither on the back, nor on the palms, nor on the soles, nor on the side ... his skin was soft, elastic and mobile. When it was pressed with the fingers, there was no evidence of dermal or subcutaneous collapse. There was also no evidence of signs of progressive incision, laceration, injury, wounds, or inflammation. Such symptoms and behavior ... must be considered outside of every type of a clinical nature. They have an extra-natural character. ... "

What to make of the Stigmata of Blessed Padre Pio and the final touch of the Almighty, their miraculous disappearance? Padre Pio patiently and heroically bore the stigmata for fifty years, fulfilling the words of St. Paul in his Epistle to the Colossians: "I find joy in the suffering I endure for you. In my own flesh I fill up what is lacking in the sufferings of Christ for the sake of His body, the Church" (Col. 1, 24). So close was his identification with the suffering Christ, it was only fitting that Padre Pio mirror in his dead body the Resurrected Christ. If we die with Christ as did Padre Pio, bearing our crosses with love, we will rise along with Padre Pio in glory.

Excerpted from the book, Padre Pio, *by Malachy Gerard Carroll, The Mercier Press, Cork, Ireland.*

The Blind See

The Girl Who "Cannot See," Yet Sees

Ask any oculist or ophthalmologist, "Can a person without pupils see?" He will answer without hesitation, "There is no way possible for a person without pupils in his eyes to see." Yet, Gemma de Giorgi of Ribera, Sicily, who is now over 55 years old, was born without pupils and now sees.

There was a time, however, when she could not. Up to the age of seven Gemma de Giorgi was completely blind. Although she was miraculously given her sight in 1947, her eyes are still without pupils. In fact when anyone looks into her eyes today he still gets the distinct feeling they are sightless, like those of any other blind person. Gemma has undergone eye examinations by well-known eye specialists, who all agree that according to all the known laws of nature, sight for her is impossible. "She has to be blind," they conclude. There have been innumerable accounts written about this outstanding miracle which is attributed to Padre Pio, but the most accurate account was written by Gemma's grandmother. It was this venerable lady with the faith that moves mountains who took the blind child to San Giovanni Rotondo, fervently praying and hoping for a miracle.

It was she who actually witnessed the miracle take place, though due to extreme anxiety and fatigue she was unable to comprehend the full reality of what she witnessed at the time. About halfway to Foggia from Sicily, Gemma's grandmother tells us, Gemma began to see the sea and a steamboat. When she identified these things to her grandmother and other pilgrims who were accompanying them, they began to speak of a miracle. Yet due to the long trip in a country ravaged by World War II and her exhausted condition, it all seemed to the grandmother to be only a dream. Hence she hastened to Padre Pio still obsessed with the idea of begging him for the much desired miracle.

Immediately after her confession she asked Padre Pio to give Gemma the eyesight the child had already begun to enjoy. The grandmother's own written account completes the story:

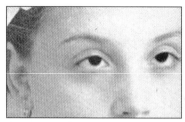

Gemma de Giorgi. Up to the age of seven she was totally blind, her eyes having no pupils. Oculists who have examined her say she cannot see, but she sees.

"I asked the grace for Gemma and I told him that the child was weeping because, in her confession with him, she had forgotten to ask this grace. I will never forget his soft and tender voice as he answered me with these words: 'Do you have faith, my daughter? The child must not weep and neither must you for the child sees, and you know she sees.' I understood then that Padre Pio was alluding to the sea and ship Gemma had seen during the trip and that God had used our saintly Padre Pio to break through the darkness that covered Gemma's eyes.

"After Padre Pio had given Gemma her first Holy Communion before all the populace that filled the church, with the same fingers that had held the Holy Eucharist he again made, for the second time, the sign of the cross over each of Gemma's eyes. And so, finally we started our return trip home but, since the whole trip had been, for me, extremely wearing and exhausting, I was taken by a very high fever and sent to the municipal hospital of Cosenza. As soon as I recovered, I had Gemma's eyes examined by an eye specialist who immediately declared Gemma blind and without pupils. I, poor ignorant person that I am, imagined that now that Gemma could see she should also have pupils in her eyes. I did not understand that even without pupils the child could, through the will of God, be enabled to see just the same. I therefore became confused and worried when I heard the oculist declare Gemma blind. But Gemma even though without pupils, had her eyesight and could see and so I insisted to the doctor that the child could see.

"In order to persuade me, the doctor showed Gemma some objects and when she recognized them and showed distinctly and without difficulty that she saw these things, the doctor stamped his foot on the floor and said, 'Without pupils, one cannot see. The child sees; therefore it is a miracle.' Since that time many eye doctors from all over Italy have contacted me requesting to examine Gemma's eyes. Many have even come here to our home and all have declared the same thing: 'That without pupils in one's eyes one should not be able to see and that, therefore, this is a miracle.'"

The above account of the grandmother was excerpted from the book, Roads to Padre Pio, *by Clarice Bruno*

A Case of Spiritual Blindness

by Malachy Gerard Carroll

Those who don't believe in miracles cannot deny that the case of Gemma de Giorgi is an unusual one. It is unique inasmuch as it is an "ongoing" miracle. Yet, Padre Pio cured another kind of "blindness" which is comparable to raising the dead to life. Sinners who came to his confessional to poke fun at him or to "expose" him were liberated on the spot from the spiritual blindness that had afflicted them for many years. An outstanding case in point is that of a distinguished photographer, Signor Frederico Abresch, which occurred in 1928. He was thoroughly converted from a skeptical curiosity seeker to an ardent and lifelong supporter of Padre Pio.

Abresch was baptized a Lutheran in Germany. As a young man he moved to Bologna where he set up a photography studio. At the time of his marriage to a Catholic girl he became a Catholic more as an accommodation to his wife's religion than out of sincere conviction. Later, his shaky religious commitment gave way to spiritualism, and then to "occultism and magic of every description." In his own words, "I made the acquaintance of a gentleman who with a mysterious air declared himself the possessor of the only truth—'Theosophy.' I soon became his disciple. ... "

When he first heard of the Capuchin priest who was described as enduring a living crucifixion and who was capable of working many miracles, he decided to see him even though he had a great antipathy for anything "Catholic." His first encounter left him cold as he expected a warmer welcome after his long journey. Soon after this brief encounter he was kneeling at the feet of the famous confessor. His own words describe what happened:

"It was not I, but Father Pio who spoke. He told me of certain grave sins I had committed in my previous confessions and asked if I had been in good faith. I said in reply that I thought confession was good 'psychologically' but that I did not believe in the divinity of the Sacrament. But, deeply moved by the fact that he had read my past life, I exclaimed, 'Now, however, I do believe.'

"'These are all heresies,' he said, with an atmosphere of great pain. 'All your communions have been sacrileges. You must make a general confession. Make your examination of conscience and try to remember when you last made a sincere confession. Jesus has been more merciful with you than He was with Judas.' He dismissed me with the words: 'Jesus and Mary be praised.'

Frederico Abresch, converted from spiritualism through a confession to Padre Pio.

"My head was in a turmoil, I kept hearing those words over and over again: 'Remember when you last made a sincere confession.'"

Abresch went through an agonizing examination of conscience and decided to review his whole life in a general confession. But when he was once again alone with the priest in the confessional, Padre Pio asked him: "When did you last make a good confession?"

"Father, as I happened to be ... " The priest interrupted him, saying: "Yes, you made a good confession that time when you were returning from your wedding trip, let us leave out all the rest, and begin from there." Abresch goes on to say, "I was struck dumb with the overwhelming realization that I had come in contact with the supernatural. Then concealing his knowledge of my entire past under the form of questions he enumerated with precision and clarity all of my mortal sins. He made me understand, with most impressive words, the whole of their gravity, adding in a tone of voice that I shall never forget:

"'You have launched a hymn to Satan, whereas Jesus, in his tremendous love has broken himself for you.' He then gave me a penance and absolved me. But to further emphasize the prodigious thing that happened to me ... and which, of course, only I could tell ... may I repeat that it was impossible for Father Pio to know that I had made that wedding journey, and that the confession that I had made on my return was indeed a good one. It actually did happen just as he said. The day after we returned from the trip my wife expressed the desire that we should both approach the Sacraments. I complied with her wish. I went to confession to the same priest who had prepared me to be a Catholic before the wedding. Knowing I was a novice, little accustomed to such things, he had helped me with many questions ... and that is why I had made a good confession. ...

"To complete this story of my conversion: From that day to this I have been to daily Mass and Communion. Both my wife and I have become Franciscan tertiaries. Not only do I believe in the dogmas of the Catholic Church, but in everything she teaches. And I would not lose this faith without also losing my life."

Signor Abresch, like so many other converts of Padre Pio, decided to move to San Giovanni Rotondo where he could be near to the man who had completely changed his life. He became, so to speak, the official photographer of Padre Pio, and most of the pictures one sees of the famous stigmatist were taken by him. Both he and his son, Pio, served his Mass many times. Eventually his son became a priest in fulfillment of a prophecy of Padre Pio. According to this prophecy the boy was not only to be a priest but would some day be placed in a high position in the Church. Msgr. Pio Abresch ended up working in the Vatican. Frederico Abresch died in August, 1969, within a year of the death of his great spiritual father.

Excerpted from the book, Roads to Padre Pio, *by Clarice Bruno*

Prayer is the best weapon we possess, the key that opens the heart of God. Have patience and persevere in the holy exercise of meditation; be content to begin with small steps till you have legs to run, better still wings to fly. Be content to be obedient, which is never a small thing for a soul which has chosen God for its portion. And be resigned to be, for the present, a little bee in the hive which will soon become a large bee capable of making honey.

The most beautiful Credo is that which comes from your lips in darkness, in sacrifice, in pain, in the supreme effort of an unbending will for good. It is this which, like a stroke of lightning, penetrates the darkness of the soul; it is this which in the flash of the tempest lifts you and leads you to God.

The prayers of the Saints in heaven and of the just on earth are a perfume which will never be lost. Pray, hope and don't worry. Anxiety doesn't help at all. Our Merciful Lord will listen to your prayer. Let us bind ourselves tightly to the Sorrowful Heart of our heavenly Mother and reflect on its boundless grief of how precious is our soul.

A Pen Sketch by One of His Friars

by Padre Giovanni

A great deal of light is thrown on Padre Pio's life in community by a friar from another province of his order, Padre Giovanni of Baggio, who made his acquaintance in 1934 when Padre Pio was nearly fifty years of age. A man of deep piety, fully committed to the quest for evangelical perfection in the footsteps of St. Francis of Assisi, he was sought by many as a spiritual guide. Such a priest could not fail to appreciate Padre Pio's spiritual worth.

Over a period of about fourteen years Padre Giovanni visited San Giovanni Rotondo a number of times, whenever his preaching commitments took him to that region. He wrote a small book, entitled, *Padre Pio Seen From Within,* in which he gives an account of his private conversations with Padre Pio. From their very first meeting he found in Padre Pio a great-hearted brother who opened wide his arms to him and laid bare his soul. Padre Pio called this friar his "dear little John" and used to joke with him and tease him, while he enjoyed being teased in return. To Padre Giovanni he revealed the sorrows and joys of his heart and several times he made his confession to him, although Padre Giovanni was only an occasional visitor. The Tuscan friar gives us a revealing pen-picture:

"Padre Pio had the ingenuous candor of a little child, and he opened his heart with unspeakable affection to those who approached him in a frank and sincere spirit. On the other hand, he was relentless in dealing with any one who was shamming, who showed craftiness in his presence or did not act with a pure intention. Any slyness or duplicity was immediately evident to him and no one of this kind was well received by him, just as he rid himself (and in no uncertain terms) of visitors in search of a religious thrill or those who came from mere curiosity.

"He certainly possessed uncommon human qualities. His fine well-marked features, his large bright eyes which looked into the depths of the soul, his melodious voice, his sense of humor which was enhanced by his accent and the dialectal expressions he used, and above all his keen intelligence gave him a particular charm. But all these exterior qualities amount to very little when compared to the interior worth and beauty of this friar."

Padre Giovanni goes on to describe his affability in the midst of his community:

"After evening devotions we all went to the hall for a show prepared by the young tertiaries in honor of Father General. At the end of the show, when Father General had left, the young people surged excitedly around Padre Pio, who continued to smile and joke with them. He is always cheerful, jovial and most affable. You would take him to be the happiest man in the world. In the depths of his soul he is the happiest man, but he admitted to me that he suffers terribly from constant headache, which is worsened by almost habitual insomnia and by the summer heat."

In 1935, as Padre Giovanni continued on his journey after a visit to Padre Pio, his mind kept returning to him.

"I was still thinking of the happy days spent there close to him. I recalled the stigmata, the spiritual radiance which seemed to shine out of him and overpower those around him. At the same time I noticed certain defects in him, genuflections badly made, drumming with his fingers during meditation, letting his eyes stray towards those who came into or out of the church ... I thought of his outbursts which at least at the moment seemed to indicate impatience. They were quite public and he didn't hide or check them.

"I concluded that he acted with the maximum simplicity and naturalness and this convinced me more fully of his holiness. The saints are human beings, they have their defects and weaknesses. They aren't as we somehow expect them to be. They are neither formal nor stiff, like Byzantine or Baroque statues. They are simple, straightforward and spontaneous."

In November, 1946, Padre Giovanni of Baggio visited him again.

"I was to see him in the evening, but he felt so bad that he couldn't receive anyone. Next day at lunch he was as jovial as ever. Later that day I went to his cell. He opened the door but went back to bed at once, as he had pains in his whole body. He said to me: 'For some time when I lie down on the bed I feel that my body receives a certain satisfaction. I hope I am not giving in too much to nature.' I admired the delicacy of his virtue: he would therefore like to keep his body stretched out on the cross all the time and never allow it any relief. I said to him: 'Stay there in bed, don't come down for the sermon' (I was preaching the community retreat). But he answered: 'Pray that I may be able to follow this holy retreat,' and he arrived down for the sermon. That evening he came to me for confession and I felt thoroughly ashamed in face of his delicacy of conscience."

Excerpt taken from the book, Padre Pio: His Life and Mission, *First published by Veritas publications. Used with permission.*

A Capuchin Friar for sixty-five years, Padre Pio embodied Franciscan peace and joy based on identification with Christ—Christ crucified. He radiated the merciful love of Christ and thus attracted thousands upon thousands to his confessional.

PART V

The young priest, Padre Pio, suffered severe bouts of extreme fevers which ran as high as 125 degrees Fahrenheit. Documents and broken thermometers attest to that which medical science can offer no explanation. It certainly was not of an exclusively physical nature. In the mystical life it is known as "fires of love," experienced also by other mystics. He wrote once: "I am aflame, though there is no fire. A thousand flames consume me; I feel I am dying, yet I am still alive." In 1921 he wrote to his superior: "I confess that for me it is a great misfortune to be unable to express and pour out the ever active volcano which burns me up and which Jesus placed in this very small heart. It can all be summed up as follows: 'I am consumed by love of God and love for my neighbor.'"

Padre Pio once said: "It would be easier for the earth to exist without the sun than without the Holy Mass." When one understands that it is Jesus, both victim and priest, offering Himself in expiation for the sins of mankind, this is no exaggeration.

How the Forgiones Raised a Saint

Mary Ann Budnik

*"Choose this day. ... whom you would rather serve. ... ;
but as for me and my house we will serve the Lord"(Joshua 24:15).*

The above quote from the *Book of Joshua* describes the lives of
Grazio Maria Forgione and Maria Giuseppa De Nunzio, the parents of
Padre Pio. Before work, leisure, or personal desires they served God.
Neighbors called them the "God-Is-Everything Family." This is the sim-
ple formula of how to raise saints and foster vocations.

Padre Pio's father, Grazio Maria Forgione, was born October 22,
1860, to Michele and Felicita D'Andrea Forgione. When he was but
seven years old, his father died suddenly. His mother remarried and
Grazio and his brother, Orsola, were raised by their kind stepfather,
Celestino Orlando. The family, while happy, lived in poverty. As he
matured, Grazio was known not only for his piety but also for his lead-
ership and strong sense of justice. While still in his teens, he was honored by being named a "Master of the Feast"—a committee member that
planned the annual festivities for Pietrelcina. "Gra," as he was affectionately called, had fair skin, dark eyes and chestnut hair. Of medium
height, he was strong, supple, and wiry with handsome features and a
strong voice which he used to serenade the young ladies of the village.

Grazio was a man of action. He faced his problems, resolved them
the best way he could and then moved on. He trusted that God would
give him the wisdom to do the right thing. This attitude of personal
responsibility and trust in God he likewise instilled in his children. Six
adjectives aptly describe him: he was simple, enthusiastic, intelligent,
full of life, holy and hardworking. Gra's conduct was virtuous and his
speech free from oaths or foul words. His struggle to live the different
virtues (good habits) was the root of his joyful personality which expressed itself in singing and storytelling. It is said that he radiated "a
contagious joy about him which communicated itself to others." He
instinctively knew that personal happiness consists in developing and
living the virtues while at the same time learning to deal with suffering
in a positive manner.

June 8th, 1881, at the age of twenty, Grazio Forgione married Maria Giuseppa De Nunzio. By law, the couple first married in a civil ceremony at the town hall and then in church. Although Maria's relatives initially disapproved of her marriage to the "humble" Grazio, it was a love match that endured for forty-eight years. Their marriage produced eight children, five of whom survived, including two religious vocations, one who has been beatified. Padre Pio's mother was likewise a virtuous woman. Born March 28, 1859, Maria Giuseppa De Nunzio was the only child of Fortunato De Nunzio and Maria Giovanna Gagliardi. A year and a half older than her husband, she was as tall as her husband with light blue eyes. Maria Giuseppa was called "The Little Princess" because of her grace, elegance, and sharp intelligence. She was as petite and dainty on the day that she died as she was on her wedding day.

Maria Giuseppa matched her devout husband in putting God in the first place. Even as a young woman she always prefaced her plans by saying, "If God is willing." When Francesco was born the midwife told her, "...your son has been born wrapped in a white veil. This is a good sign because he will be either great or fortunate." Maria simply replied, "Let the will of God be done." Despite her work load at home and in the fields, after morning prayers with the family, Maria always attended daily Mass. Known in town as Zia Beppa, she refused to criticize or gossip. Even when her beloved son, Padre Pio, was under attack she would cut short any criticism of his attackers by saying: "Who are we to permit criticism of the ministers of God? The Lord said that we ought not judge if we do not wish to be judged ourselves, and this means that we should judge neither the good nor the evil, because we can see only what people are doing, while God alone can see into men's hearts the reason why they do such things."

She mortified herself by abstaining from meat not only on Friday but also on Wednesdays and Saturdays in honor of Our Lady of Mount Carmel, but this did not stop her from exercising the virtue of hospitality. It is said that, "She was happier when she could give than when she could receive." Later in life Saint Padre Pio referred to Maria Giuseppa as "my holy mother," quite a compliment coming from a saint!

St. Augustine advises: "As regards the offspring it is provided that they should be begotten lovingly and educated religiously." This was the case in the home of Padre Pio. Of the five children who survived to adulthood, Michele the eldest was born on June 25, 1882. He married and eventually took over the family farm. On May 25, 1887, a third son was born and given the name of his short-lived brother, Francesco. This son would be known to the world as Padre Pio. His sister Felicita was born on September 15, 1889. She married the town clerk and had three children. Pellegrina was born three years later and was a source of sorrow to the Forgione family because of her loss of faith and scandalous behavior. Despite her devout upbringing, she gave birth to an illegitimate son, Alfredo, who was rumored to have been fathered by Felicita's husband Vincenzo Masone. Felicita forgave her sister and on her deathbed urged her husband to marry Pellegrina. Through the prayers of her family Pellegrina was reconciled to God before she died. Grazia (or Graziella) was born on December 26, 1894, and became Sister Pia of the order of St. Bridget in Rome.

The Forgiones not only taught the Catholic faith to their children but more importantly they *lived* their faith. The family attended Sunday Mass together at a time when many men stayed outside chatting while their wives and children attended Mass. Weekdays, after walking a half hour home from their farm fields, the family would stop into church to thank God for His blessings and present their needs to Him. Grazio was never without a rosary in his hands which he prayed continuously. From his example his children also developed devotion to the rosary. The Forgione children were strongly influenced by their parents mortified example in regard to food and drink. Imitating their example, young Francesco would also secretly deprive himself of food and drink for the love of God. The children were disciplined by persuasion and scoldings, never by spankings. They were taught to avoid blasphemy and crude language. Working on Sunday was forbidden.

The Forgione family lived simply. Originally their home seems to have been two small houses since one has to go out the door of Number 27 to get into Number 28. As Padre Pio would reminisce: "We had little. But thank God, we never lacked anything." The only decorations in the home were a crucifix and lithographs of Our Lady and the saints. These lithographs were more than decorations. The Mother of God and the various saints were considered important members of their family. It was in this atmosphere that Saint Pio developed his fervent love of the Madonna.

A typical day began for the Forgione family at daybreak with morning prayers. Then the family would set off for a half hour walk to their five acres in Piana Romana where they tended their sheep, goats, hens, ducks, rabbits, some hogs, and occasionally a milk cow. On the land itself they raised grapes, wheat, Indian corn, olives, figs, and plums. There was a cottage with a dirt floor located on their land where they kept their animals, stored their equipment, and ate and slept in summer. The crops were picked or reaped by hand and the threshing was done by animals dragging a stone behind them on the threshing floor. Once a crop was harvested, another was planted. Later in the season the grapes and olives were gathered. The workday would end for Gra at sundown. Maria Giuseppa, on the other hand, would rise in the middle of the night to begin baking bread. Three times a day Maria would have to climb up and down twenty steps to carry home water for the family's needs. Although it was an exhausting life, she and her husband were content.

On winter evenings, the children would listen to stories told by their father or their maternal grandmother, Giovanna Gagliardi, who lived close by. Most of the stories came from Scripture which Grazio had memorized, since he was unable to read. The day would always end with the family saying the rosary on their knees. Graziella, later Sister Pia, related that prayer was given the first priority in their family.

Maria Giuseppa was frugal, industrious and generous, always donating a portion of their farm products as alms for the Poor Souls in Purgatory. She also gave the first fruits of the family harvest to the poor. It was after Mamma Giuseppa donated an abundant amount of wheat to a questing friar that Francesco told his father, "I want to be a religious." Immediately his father gave his consent. Pio's vocation necessitated heroic sacrifices for his mother and father. They would have to forgo his help on the farm while he went to school. Grazio would have to procure a job in the United States to earn money for his son's education. Mamma Giuseppa was left to care for five children and the farm while her husband was thousands of miles away. Their only means of communicating was by letters written by Francesco to his father. Until an American taught his father to read and write, Grazio had to rely on strangers to read his son's letter to him and write letters for him to his family. Blessed Pio relates: "My father crossed the ocean twice in order to give me the chance to become a friar." Francesco began his junior high studies with Dominic Tizzano, but he did poorly. Later Grazio admitted, "Our choice of a teacher for our son was poor. Sending him to a former priest who had left the Church and married was an error on our part."

Each Sunday evening the children attended catechism classes in preparation for their First Holy Communion at the age of ten and confirmation at the age of twelve.

Grazio and Maria passed on to their children the Catholic tradition of making pilgrimages to various shrines. It was on one such pilgrimage with his father that the future Padre Pio witnessed a miracle at the Shrine of St. Pellegrino which taught him the power of prayer (see page 10).

Heroic sacrifice was part of this family's everyday life. It broke the hearts of both parents and children when one left home to follow a religious vocation. Grazio was unable to even attend his son's ordination, Aug. 10, 1910, since he was in the United States earning money for his son's education. He had to rely on details in a letter written by Don

Little did the parents of Padre Pio realize that some day people would pilgrimage to shrines in honor of their son.

Salvatore, the parish priest, describing his son's great day for which he had labored so diligently for years.

In 1928, when she was nearly seventy years old, Maria Giuseppa came to San Giovanni Rotondo to spend Christmas near her son. In a short meeting with her son, Giuseppa fell to her knees and asked: "Padre Pio, how can we know if before God we are not great sinners? We confess everything that we can remember or know, but perhaps God sees other things that we cannot recall." Pio replied: "If we put into [our confession] all our good will and we have the intention to confess everything—all that we can know or remember—the mercy of God is so great that He will include and erase even what we cannot remember or know." She attended his Midnight Mass but was not dressed warmly enough for the weather. She refused an offer of a fur coat saying, "Oh, I don't want to look like a great lady, my dear." She caught double pneumonia and died January 3, 1929. Francesco Morcaldi relates that "her death was truly beautiful. She breathed her last serenely while they were praying [around her bed]. Unaided, she raised the crucifix, pressed it to her lips, [and died]." Upon her death Padre Pio collapsed. For hours he sobbed, "Mammella! Mammella! My beautiful Mammella! My sweet, darling Mammella!" He was unable to return to the friary or even attend her funeral. For days he wept as did his younger sister, Sister Pia, in her cell in Rome.

In 1938, Grazio moved to San Giovanni to be near his son until his death. When people complimented Grazio on his son, he would humbly reply, "I didn't make him. Jesus Christ did." On October 7, 1946, Gra died at the age of eighty-six. Upon the death of his father, Padre Pio again collapsed in sorrow.

Grazio and Maria Giuseppa knew the formula for raising a happy, holy family. It consists in the four S's. By serving God they became Christ-like. Their son, Padre Pio, even bore the wounds of Christ. Daily they struggled to grow in the various virtues. They suffered with acceptance. They sacrificed themselves for family members and strangers alike. By living this simple formula they gave the world a great saint. Can we not imitate their example? John Paul II reminded us in New Orleans: "Holiness is not the privilege of a few; it is a gift offered to all."

"L'Americana" Collaborator

Madeline Pecora Nugent, SFO

Nearly all those who knew Padre Pio from shortly after he received the stigmata to shortly before his death knew in some way "L'Americana." A rotund, jovial woman with a red-cheeked, fair face that radiated peace and welcome, Mary Pyle's name became almost synonymous with that of the famous friar.

Early in their friendship, Padre Pio, knowing that Mary hated to take orders, had told Mary Pyle that God had no intention of her becoming a nun. Instead the Padre told her to join the Third Order of Saint Francis. With great enthusiasm Mary did so, immediately begging the friars to allow her, as a tertiary, to wear the Capuchin habit, a penitential garb worn by tertiaries in earlier centuries. Mary's persistent winsomeness won approval for this distinctive favor. Decked out in a Capuchin habit complete with rope belt, rosary, and large crucifix, Mary daily climbed the steep hill from her house to the friary church to participate in the Divine Office and to assist at Padre Pio's Mass, sitting always in the back so that others might have the front seats. "I want only to be in church with him," Mary said with devotion. So often was she in church, and so much did she resemble a friar that a visitor once dubbed her "Brother Mary."

This joyful American devotee of the good padre welcomed visitors to San Giovanni Rotondo, entertained them at her house which she had built herself, and answered in Padre Pio's name many of the endless letters he received. For all this she asked nothing more than to attend Padre Pio's Mass, to assist with whatever clerical or charitable works he asked of her, and to receive his spiritual direction which not infrequently included some of the friar's harsh admonitions.

How did this fair haired "L'Americana," who dressed like a friar yet carried herself like a society dame, come to be living in San Giovanni Rotondo? Mary Pyle's story is one of God's grace. On April 17, 1888, Frances Adelaide Pyle, wife of tobacco and real estate magnate James Tolman Pyle, gave birth to her third child and first daughter. Five months later, Adelia McAlpin Pyle, one day to become Mary Pyle, was baptized at the Presbyterian Church of the Covenant where her mother was a member. In time three more children came along, giving Adelaide and James four sons and two daughters who traveled back and forth with their parents from their grandparents' house, 'Glen Alpin,' in Morristown, New Jersey, to the family house at 673 Fifth Avenue, Manhattan. Adelia grew up with a staff of eight servants who did everything including "light a match" for her.

Adelia's father James was kind and easy going, fond of high living and a spendthrift. Her mother Adelaide, who could be impulsive in the worst sense of the word, loved to live in grand style with her beribboned lap dogs, made frequent trips to Europe, and desired to become an American millionaire. A brilliant linguist who spoke several languages, Adelaide promoted the teaching of foreign languages in the schools and hired language instructors for her children. The youngsters were not permitted to speak any language but the one being taught, and this until they had learned it. Thus Adelia was educated at home, then sent to two finishing schools where she studied music, dancing, and singing.

By age fifteen, Adelia was expressing her desire to become a Catholic, an idea that horrified her mother. So she called in the pastor of her church to have him talk some sense into the blond teen who asked, "Are you really sure of the truth of the Westminster Confession?" When he admitted that he was not, Adelia asked, "Why, then, do you want to impose it on me?"

In 1912, shortly after the sudden death of her father, Adelaide's interest in early childhood education marked a turning point in Adelia's life. Making the acquaintance of Maria Montessori, a famous but controversial childhood educator, Adelaide set up the Montessori Education Foundation to found American schools based on the Italian educator's methods. When Dr. Montessori visited the Pyle home, Adelia's fluency with languages impressed her, and she asked Adelia to become her interpreter. Before Adelaide could stop the transaction, Adelia had left for Europe with Maria Montessori.

Montessori's Catholic faith drew Adelia spiritually until Adelia was conditionally baptized by a Capuchin priest in Rome, taking the name Mary. From this time on, Adelia McAlpin Pyle answered only to Mary Pyle. To this act of grace, Adelaide responded with characteristic, impulsive anger. She stopped funding Montessori's work and cut off her daughter's allowance, declaring that she never wanted to see her child again.

After reading the book *Self-Abandonment to Divine Providence* by Father Jean-Pierre de Caussade, Mary began to search for a spiritual director like Father Caussade who wrote "We have to do nothing except allow His Holy Will to work within us and surrender ourselves to it blindly and with absolute confidence." Sometime in the early 1920's, Mary became aware of Padre Pio. Suffering what she called "spiritual lethargy," Mary desperately wished to visit the humble Capuchin who had been branded with the wounds of Christ. Mary wanted the friar to guide her out of her uncomfortable spiritual morass which was, unknown to her, God drawing her out of her current lifestyle into another one of poverty, simplicity, faith, and abandonment of the world.

In early fall of 1923, Mary's friend Rina d'Ergiu persuaded Mary to accompany her to San Giovanni Rotondo to see Padre Pio. Rina wanted to ask the Padre if she should become a Roman Catholic. To Rina's tearful response that she was not a Roman Catholic, Padre Pio said bluntly, "Who's stopping you?" To Mary Pyle he said nothing at first. Gazing at the Padre, Mary fell to her knees at his feet, saying, "Father." He touched her head and said, "My child, stop traveling around. Stay here."

But true to her nature of not slavishly following instructions, Mary returned to Maria Montessori to persuade her to meet the Padre. After the meeting, when both women went to board the bus to return to Rome, Mary literally could not move. It was as if, she later declared, "someone had nailed my feet to the ground." Montessori boarded the bus while Mary remained behind where the good friar told her to join the Third Order of Saint Francis. Soon Mary, dressed like a Capuchin friar, had rented a room in town and had joined the Padre's other spiritual daughters who climbed the hill daily for Mass.

In time, through Padre Pio's efforts, Mary and her mother Adelaide were reconciled, although to Mary's dismay Adelaide never joined the Catholic church. When Mary voiced to Padre Pio her concern over her mother's salvation, the friar pointedly told her, "Who told you that your mother could not be saved?" At Padre Pio's insistence, Mary made one last trip to see her ill mother in London in 1937. Soon after the visit, Adelaide died.

While still alive, after she had reconciled with Mary, Adelaide had reinstated Mary's allowance in the amount of five to seven thousand dollars yearly. Mary, who lived like a pauper herself, would use this money to build a two story house in which she lived and which was open daily to pilgrims to San Giovanni Rotondo. Some of the funds went to feed the many pilgrims, and during World War II, soldiers, all of whom always had ample food to eat at that house. With the rest of the monthly stipend Mary gave alms and assistance to the village ill and poor. In addition, she used the money to build a friary at Pietrelcina dedicated to the Holy Family, and to fund the seminary education of about ten young men who became priests.

Above, left: Mary Pyle, the American collaborator and spiritual daughter of Padre Pio in her Franciscan tertiary habit. Below: as a New York socialite. Above, right: The house Mary built near the monastery. The parents of Padre Pio spent their last days and died here.

For over forty years Mary Pyle labored with love in San Giovanni Rotondo. She visited the poor and ill, bringing them material and spiritual solace. She took sick, needy women into her home to care for them. To all who knocked at her door for assistance, Mary gave aid. So generous was she with her money that she sometimes was tricked by swindlers into giving funds to bogus causes. She never worried about these dishonest folks, preferring to give to all who asked, even though at the end of every month she was penniless as she awaited her next monthly allowance. Around her Mary gathered a community of local women who lived poor, chaste lives and who helped Mary in her many charitable works.

Some of Mary's acts of kindness became legendary. Several people recalled her tender care of Emerenziana, a woman suffering from a form of facial cancer so hideous that few people could overcome their revulsion to visit her. Mary visited Emerenziana weekly and even kissed her face. After these visits, she would joyfully tell her companions that the poor invalid was "so nice, so very nice. She certainly knows how to suffer." Mary also took into her home Padre Pio's parents, nursing them both through their final illnesses and watching the Padre weep at their deathbeds.

Mary's many charitable works were surpassed only by the depth of her faith. She daily attended Mass and the praying of the Divine Office. Frequently she made long visits to the Blessed Sacrament, remaining before It in silent prayer and adoration. She prepared hosts for the altar, cared for the altar linens, and was, at Padre Pio's request, the official organist at the Sanctuary of Our Lady of Grace, the church from which she was buried. During her final illness, when she could no longer attend Mass, Mary asked for and was granted permission to receive the Eucharist at home. Padre Pio once commented to her that not a day had gone by since she had come to San Giovanni Rotondo that Mary had not received the Eucharist.

Mary's own final illness was painful and prolonged, yet she bore her sufferings with patience and serenity. When Mary died in 1968, Padre Pio, himself very ill, watched her funeral from the balcony of the church. At her own request "Brother Mary" was buried in her habit in the Capuchin chapel in the cemetery at San Giovanni Rotondo where the Capuchin priests and brothers had their final resting place.

Those who remember Mary describe her as "a beautiful soul," "always smiling," "serene," "generous ... in a very rare, evangelical manner." Of her Padre Pio once said, "The earth is much more beautiful because of her presence!" She would have liked that as her epitaph.

Do not be so given to the activity of Martha as to forget the silence of Mary. May the Virgin who so well reconciled the one with the other be your sweet model and inspiration.

Some persons when they are with the good, are good; when they are with the bad they follow evil. This is to have half a conscience; it is to act like children who, in the presence of strangers, abuse the occasion to do things that please their taste, certain that the parents will not reprove them.

If we wish to reap it is necessary not so much to sow abundantly as to spread the seed in fertile soil, and when this seed becomes a plant, our chief anxiety should be to watch that the weeds do not suffocate the tender plants.

— *Padre Pio*

A Padre Pio Family Begets Another Franciscan Family

Franciscans of the Immaculate

Settimio and Licia Gualandris Manelli were not only the proud parents of 21 children, but were given the distinction by Padre Pio of being referred to as: "This is my family." One of their sons, Stefano, in particular had the privilege of having Padre Pio as his spiritual director for many years. And it is this Franciscan priest, Fr. Stefano Manelli, the founder of a branch of the Franciscan Order known today as the Franciscans of the Immaculate whom the following story is about.

The Manellis, parents of Stefano and their twenty other children, would make a pilgrimage to San Giovanni Rotondo from their home in northern Italy every year. On their way and on their return trip to visit Padre Pio they would stop at the great Marian Shine of the Holy House of Loreto. How special was their trip in 1933, as Licia was carrying a baby in her womb to be blessed by Padre Pio and the Holy Virgin Mary at the Holy House of Loreto, where Mary conceived the baby Jesus in her womb. In August of the same year the Manellis returned to thank Padre Pio for his prayers for a safe delivery and to entrust their little Stefano to the care of Our Lady of Loreto.

Stephanuccio (little Stephan) as he was affectionately called, was a spiritual child of Padre Pio from his earliest years right up to the day the holy friar died in 1968. Raised in a devout Catholic home, he learned early in life the importance of prayer and sacrifice. This was enhanced and further developed by direct contact with the saintly Franciscan, recently canonized, Saint Padre Pio. While Stefano was still a small child, the family was able to move a short distance from San Giovanni Rotondo, to Lucera where his father obtained a position as professor of literature.

At the age of five Stefano received his First Holy Communion from the hand of Padre Pio, and from the age of six on he frequently had the privilege of serving Padre Pio's Mass (in Latin). From then until his twelfth birthday when he entered the Franciscan minor seminary, he would serve his Mass and according to the custom of that time he would kiss Padre Pio's stigmatized hands after Mass. He frequently went to confession to him and on occasions when his father would visit Padre Pio, he would sit near him as they conversed on such themes as the Gospels, the writings of St. Augustine, St. Teresa of Avila, and St. John of the Cross. There were times when the boy would begin to nod resting his head upon the breast of Padre Pio.

Stefano also served Mass in his home parish of St. Francis in Lucera, where the body of St. Francis Anthony Fasani is laid out under the high altar. Both the Saint and the custodians of the Church were Conventual Franciscans. Noticing his reverence and seriousness, the pastor suggested he become a *fratino* in their minor seminary. Stefano gladly accepted the invitation, though at the time he didn't have a clear idea of the distinction between the various branches of the Franciscans. He was simply attracted to being a friar and studying for the priesthood.

When he told his father his desire to enter the seminary, his father took counsel with Padre Pio. One might expect that Padre Pio would advise Mr. Manelli to send his little friend, Stefano, to the Capuchin seminary. Yet instead Padre Pio indicated that the boy should enter the Friars Minor Conventual. So on December 8, 1945, at the age of 12, Stefano entered the Conventual Friars' minor seminary. There he distinguished himself for his fidelity to the routine of seminary life. Ordained a Conventual Franciscan priest in 1955, Fr. Stefano Manelli continued receiving spiritual direction from his friend, the holy Capuchin of the

Settimio and Licia Manelli, parents of 21 children, one of whom, Fr. Stefano, became a Franciscan priest and eventually received direction from Padre Pio on founding a new branch of the Franciscan Order.

Gargano. On occasion he was able to spend several days in the Friary of Our Lady of Grace sharing the common table with Padre Pio. Once he saw Padre Pio with his face aglow with the light of the blessed. Another time when the door of his cell was locked, Padre Pio came in to awaken him at 3:45 for his Mass at 4:00 am.

Five years before Padre Pio's death, Fr. Stefano began an in-depth study on Franciscan sources, in the light of the Conciliar document *Perfectae Charitatis*, which called for the renewal of Religious Life. He found that the much heralded "renewal" and "updating" at that time had begun to take on features which had little to do with the genuine Seraphic spirit of the founder of the Franciscan Order, St. Francis of Assisi. Among the writings he studied carefully were those of St. Maximilian Kolbe, though at the time he was not yet canonized. He made St. Maximilian's spirituality his own. Kolbe's interpretation of the Franciscan charism went back to the original Franciscan spirit and life of the early Franciscans, applying that life and ideals to the present time yet without compromises with the spirit of the world.

The last years of Padre Pio's life were decisive in maturating and preparing for Fr. Stefano's experience in establishing Casa Mariana on August 2, 1970, at Frigento, Italy. Even before this period, Padre Pio was offering valuable suggestions to help polish up and fill in details of the plan (the Traccia) to live a renewal of Franciscan life in Frigento, modeled on the lives of Franciscan saints, past and present. This plan and experience of Franciscanism was to be essentially Marian and Seraphic in its orientation.

In regard to its Franciscan dimension, Padre Pio recommended above all the "perfect observance of religious life thus fostering all that is necessary to become a saint." He pointed out that perfect observance referred to conforming one's life to the Constitutions of the Institute. He warned that, "At the judgment seat of God our Constitutions and our lives will be compared with one another." Faithful observance must include both body and soul, that is, it must touch both the interior and exterior, as Padre Pio recommended with these enlightening words: "We must carve on souls and bodies our Franciscan vocation ... my little brother, do this as God wills!"

Saint Pio was even more concise and brief on the Marian dimension of the Casa Mariana, emphasizing this by the significant tone of his voice and his facial expression: "I recommend you to Our Lady!" It was the mystery of Mary, in particular her Immaculate Conception, the sublime glory of the Franciscans, which Padre Pio recommended to Fr. Stefano. The continuous praying of the Rosary is the inheritance and example that Padre Pio has left to all his spiritual children, especially a

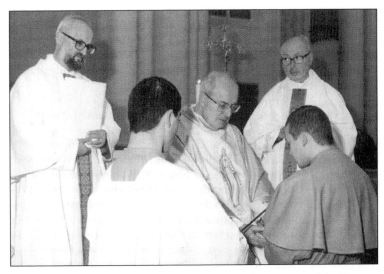

Fr. Stefano receiving the vows of a member of the Franciscans of the Immaculate (F.I.). Standing to the right of him is Fr. Gabriel M. Pellettiere, the cofounder of the new community.

spiritual son so dear to him as Fr. Stefano.

To understand these Marian teachings and directives of Padre Pio better, one must consider how this Marian dimension in Fr. Manelli's life parallels his Franciscan vocation. Providentially Fr. Manelli was stationed in Assisi in 1967 and 1968. He had ample opportunity to visit and make long meditations in the places most sacred and dear to Franciscans, especially the Portiuncula at St. Mary of the Angels which is considered the womb and cradle of the Franciscan Order. The fruit of his meditations was a long article in homage of Padre Pio, entitled, "The Signs of Being in Padre Pio," which eventually was published in the review *"La Casa Sollievo della Sofferenza."* It was on September 20, 1968, the golden jubilee of Padre Pio's Stigmatization, that Fr. Stefano placed the manuscript in the hands of Padre Pio.

The first fruit of this prayerful study resulted in Fr. Stefano's consecrating himself in a special self-offering to God, "through the Immaculate," using the solemn act of consecration to Mary Immaculate composed by St. Maximilian Kolbe. From this it is clear that Padre Pio's example of Franciscan and priestly life forged and formed the life and apostolic labor of Fr. Stefano. It guided him to the goal of sanctification to which God directed him for the benefit of the entire Church. Among its fruits are the Franciscans of the Immaculate, both friars and sisters.

137

The founding of the Sister's community was understood fully only after the fact. Once, after a confession Fr. Stefano lamented the fact that no one in his family or among his relatives was inclined to the religious life, in particular the sisterhood. Padre Pio fixed his eyes on Fr. Manelli and smiled as if looking far into the future and said joyfully: "Let us hope, let us hope, let us hope. ... " At the time it was impossible to conclude anything, but the joyful and confident tone of his voice indicated what would happen in the future.

During the years that followed, Fr. Stefano had no clue as to what would later transpire in regard to Frigento. He received an obedience to preach a retreat at the friary there to a group of Franciscan clerics preparing for solemn profession. He stopped by San Giovani Rotondo commending the retreat to the prayers of Padre Pio. He was puzzled when Padre Pio said, "So at Frigento, Frigento." Pausing and as if looking far ahead for a few moments he said, "You are going to make a retreat." Fr. Stefano thought Padre had misunderstood him and so repeated, "Father, I'm to give a retreat." Padre Pio with even greater insistence said again: "You are going to make a retreat."

Thus the conversation ended without a common understanding. It was only later that Fr. Stefano realized that Padre Pio had foreseen how Frigento would become the center for the renewal of the Seraphic life at which he and the cofounder, Fr. Gabriel M. Pellettiere, and their followers would begin what was to become the "Franciscans of the Immaculate."

Another delicate affirmation of Padre Pio's presence, interest and intervention in the founding of this new Franciscan family took place on August 2, 1970, the day the friars took over the Frigento friary. The light scent of perfume, distinctive of Padre Pio, was experienced in the corridors of Our Lady of Good Counsel friary.

With Padre Pio's example of a genuine Franciscan and a priestly priest who identified with Christ and His Immaculate Mother, Fr. Manelli was guided toward that holiness which would benefit him and the whole Church. The General Council of the friars and sisters of the "Franciscans of the Immaculate" has acknowledged his role, recently adding this spiritual father, Saint Padre Pio, along with St. Joseph, St. Clare, St. Francis and St. Maximilian as a special patron of the community, trusting that he who was so instrumental in bringing about its very existence will continue to guide, protect and illumine them.

A Man Become Prayer

Eusebio Notte

The attitude in which we were used to seeing Padre Pio was that of prayer. It was his bond with God and at the same time brought him closer to man.

For many people Padre Pio is the "crucifix of the century," for others the first priest to bear the stigmata, the man who has worked and still works wonders, the consoler of suffering humanity, the intermediary between God and man, and so on. Certainly, the one who knew him like that is not mistaken but has an incomplete or imperfect knowledge of the Padre, understanding only one aspect of his great soul.

If instead we try to obtain in a few words the complete portrait of Padre Pio, I think we should describe him as "a man become prayer," just as his father Saint Francis was described.

For me this is the most exact description of Padre Pio and also the most realistic, as I was able to ascertain during the long years that I was at his side night and day. With these three words, in fact, we summarize the life and the mission of the Padre and we have a precise picture of his character whose features depart from the earth and lose themselves in Heaven. Everyone who has met Padre Pio remembers him as always in an attitude of intimate union with God. This is how the world saw him and he was always like that at every moment. Therefore each time one met him he was always praying.

Many, in fact, only saw Padre Pio during Mass; and the Mass is the most sublime act of our community prayer, when we renew the Sacrifice of Golgotha and offer it again to God.

Padre Pio was deeply convinced of this, which is why he wanted to say his Mass in the early hours of the morning, to give our Lord the first fruits of the day. And how many conversions, how many graces there were during his Mass, the memory of which not one of us will be able to cancel? Many have met the Padre only in the confessional and what is the Sacrament of Penance if not prayer become repentance-pardon? At that moment the Padre was for us the channel through which grace returned to our souls.

Many men have had the good fortune to see Padre Pio a bit closer, that is in the sacristy, on the stairs of the friary, in the corridors, on the verandah, etc. In what attitude did they find the Padre? Always in an attitude of prayer. Besides external recollection and the edifying composure which showed in his whole person, he always kept a hand hidden in his pectoral pocket where he kept a rosary. Most pilgrims saw Padre Pio only in the church and precisely in that corner of the gallery; he seemed then to be raised between heaven and earth, intent on receiving the requests of the people to present them to Jesus, or the Heavenly Mother, whose image dominated his eyes.

And this "corner" was the place where we were used to seeing him. We had the sensation that the Padre was there waiting for us, at every moment, to invite us to unite our prayers to his, and all together make "gentle pressure on the Heart of God" as he used to say. And even today, entering the church of San Giovanni Rotondo, our eyes instinctively search that angle of heaven; but we look away dismayed and a new sorrow pierces our hearts!

Oh, dear Padre, even though we cannot see you with our eyes, let us find you again up there with our spirits, in that "corner." Your presence will be a call for us and an invitation to pray together with you under the vigilant gaze of our Lady. The attitude in which we were used to seeing Padre Pio was the attitude of prayer, but if this was the bond which kept him bound to God, it was at the same time the bond that brought him closer to man.

When people turned to him for help, advice, comfort, the first thing he did was to assure them of his prayers and to exhort them to pray also.

And how many of these people must be grateful to him after having experienced the efficacy of this most powerful weapon of his that benefits bodies and souls. His prayers were answered because he knew how to ask without ever giving up. His life was a continuous prayer as could be seen outwardly. Even when he took a bit of recreation with his confreres or his spiritual children, he always continued to pray his rosary. (Oh, what blessed moments those were when the Padre entertained his children with his witty remarks as well as instructing them.)

The same thing happened at the refectory: the plate would be steaming in front of him, but he would not touch it before he had said the fifteen decades of the Rosary; and he did the same thing after the meal. You can imagine what his meal was reduced to! At night, he did not go to sleep (if he slept at all!) without first having prepared at length for holy Mass, which he did again in the middle of the night as well as saying many Rosaries. And if he happened to doze off while saying the

Rosary, he would hold the rosary firmly at the bead where he had left off and when he woke up he would continue from there.

It is known that the Rosary of our Lady was the Padre's favorite prayer. How many must he have said during his life? Sometimes, in one day, he said sixty rosaries of fifteen mysteries! But the usual number was never less than forty. And what about those short exclamation prayers, poignant sighs and those moans every moment of the day and night? When he passed in front of a picture of Jesus or our Lady, he was transfigured; his face lit up with a heavenly smile or was clouded with visible suffering, while more than once his eyes became moist with tears.

But up till now I have spoken only of "external" prayer; unfortunately his long meditations, his intimate conversations with our Lord escaped our attention. All the same we can suppose that if the "external" prayer was so sublime, then the internal prayer must have been celestial!

It is a pity we cannot penetrate into the mystery which surrounded Padre Pio's contemplation! I think that if we had been able to satisfy this desire, we would have been dumbfounded and left breathless! We must not think, however, that the Padre's prayer was a continuous ecstasy; nothing could be further from the truth! Indeed, I know for a fact that often when Padre Pio prayed his spirit was restless, arid and frozen. How many times, before praying or during prayer itself he was obliged to renew his act of faith, because he could not see or feel anything: the One to whom was directed so much moaning was hiding from the eyes of the spirit while remaining intimately united to his creature.

Therefore, prayer for the Padre was not always an ecstatic conversation with our Lord, but often a tremendous effort of the will, a continual act of faith to the "One" whom he knew was close to him, but whom he felt to be terribly far away. And since the Padre prayed under difficult conditions all his life, one can deduce that his prayers were meritorious beyond words, because devoid of sensible consolations that could captivate him.

One day at the top of the stairs one of his spiritual sons posed him a question that was very embarrassing for the Padre, he said: "Padre, which is most acceptable to God: the prayer of a saint in Heaven, or a man on earth?" After a few moments of silence he replied: "I think the prayer of man on earth, because his prayer is accompanied by a sigh!" With this marvelous reply the Padre did not in the least minimize the greatness of the prayers that the Saints raise to the throne of God as they plunge into that ocean of light and love; instead he wanted to exalt the value of prayers that men send up from the earth while their hearts weep and their spirits are overcome by the deepest obscurity. These words of the Padre are a call for us, men of his period, who no longer feel drawn to pray because distracted by a thousand preoccupations, or slaves of a spiritual dryness, which withdraws us from God always more.

The thought that our prayer is more acceptable to our Lord the more difficult it is, should urge us to raise our eyes towards Heaven and tear open that sky which seems deaf and insensible to our entreaties. Probably, from behind those clouds a ray of sunlight will not delay to appear, which will enlighten our path and warm our heart. This is what Padre Pio teaches us with his life of prayer and intimate union with God.

Prayer remains still today the only means to reach the Heart of God and snatch from Him what humanity most needs. The progress of science and technology has not succeeded in taking its place; indeed, it teaches us that the more man advances in the achievements of his intelligence, the more he needs to bow his head before God and humbly implore his help.

Padre Pio, noble creature of our century, gives this very message to humanity: To return to God by means of prayer.

He consumed his long existence (although too short for those who knew and loved him) immolating himself for the good of the Church, priests, and all his brethren scattered in the world, and that when dying he left as his testament an accent of prayer and blessing for everyone. He now reminds us that we must not live forgetting God, but we must remain closely united to Him, as children with their Father.

Only in this way will we have nothing to fear from the days that are coming; indeed, we will be able to confront them with great hope in our hearts. And Padre Pio will not have lived in this world in vain, but will have the great merit of having brought men back to God by means of prayer.

Reprinted from the Voice of Padre Pio *magazine, San Giovanni Rotondo.*

The final purpose of meditation is the love of God and one's neighbor. Love the first with all your soul and without reservation, love the second as another self, and you will have arrived at the final purpose of meditation.

Ahead! Courage! In the spiritual life he who does not advance goes backward. It happens as with a boat which always must go ahead. If it stands still the wind will blow it back.

When you do not succeed in meditating well do not for this reason cease to do your duty. If there are many distractions do not lose heart. Make a meditation on patience; you will profit all the same. Fix the time, the length of your meditation, and do not rise from your place until you have finished it even at the cost of being crucified.
— *Padre Pio*

Mystical Ascent

Mary E. Ingoldsby

"I believe that the true story of Padre Pio's spiritual life is to be found in his Letters, of which the first volume appeared very recently. Those who want to understand Padre Pio of Pietrelcina, rather than reading a biography written by someone else ought to read his Letters." This statement was made by Joseph Cardinal Siri, Archbishop of Genoa, in an address to a large meeting of Padre Pio's devotees assembled in that city in September, 1973 to commemorate the fifth anniversary of his death. The Cardinal was referring to the young friar's correspondence with his spiritual directors during the years of his enforced absence from his community.

Another prelate, Most Rev. Msgr. Paolo Carta, formerly Bishop of Foggia and at present Archbishop of Sassari (Sardinia) stated:

"On reading the first volume of his letters, which contains his correspondence with his spiritual directors from 1910 to 1922, I was deeply impressed and moved. Although I already held Padre Pio in great esteem, I should never have imagined that his union with God and his prayer life had reached those sublime heights of mysticism which I admired in St. Teresa of Avila. For me this was a wonderful discovery. I rejoiced to think that I had known him, had made my confession to him, had taken part in great events of his life and had embraced him many times. In his intimate relations with God he reached the summit of transforming union and mystical experience."

In those very early days of his priesthood, during which he wrote the letters to which both of these prelates refer, Padre Pio climbed the "mountain of perfection" with rapid strides. It is not given to many souls to progress so quickly on the path of mysticism. Before he was thirty years of age Padre Pio had already "reached the summit of transforming union and mystical experience." The best way to trace his mystical ascent is to let him speak for himself, in the letters he wrote during that period. At most we add an occasional explanatory comment borrowed from the introduction to the first volume of his Letters, where an attempt is made to classify the phenomena to which he refers. Adopting the generally accepted terminology in this field, his biographers speak of *impulses or transports of love, divine touches, strokes and wounds of love, transverberation and Stigmatization.*

Padre Pio's love for God was so strong that it sometimes exploded without warning in surprising transitory effects which were reflected in some way in his whole person. What the specialists describe as impulses of love were transports inspired by the intensity of his love for God. He yearned with all his heart to correspond to divine love and when he found himself unable to satisfy this desire he either fainted or burst into tears. The loving impulse, while increasing his spiritual powers, produced the effects of a genuine illness and his body became quite weak. Acute pain was counterbalanced by ineffable spiritual delight. He yearned intensely to be united with God forever.

On January 30, 1915, he wrote: "I feel my heart and whole interior permeated by the flames of an immense fire. Along with the atrocious agony caused by these flames, my soul experiences an exceeding sweetness which makes me burn with love of God. I feel annihilated and I find no place in which to hide from this gift of the divine Master. I am ill with an illness of the heart and I can bear it no longer. It seems as if the thread of life is about to snap at any moment, yet that moment never comes. My dear Father (he is writing to Padre Benedetto), how sad is the state of a soul which God has wounded by his love. For pity's sake, pray to the Lord that he may put an end to my days, for I just haven't the courage to go on in such a state. I see no other remedy unless that of being consumed once and for all by these flames which burn yet never consume me. Do not think that it is merely my soul which experiences this martyrdom. My body also, even though indirectly, shares in it to a very great extent. While this divine operation continues, my body is becoming utterly powerless."

Divine touches, a delightful contact which God produces on "the point of the soul," at the "apex of the spirit" are described in the writings of many of the great mystics. These touches are sometimes referred to as substantial because they seem to take place between two substances. Such experiences are not reached by human efforts, but are a free gift of the divine benevolence. In Padre Pio's letters we find a description of a fusion of hearts and a substantial touch or kiss of love. On April 18, 1912, he wrote to Padre Benedetto:

"There are some things which cannot be translated into human language without losing their deep and heavenly meaning. This morning the heart of Jesus and my own—allow me to use the expression—were fused. No longer were two hearts beating, but one alone. My own heart had disappeared as a drop of water is lost in the sea. My joy was so intense and profound that I could not contain myself. My dear Father, man cannot understand that when paradise is poured into a heart, this afflicted, exiled and weak mortal heart cannot bear it without weeping. The very joy that filled my heart was what made me weep for so long."

On March 8, 1916, he wrote to his spiritual director: "Once only did I feel in the secret depths of my soul something so delicate that I cannot describe it. First of all, without seeing anything my soul felt his presence. Then, let me put it this way, he came so close to my soul that I felt his touch, exactly as happens—to give you a faint idea—when one body touches another. I can say no more about this. I can only confess that I was seized at first with the greatest fear, which changed a little later to heavenly exultation. ... I cannot tell you whether, when that happened, I was aware or not of still being in the body. God alone knows this. I am unable to say anything more to give you an understanding of this important occurrence."

Two years later, on July 27, 1918, we find him describing a further experience of this divine touch: "Here is how it came about. I call to mind that on the morning of Corpus Christi, a breath of life was offered to me during the Offertory of the Mass. I cannot give you the remotest idea of what occurred within me in that fleeting moment. I felt utterly shaken, I was filled with extreme terror and I very nearly died. There followed a complete calm such as I had never before experienced. All this terror, agitation and calm one after the other was not caused by the sight of anything, but by something I felt touching the most profound and secret depths of my soul. I can say no more as to how it really happened."

The intensity of divine love which develops gradually and destroys everything opposed to full and total transformation into the Beloved produces another marvelous effect which the mystics call strokes and wounds of love. Some of these are purely spiritual and interior, while others are manifested externally. Padre Pio, who was wounded in both ways, described them vividly and realistically, although he spoke, as usual, of his inability to give an accurate description of such things. At intervals, from 1912 onwards, he described the "interior strokes and wounds of love" to which he was subjected.

On August 26, 1912, he wrote: "I was in church last Friday making my thanksgiving after Mass when I suddenly felt my heart pierced by an arrow of such living and ardent fire that I thought I should die. I have no adequate words to convey to you the intensity of that flame. The soul that is a victim of these consolations is struck dumb. It seemed to me as if some invisible force had plunged me entirely into this fire. I had experienced these transports of love before, but on the other occasions the fire was less intense. This time a second more would have been sufficient to separate my soul from my body."

On January 24, 1915, his description of an interior wound of love was even more graphic:

"The agony I am experiencing is so great that I do not believe I shall suffer more at the supreme hour of death. I feel that someone is plunging a knife into me time after time, a knife with a very sharp point and as if it were emitting fire, which passes through my heart and searches its very depths. Then with all his might this person pulls it out, to repeat a little later the same operation. All this, as these knife thrusts are repeated, causes my soul to blaze up more and more with exceeding love of God."

The mystical writers describe the wounds of love as being deeper and more lasting than what they describe as strokes of love. Moreover, the former are manifested in some external manner, either by a physical piercing of the heart (transverberation) or else by appearing in some parts of the body, such as hands, feet or side (stigmatization). St. Teresa of Avila experienced the extraordinary mystical phenomenon of transverberation, sometimes called "the seraph's assault."

According to the classic doctrine of St. John of the Cross, "the soul inflamed with love of God is interiorly attacked by a seraph," who sets it on fire by "piercing it through with a fiery dart." The soul thus wounded is filled with a delightful sweetness.

Padre Pio of Pietrelcina received this extraordinary grace on August 5, 1918. He was already nearing the summit of the mystical mountain which he had begun to climb from the moment of his entry into the Capuchin order. The letter in which he relates this happening to his spiritual director is one of the most extraordinary in the whole volume and the terms in which he describes it are not far removed from St. Teresa's description of the same phenomenon. Padre Pio wrote on August 21, 1918:

"By virtue of obedience I have made up my mind to reveal to you what happened to me on the evening of the 5th and for the entire day on the 6th of this month. ... I was hearing our boys' confessions on the evening of the 5th when I was suddenly filled with great terror at the sight of a heavenly person who presented himself to my mental gaze. He held in his hand a kind of weapon, like a very long sharp pointed blade which seemed to emit fire. At the very instant in which I saw all this, that person hurled the weapon into my soul with all his might. I cried out with difficulty and thought I was dying. I asked the boy to leave because

Padre Pio receives the mystical dart of love or the transverberation. Painting by Koó.

I felt ill and no longer had the strength to continue. This agony lasted uninterruptedly until the morning of the 7th. I cannot tell you how much I suffered during this period of anguish. Even my entrails were torn and ruptured by that weapon and nothing was spared. From that day on I have been mortally wounded. I feel in the depths of my soul a wound that is always open and causes me continual agony."

In reply to this dramatic account of the transverberation, his spiritual director, a genuine master of the spiritual life, wrote him a beautiful and reassuring letter. "All that is happening to you," he said, "is the effect of love ... Your trial is not even a purgation, but a suffering union. The fact of the wound completes your passion just as it completed the Passion of your Beloved on the Cross ... Kiss the hand which has transfixed you and cherish tenderly this wound which is the seal of love."

Excerpt taken from the book, Padre Pio: His Life and Mission, *First published by Veritas publications. Used with permission.*

Padre Pio told the story:

News had spread that he was going to build a hospital, and a poor old woman came to him in front of the confessional, wishing to give him an offering. It was one of the first mornings after the news was released.

Knowing how poor the old woman was, Padre Pio said to her: "Thank you! But keep that money for yourself. You need it." And the old lady said: "Padre take it!" And Padre Pio said again: "No. Why should you take the bread from your mouth? Do as I say. Keep it for yourself, as you need it." So the poor woman said: "You are right, Padre. It is too little." And Padre Pio concluded: "On hearing her say that, I understood the poor woman felt almost humiliated. I was moved, and said: 'Give it to me, and may God bless you!' and I took out my handkerchief so she wouldn't see the tears which were already running down my face."

Four Steps to God

John Schug

A genius isn't always a good teacher. One of the greatest moral theologians in the Church went to pieces whenever he tried to hear confessions. But in spiritual matters Padre Pio was both a genius and an expert teacher. Often he himself would be swept away by God from the prayer of words and plunged into the wordless, contemplative prayer of union with God. But when his spiritual children were earthlings, he knew how to guide them gradually from avoidance of sin, to prayer, to meditation, and finally to contemplation.

Pietruccio, his blind friend, told me that he once asked Padre Pio what he had to do to be saved. Padre Pio answered him: "It is enough if you keep the commandments of God and of the Church. That is enough to save your soul." Consciously or not, Padre Pio was quoting the words of Jesus to the rich young man who asked Him how to be saved.

If his spiritual children continued to run with him, he would have them take a second step, that of prayer. "Pray with your heart and with your mind," he told Pietruccio. "It is useless to pray with the heart if you pray without the mind. If we pray without paying attention to what we are saying, we'll have the curse of our Lord, not His blessing. So when you pray, be very careful to pray with your heart and your mind, with all your soul."

Without laying down any rules and regulations, Padre Pio let his spiritual children know exactly what he expected of them in this second stage of the spiritual life. He insisted that they go to Mass and Holy Communion every day. Also that they pray the rosary daily. These were their basic prayer-tools. Then Padre Pio would initiate them into the third stage of the spiritual life—meditation.

Their introduction to meditation would begin with the suggestion that they spend a half hour a day in meditation, reflecting on the truths of our Faith, especially on the Real Presence of Jesus in the Blessed Sacrament. He said that if they would spend that much time in meditation, they would soon see the need for more time. In counseling his spiritual children this way, the master was showing his wisdom and prudence. He would not let a fledgling try to soar from the moment he was hatched.

In this third stage of the spiritual life, too, Padre Pio didn't prescribe a rule book. But he did offer much helpful advice. "You can meditate on any of the truths of our Faith," he said. "By using a book, you can help your mind to single out a specific, graphic topic for meditation."

A common symptom of this stage of spiritual progress is dryness. The mind goes blank. When Pietruccio complained of not being able to keep his mind on his prayers, Padre Pio offered him some very down-to-earth counsel. "In that case, go near our Lord in the church anyway, without saying anything or doing anything. It is sufficient if you give our Lord your time. Our Lord is happy at least to receive us because of the time we give Him." After one of the boys in the seminary at San Giovanni Rotondo spent the whole time of meditation fighting off distractions, Padre Pio, who was the spiritual director at the time, came up to him and patted him on the back and said: "Bravo!"

Meditation, he warned Raffaelina Cerase, a spiritual daughter, must be relaxed and not forced. "If I am not mistaken, the real reason you don't experience the presence of God, or rather, the reason you don't succeed in praying well, is because you do the following: you approach prayer with a kind of arrogance, with a great anxiety to find some subject that will please and console yourself.

"It is enough for you never to find what you are looking for. Your mind does not deal with the truth in which you are meditating on, and your heart is empty of affection. My daughter, when someone is looking for something anxiously and hurriedly, he will touch it a hundred times without noticing it. By the useless anxiety, you will only become spiritually very tired, and your mind will not be able to rest on the subject in which you are considering. For this reason, your soul itself is responsible for becoming cold and stupid.

"The only remedy I know of is this: Get rid of this anxiety, because it is one of the worst traitors to real virtue which devotion can have. It pretends to warm us up for good works, but it doesn't. Rather, it chills us, and only makes us run in order to stumble. So you must, as I have often told you, always be careful, especially in prayer. To succeed better, remember that grace and the taste of prayer are not drawn from earth but heaven.

"It is necessary that we use the greatest care and every effort to dispose ourselves, but always humbly and calmly. Even if we should use all our strength, we are not the ones who pray and draw grace by our own efforts. It is necessary that we hold our hearts open to heaven and wait for the heavenly dew to descend. Don't forget this, my daughter. How many courtiers come and go in the presence of the king, unable to speak to him or hear him. They are only seen by him. In this way, we show ourselves as the king's true servants. This is the way to be in the presence of God, just by declaring with our will that we want to be his servants. This is a holy and excellent way, pure and perfect. You may laugh, but I am speaking seriously.

"We put ourselves in the presence of God to speak to Him and to hear his voice by means of his internal inspiration and illumination. Usually this gives us great pleasure, because it is a significant grace for us to speak to so great a Lord; when He replies, thousands of perfumes descend on the soul and cause great joy.

"If you can speak to our Lord, praise Him, listen to Him. If you cannot speak because you are uncouth, don't be unhappy. Shut yourself up in a room, and similar to a courtier, pay Him homage. He who sees you will be pleased with your patience. He will prefer your silence.

"On some other occasion He will prefer to console you. Then He will take you by the hand, speak to you, and walk a hundred times with you along the paths of his garden of prayer. Even if that never happens, which is really impossible, because the Father cannot bear to see his creatures in perpetual turmoil, be content all the same. Our obligation is to follow Him. Consider it a great honor and grace that He should take us into his presence.

"In this way, don't bother yourself about speaking to Him. The other way, just standing by his side, is no less useful. Perhaps it is even better, although less to our taste. So when you find yourself with God in prayer, reflect on the truth, speak to Him if you can. If you cannot, remain there. Put yourself into this state. Lucky soul! Even when the soul is plunged into this dense darkness, it can still receive a little light so as not to fall into despair.

"When God sees that the soul has become strong in his love, affectionately united to Him, and already withdrawn from earthy things and from the occasion of sin, and has acquired sufficient virtues to stay in his service without all these attractions and tangible sweetness, then He takes away the sweetness of the affections which until that time have been felt in all devotions and meditations.

"What is even more painful for the soul, He takes away the power to pray and to meditate, and He leaves the soul in the dark, in complete and painful dryness. In the face of such a change, the soul is at first terrified. A person might think that this fear is due to some mortal sin into which he has fallen. He is afraid of being in disgrace before God. What a mistake! What the soul thinks is abandonment is nothing other than exceptional grace of the heavenly Father. This is the transition to the capacity for contemplation. It is dry at the start, but afterwards, if a person perseveres, the soul will be lifted from meditation to contemplation, and everything becomes sweet and pleasant.

"The soul is then preoccupied with a sense of love, and that is the reason for its pain. But the poor soul can't become comforted. It thinks that nobody knows the real condition. If only the soul could realize that the impossibility of centering the imagination on a point of meditation is due to God. He subtracts from the imagination that bright light which had previously been helpful in working on supernatural things.

"Now God infuses a better light into the intellect, a much more spiritual light, a purer one which enables the soul to fix the mind on God and on divine things without any discursive reasoning; now the soul can contemplate God with a simple vision, ever so sweet, delicate and divine."

In another letter Padre Pio elaborates on the sweet and simple vision of God and the price which must be paid for it. Again we quote a letter to Raffaelina Cerase:

"Remember that the love of God is continuously growing in the soul. You can watch it. You will always feel ready for anything in the service and honor of God, even though your soul will not feel an attraction and your spirit will be completely empty of any feeling. On the contrary, you will feel surrounded by darkness, and everything you do will be done with great difficulty and repugnance.

"After all this, I don't know if the purge will end. It seems to me that there is another grade of contemplation to which our Lord invites us. If it is true, and I hope and am firmly convinced that the Divine Doctor will lift you still higher, then I'll not add another word, except to urge you to be faithful and humble. Keep the great Mother of God before your mind. The more she was exalted, the more she humbled herself.

I'll warn you that at this point, dryness alone is not sufficient for the purging of the soul. There is need of another interior cause of pain, which penetrates the whole soul, piercing it intimately and renewing it completely.

"This light transfixes the soul in its sins and upsets the poor soul as if to put it into a state of extreme affliction, with interior pains of death. Yet, in this light, which at first surrounds the soul with such abandonment and pain, there is something which eventually transforms the soul and lifts it up into mystical union.

"How that happens, I don't understand. Only, I tell you without fear of making a mistake, or of telling you a lie, that it will happen this way, and not in any other way. The soul will experience atrocious pains, as if penetrating the sufferings of the damned in hell. The light which is the cause of this horrible suffering will render the soul capable of receiving the kiss of perfect union of love and clothe it with a brilliant light."

Any commentary on these sublime thoughts would be an anticlimax. I will only say that any Christian who wishes to progress from obligation to love, from purgation to contemplation, has not only Padre Pio's words of wisdom, but through his stigmata we may rightly judge that we also have God's own stamp of approval on the guidance offered by this Wise Man of Gargano.

Reprinted from the Voice of Padre Pio *magazine, San Giovanni Rotondo*

I'll not add another word, except to urge you to be faithful and humble. Keep the great Mother of God before your mind. The more she was exalted, the more she humbled herself. — *Padre Pio*

May 2, 1999, St. Peter's Square, Rome. The bishops in union with the Holy Father give their episcopal blessing to the people at the beatification ceremony of Blessed Padre Pio.

PART VI

Love At the Foot of the Cross

The Charismatic Padre Pio

The Eucharist in Padre Pio's Life

Padre Pio Helps the Poor Souls

Why He Could Embrace Suffering

New Saint's Life, a Replay of the Glory of the cross

Love At the Foot of the Cross

His Holiness Pope John Paul II

An estimated 300,000 faithful gathered in St. Peter's square on Sunday, May 2, for the solemn Mass at which Pope John Paul II beatified Padre Pio of Pietrelcina. The Holy Father stated that Padre Pio "shared in the Passion with a special intensity: the unique gifts which were given to him, and the interior and mystical sufferings which accompanied them, allowed him constantly to participate in the Lord's agonies, never wavering in his sense that 'Calvary is the hill of the saints.'" The following is a translation of his homily which was in Italian.

"Sing a new song to the Lord!" The summons of the entrance antiphon captures well the joy of so many of the faithful who have long awaited the beatification of Padre Pio of Pietrelcina. By his life given wholly to prayer and to listening to his brothers and sisters, this humble Capuchin friar astonished the world. Countless people came to meet him in the friary of San Giovanni Rotondo and, since his death, the flow of pilgrims has not ceased. When I was a student here in Rome, I myself had the chance to meet him personally, and I thank God for allowing me today to enter Padre Pio's name in the book of the blessed.

Guided by the texts of this Fifth Sunday of Easter, which provides the context for the beatification, let us this morning trace the main features of his spiritual experience. Padre Pio's life was a constant act of faith.

"Do not let your hearts be troubled. Believe in God and believe also in me" (Jn. 14:1). In the Gospel just proclaimed, we heard these words of Jesus to his disciples who were in need of encouragement. In

157

fact his allusion to his imminent departure had thrown them into turmoil. They were afraid of being abandoned, of being alone, and the Lord consoled them with a very specific promise: *"I am going to prepare a place for you,"* and then, *"I will come again and will take you to myself, that where I am you may be also"* (Jn. 14:2-3).

Through Thomas, the Apostles reply to this reassurance: *"Lord, we do not know where you are going, how can we know the way?"* (Jn 14:5). The remark is apt, and Jesus does not avoid the question which it implies. The answer he gives will remain for ever a light shining for generations still to come: *"I am the way and the truth and the life; no one comes to the Father but by me"* (Jn 14:6).

The "place" that Jesus goes to prepare is in "the house of the Father"; there the disciple will be able to be with the Master for all eternity and share in his joy. Yet there is only one path that leads there: Christ, to whom the disciple must be conformed more and more. Holiness consists precisely in this: that it is no longer the Christian who lives, but Christ himself who lives in him (cf. Gal 2:20). An exhilarating goal, accompanied by a promise which is no less consoling: *"Whoever believes in me will also do the works that I do, and greater works than I will they do, because I am going to the Father"* (Jn. 14:12). We hear

these words of Christ and think of the humble friar of Gargano. How clearly were they fulfilled in Bl. Pio of Pietrelcina!

"Do not let your hearts be troubled. Believe. ... " What was the life of this humble son of St. Francis if not a constant act of faith, strengthened by the hope of heaven, where he could be with Christ? *"I am going to prepare a place for you ... that where I am you may be also."* What other purpose was there for the demanding ascetical practices which Padre Pio undertook from his early youth, if not gradually to identify himself with the Divine Master, so that he could be "where he was?"

Vera Calandra, director of the National Center for Padre Pio Inc. did the English reading at the Beatification Mass.

Those who went to San Giovanni Rotondo to attend his Mass, to seek his counsel or to confess to him, saw in him a living image of Christ suffering and risen. The face of Padre Pio reflected the light of the Resurrection. His body, marked by the "stigmata," showed forth the intimate bond between death and resurrection which characterizes the paschal mystery. Bl. Pio of Pietrelcina shared in the Passion with a special intensity: the unique gifts which were given to him, and the interior and mystical suffering which accompanied them, allowed him constantly to participate in the Lord's agonies, never wavering in his sense that "Calvary is the hill of the saints."

No less painful, and perhaps even more distressing from a human point of view, were the trials which he had to endure as a result, it might be said, of his incomparable charisms. It happens at times in the history of holiness that, by God's special permission, the one chosen is misunderstood. In that case, obedience becomes for him a crucible of purification, a path of gradual assimilation to Christ, a strengthening of true holiness. In this regard, Bl. Pio wrote to one of his superiors: "I strive only to obey you, the good God having made known to me the one thing most acceptable to him and the one way for me to hope for salvation and to sing of victory" (Letter I, p. 807).

When the "storm" broke upon him, he took as his rule of life the exhortation of the First Letter of Peter, that we have just heard: *Come to*

Christ, a living stone (cf. I Pt 2:4). He himself thus became a "living stone" for the building of that spiritual house which is the Church. For this we today give thanks to the Lord.

"You too are living stones, built into a spiritual house" (1 Pt. 2:5). How fitting are these words if we apply them to the extraordinary ecclesial experience which grew up around the new Blessed! So many people, meeting him directly or indirectly, rediscovered their faith; inspired by his example, "prayer groups" sprang up in every corner of the world. To all who flocked to him he held up the ideal of holiness, repeating to them: "It seems that Jesus has no interest outside of sanctifying your soul" (Letter II, p. 155).

If God's Providence willed that he should be active without ever leaving his convent, as though he were "planted" at the foot of the Cross, this is not without significance. One day the Divine Master had to console him, at a moment of particular trial, by telling him that "it is under the Cross that one learns to love" (Letter 1, p. 339). The Cross of Christ is truly the outstanding school of love; indeed, the very "wellspring" of love. Purified by suffering, the love of this faithful disciple drew hearts to Christ and to his demanding Gospel of salvation.

At the same time, his charity was poured out like balm on the weaknesses and the sufferings of his brothers and sisters. Padre Pio thus united zeal for souls with a concern for human suffering, working to build at San Giovanni Rotondo a hospital complex which he called the "House for the Relief of Suffering." He wanted it to be a first-class hospital, but above all he was concerned that the medicine practised there would be truly "human," treating patients with warm concern and sincere attention. He was quite aware that people who are ill and suffering need not only competent therapeutic care but also, and more importantly, a human and spiritual climate to help them rediscover themselves, in an encounter with the love of God and with the kindness of their brothers and sisters.

With the "House for the Relief of Suffering," he wished to show that God's "ordinary miracles" *take place in and through our charity.* We need to be open to compassion and to the generous service of our brothers and sisters, using every resource of medical science and technology at our disposal. The echo stirred by this beatification in Italy and throughout the world shows that the fame of Padre Pio, a son of Italy and of Francis of Assisi, has gone forth to embrace all the continents.

Let me conclude with the words of the Gospel of this Mass: "Do not let your hearts be troubled. Have faith in God." There is a reference to this exhortation of Christ in the advice which the new Blessed never tired of giving to the faithful: "Abandon yourselves fully to the divine

Though the mayor of Rome made every effort to keep the crowd of pilgrims down for fear that the city could not handle such a large number of people, at least 300,000 converged on St. Peter's Square and overflowed down the Via della Conciliazione. Another 180,000 gathered in the square before St. John Lateran to watch the ceremony on large TV screens.

heart of Jesus, like a child in the arms of his mother." May these words of encouragement fill our hearts too and become a source of peace, serenity and joy. Why should we fear, if Christ is for us, He who is the Way, and the Truth and the Life? Why should we not trust in God who is the Father, our Father?

May "Our Lady of Graces," whom the humble Capuchin of Pietrelcina invoked with constant and tender devotion, help us to keep our gaze fixed on God. May she take us by the hand and lead us to seek wholeheartedly that supernatural charity flowing forth from the wounded side of the Crucified One.

And you, Bl. Padre Pio, look down from heaven upon us assembled in this square and upon all gathered in prayer before the Basilica of St. John Lateran and in San Giovanni Rotondo. Intercede for all those who, in every part of the world, are spiritually united with this event and raise their prayers to you. Come to the help of everyone; give peace and consolation to every heart. Amen!

The homily and illustrations from pages 154-162 were taken from the English and Italian editions of L'Osservatore Romano. (with the exception of the picture on page 159)

It is necessary to guard all your senses particularly your eyes: they are the means by which all the fascination and charm of beauty and voluptuousness enter the heart. When fashion, as in our time, is towards provocation and exposes what formerly was even wrong to think about, caution and self-restraint must be exercised. Whenever necessary you must look without seeing and see without thinking about it.

Endeavor to unite the simplicity of children with the prudence of adults.

To doubt is the greatest insult to the Divinity.   — *Padre Pio*

The Charismatic Padre Pio

Augustine McGregor

When we say that Padre Pio was a charismatic figure we immediately place him in a certain category of persons who in some way are outstanding by reason of supernatural powers and gifts which they possess through the Holy Spirit. This is not to say that the gifts or "charisms" as they are called are primarily extraordinary or, in any exclusive sense, limited to a special group of persons in the Church. Indeed the gifts of God are of infinite variety and their distribution in the Church is unlimited according as the Spirit "blows wherever He pleases" (Jn 3:8).

But at the same time, the Church has always held that besides the gifts and graces received by the faithful for the living of the Christian life and those bestowed on the ordained for the stability and right order of the structures of the Church, there are others bestowed by God on certain specially—chosen individuals. Pius XII in his encyclical *Mystici Corporis,* which to a great extent paved the way for Vatican II's *Constitution on the Church*, referred to these "charismatics" as persons endowed with miraculous powers, and what is more, he said that such persons will never be lacking in the Church.

So, when we refer to Padre Pio as a charismatic we are simply saying that he belongs to a category of persons that has been present in the life of the Church since the first Pentecostal event (Acts 2:1 ff.). There can be no artificial division of the Church into her charismatic and institutional structures using the words "charism" and "charismatic" in the attempt to force a breach between the two. One is not opposed to the other. In practice the genuine charismatic accepts unhesitatingly the authority of the Church—he is, in fact, distinguished as much by this obedience to authority as by his unconditional assent to the faith. Another outstanding feature of the true charismatic will be his ability always to work within the Church structure in which he finds himself, no matter how restricting this may appear to be.

Besides the more extraordinary charisms there are in Padre Pio's life others of less striking impact, ordinary ones such as the faithful in grace possess that come from the Spirit. It is important to note this. The gifts granted to any individual must never be thought of independently of the Giver, the Sanctifier, but must always be seen as the result of God's operation through the Holy Spirit. We can say, therefore, that Padre Pio did not receive such an array of gifts for his own special benefit or, for that matter, his own sanctification. In each instance it will be found, after examination, that wherever a "good work" took place, whether of healing, of discernment, or of prophecy, the benefits always redounded beyond the immediate person of Padre Pio to the welfare and spiritual profit of those who sought his aid.

There is, however, one charism which has not received the attention it merits and that is the gift of "spiritual fatherhood." It is one firmly rooted in the New Testament. St. Paul alludes to this precious gift on a number of occasions. After detailing his personal tribulations and humiliations which he had undergone for his proud Corinthian converts Paul concluded: "I am saying all this not just to make you ashamed but to bring you, my dearest children, to your senses. You might have thousands of guardians in Christ, but not more than one father and it was I who begot you in Christ Jesus by preaching the Good News" (1 Cor 4:14-15). And grieved with his Galatians he had said: "... my children! I must go through the pain of giving birth to you all over again, until Christ is formed in you" (Gal 4:19). In another place to his Corinthians he writes: "I speak as if to children of mine" (2 Cor 6:13) while to the Thessalonians Paul even assumes the role of mother: "Like a mother feeding and looking after her own children we felt so devoted and protective towards you, and had come to love you so much. ... " (1 Thess 2:8). Timothy is referred to by Paul as "true child of mine in the faith" (1 Tim 1:2) and Onesimus he regards as "a child of mine, whose father I became" (Philem 1:10).

To all who entrusted their spiritual lives to his care and guidance Padre Pio was indeed truly a father, exercising rights, duties and responsibilities similar to those of fathers in the temporal order. He was certainly conscious of having this particular charism from an early age for, in a letter dated August 23, 1919, Padre Pio at the age of 32 wrote to one under his care: "My prayers, for which you ask with insistence, will never be lacking for you because I cannot forget what has cost me so many sacrifices and that I have given birth to you to God in extreme pain of the heart. ... "

How reminiscent that is of the manner in which Paul speaks of his converts. To another of his spiritual children, Padre Pio said: "Your goodness, your generosity have won my heart and that is why I am fond of you. Today I have spoken of you to our Lady. I desire your salvation as that of all my children. But those who wound me are ungrateful." It would seem from this that among his spiritual children there were those who caused him joy and happiness on account of their virtuous lives and prayerful progress in the Lord as well as those who were cause for disappointment. But he loved all of them, the weak no less than the strong.

Here was a father who worried about his children, always anxious that they should live their lives aright and in the sight of God. If he had a special liking for some this was because of their goodness and purity but it is true that he forgot none of them. He belonged to all, he prayed for all and for all he suffered and shed tears. Once he said to one of them: "You think you know my love for you. But you don't know that it is much greater than you can imagine. I follow you with my prayer, with my suffering and with my tears." As a father he would often rebuke and threaten his children but later would lavish on them his love and all the tenderness of his heart when they returned to the right path. For his love was directed to the spiritual interests of his children, above all to the ultimate salvation of the soul. This is the reason for that wonderful and consoling promise of his: "I shall stand at the gates of Paradise and shall not enter until all my spiritual children have entered."

The spiritual father is a master of the spiritual life. Through the guidance of the Holy Spirit he has trodden the deep and intimate paths of the interior life of prayer; through the path of suffering and self-sacrifice he has learned what it is to follow his Master, Jesus Christ. Again, spiritual fatherhood is a charism that flourished long ago in the desert. Because of its close connection with spiritual direction it was for the most part confined to religious and monastic life. In the case of Padre Pio's paternity we can certainly say that it went far beyond the usual limits to overflow in all directions. His paternity was not confined to the members of his own friary or Order but embraced all those who turned to him for help and direction.

Padre Pio has imparted to each of his children something of his own spirit. Perhaps they have received through knowing him the grace of a deeper prayer life, or seeing in his particular "passion" the grace and the willingness to unite a little more to the sufferings of Our Lord. Or to be more penitent and mortified in a world engrossed in materialism and selfishness, where daily we witness the erosion and debasement of true human values and where immorality and vice have become an accepted way of life for so many. But whatever the grace they may have received, it is for Padre Pio's spiritual children to keep alight that flame of love for God and neighbor with which he was consumed. For this he suffered and prayed, that they, following in his footsteps, might continue what he had begun in their hearts.

By their very nature the gifts enjoyed by men like Padre Pio will always be rare. Moreover, to show as we have already said that charism and institution are complementary, it will be the task of those who preside over the Church, to whose special competence it belongs, to judge the genuineness of these gifts. In the words of the Council this is done "not indeed to extinguish the Spirit, but to test all things and hold fast to that which is good" (1 Th 5:12); cf *Lumen Gentium,* (a.12).

Finally, let us recall the teaching of St. Paul, "The Christian must be ambitious for the higher gifts" (1 Cor 12:31). "The whole life of the believer must be animated by charity" (Gal 5:6). This is the gift to be desired most of all; it is the one that lasts into eternity and situates our place in the kingdom. St. Paul rises to heights of lyrical poetry in the passage which deals with the superiority and necessity of love, the greatest of all the charisms. For when all is said and done, beyond all the rare charisms and extraordinary spiritual phenomena, it was love that was the essence of Padre Pio's life and activity, the very foundation of all he taught. Let the love which he demonstrated in his life and taught to his children be the monument by which he will always be remembered. He would desire nothing else. On the fiftieth anniversary of his first Mass he said: "I desire nothing other than to love, to suffer another fifty years for my brothers; to burn for all with Thee, Lord, with Thee on the Cross."

Let St. Paul's word in this matter be final: "I may speak with every tongue that men and angels use; yet if I lack charity, I am no better than echoing bronze, or the clash of cymbals. I may have powers of prophecy, no secret hidden from me, no knowledge too deep for me; I may have utter faith, so that I can move mountains, yet if I lack charity, I count for nothing. I may give away all that I have to feed the poor; I may give myself up to be burnt at the stake; if I lack charity, it goes for nothing. Charity is patient, is kind; charity feels no envy; charity is never perverse or proud, never insolent; does not claim its rights, cannot be provoked, does not brood over an injury, takes no pleasure in wrongdoing but rejoices at the victory of truth; sustains, hopes, believes, endures to the last" (1 Cor 13:1-8).

A condensation of the article "A Charismatic in the Church," from the Voice of Padre Pio *magazine, San Giovanni Rotondo.*

Walk the way of the Lord in simplicity; do not torment your spirit. Speak the truth, always the truth.

You are trying to find the highest good but, in all truth, it is within you and holds you stretched out on the naked cross, instilling strength to sustain the insupportable martyrdom, and also to love Love bitterly. Say to our sweetest Lord, and say it always: "I want to live by dying, because from death comes life which does not die and assists life to raise the dead." — *Padre Pio*

The Eucharist in Padre Pio's Life

Tarcisio of Cervinara

Padre's favorite haunt was in front of the tabernacle. His very being depended upon Christ's presence in the Eucharist. There is no other explanation how this man could have lived for half a century without sufficient nourishment or sleep to sustain life.

According to Vatican Council II, all the spiritual goods of the Church are contained in the Most Blessed Sacrament. It is also the center and the basis for the priestly life. Padre Pio's life revolved around the tabernacle, with the Eucharist being the center of gravitation.

We learn from the testimonies of people from Pietrelcina, contemporary with Padre Pio, that as a child Francis Forgione attended church regularly. He was an altar boy; he heard Mass every day, receiving Communion frequently and showed great reverence to the Eucharist edifying the priests of the village so much so that they held him up as an example to the other boys, hoping to encourage vocations to the priesthood.

After entering the Franciscans, due to precarious health, Padre Pio was allowed to stay in Pietrelcina for several years, the superiors hoping that the native air would help restore his health.

The people of the village testified that Friar Pio spent long hours before Jesus in the Blessed Sacrament, sometimes whole nights. He would say to those who asked him for his prayers: "I will ask Jesus in the Blessed Sacrament when I am near the tabernacle!" There is documentary evidence from this period that reveals the Eucharistic fire that set Padre Pio's heart aflame. He felt an extraordinary force that drew him ever closer to the Eucharist, while at the same time he was consumed by a great desire to receive Jesus.

On March 29, 1911, he wrote to Padre Benedetto: "My heart feels drawn by ever higher attraction each morning before I am united with Him in the Blessed Sacrament. I have such a hunger and thirst for Jesus, before I receive Him, that I almost die, and precisely because I am incapable of not uniting myself with Him ... Moreover, instead or being satisfied after I have received Him sacramentally, this hunger and thirst for Him steadily increases. When I possess this Supreme Good, the abundance of sweetness from Jesus is so great that I am nearly tempted to say to Jesus: 'Enough, I can hardly bear more.' I almost forget, that while I am still in the world; my mind and heart desire nothing more and sometimes for a long time even the desire for anything else is lacking to me." He thought that this fire that burns in his chest was common to everyone.

"I often ask myself," he wrote on December 3, 1912, to Padre Agostino "if there are any people who do not feel in their breast a burning of this divine fire, especially when they are close to Him in the Blessed Sacrament; this seems impossible, especially in the case of a priest or religious. Perhaps those who say they do not feel this fire are not aware of it because their hearts are bigger than mine. I resort to this kindly interpretation of their words so as not to accuse them of shameful falsehood" (Letters 1).

Jesus is so necessary to Padre Pio he cannot live without Jesus in the Blessed Eucharist, especially when problems of conscience and afflictions of all kinds torment him: "I still feel tempted at times to neglect daily Communion, but up to the present I have always got the better of myself. May it all be for the glory of Jesus. How could I live, my dear Father, if I were to fail even for a single morning to receive Jesus?" (Letters 1). Sometimes, from one day to the next he had such temptations. In such cases Padre Pio was frequently assailed by doubting whether he had rejected the insinuations of the Evil One. On July 6, 1910, he wrote to Padre Benedetto: "I weep and moan at the feet of Jesus in the Blessed Sacrament. On this account I seem very often to be consoled, yet at other times Jesus seems to hide from me. My pen is powerless to describe what goes on in my soul in these moments when He conceals Himself" (Letters 1). At these moments the comfort of the Lord is sweet, but then it is that much harder for him when Jesus hides. The suffering he goes through when the Beloved hides, makes Padre Pio think of the many offences that Jesus receives from men especially in the Sacrament of His love. What would happen, he asked himself, if the Heavenly Father took His Son out of this world to punish ungrateful and unworthy men?

On September 8, 1913, he wrote to Padre Agostino: "Alas my Father, how many offences Jesus receives! I feel my blood freezing when I consider how wretched people respond to such great love on the part of Jesus ... How many times have I not lifted up my voice to the heavenly Father, asking Him for the sake of Jesus' meekness and the reverence due to his adorable person, either to put an end to the world or to put a stop to this wickedness. He is almighty and has the power to do this. Beseech Him without ceasing, you too, for this purpose. I am very weak and haven't the courage to implore this heavenly Father to take His beloved Son out of the world so as to spare Him so many insults.

"What would become of men if they did not have Jesus in their midst, but what would become especially of me? I am conscious of all my weakness and powerlessness. I shudder at this sad thought and I am filled with horror and fear of the chastisements which God would send our unfortunate brothers" (Letters 1). Every line of this letter is full of Padre Pio's zeal and love for Jesus. It would be just if Jesus were taken away from men because of the many offences He receives. But then what would happened to Padre Pio who felt all his weakness and powerlessness? He felt how necessary for all of us and particularly himself was the presence of Jesus in the Blessed Sacrament.

Towards the end of October, 1911, Padre Pio went to the friary of Venafro to follow a course in rhetoric ... Padre Pio's contacts with Jesus in the Blessed Sacrament at the Venafro friary were altogether unique. Falling seriously ill he had to go back to Pietrelcina on December 7 of that same year. Extraordinary phenomena took place around Padre Pio during his brief forty days stay in Venafro. Padre Agostino of San Marco recorded the ecstasies, heavenly visits and diabolical oppressions during this period. Padre Pio lived off the Blessed Sacrament alone. The conversations that took place between him and Jesus after communion are sublime. The fire of love that burns in the heart of the Capuchin in anticipation of receiving Jesus in the Blessed Sacrament is revealed in ecstasy on November 29, 1911, "Jesus... why am I so thirsty in the mornings? ... You are right," Padre Pio exclaims, "I miss You who are my Father and my Spouse."

On November 28, the Seraph of Pietrelcina said to Jesus: "Oh Jesus. ... I love You ... very much ... I want to be yours entirely ... don't You see that I burn for You? ... You ask of me love, love, love, love ... I love You ... come to me every morning ... we will be alone together ... I with You alone, You alone with me ... Oh Jesus, give me your love ... when You come into my heart, if You see something that is not pleasing to You, destroy it ... I love You ... I will hold You close, close, close to me ... I will not let You go, it's true that You are free, but I will hold You so close, close ... that I will almost take away Your freedom."

Padre Pio's fervent love for Jesus in the Blessed Sacrament is, not only a love of giving but also of intercession. During the ecstasy of November 30, he pleads with broken heart for priests who go to the altar unworthily: "You hadn't noticed? ... they even come to insult You at the altar? ... They have gone too far? ... but why don't You look at your Angels, at the good priests? ... But help these unfortunates ... they are priests' too ... You have to help the priests ... beg the Father ... especially in our days ... they are held up to ridicule, a target for everyone."

Padre Agostino also notes during that period, Padre Pio received Communion twice without realizing it when he was in ecstasy. During one of these ecstasies, when Jesus was in his heart, he said to the Lord: "I already felt You in my heart like the disciples of Emmaus ... I felt You ... with your gentleness ... I am no longer thirsty ... Ah Jesus, my love ... and how can I live without You? Come always my Jesus, come and You alone take possession of my heart ... Oh, if I had an infinite number of hearts, all the hearts in heaven and earth, even the heart of your mother, I would offer them all, all to You ... my Jesus, my sweetness, love which sustains me ... thank You ... good-bye."

This intimate contact with the Lord in the Blessed Sacrament kept increasing during the whole span of his life. When Padre Pio was not at the altar his eyes were continually turned towards the tabernacle. It is enough to think of the hours that he spent near Jesus in the Blessed Sacrament during the day. In the morning, after celebrating Mass, he heard another Mass in thanksgiving to Jesus who had entered his heart. During confessions, he did not forget the tabernacle. And what about the time his pastoral activity was restricted? During this painful period Padre Pio would spend extra long periods at the altar in the friary chapel celebrating Mass or he could be found spending hours before Jesus in the Blessed Sacrament.

On the occasion of Padre Agostino's death, May 14, 1963, after the funeral, the saddened and exhausted Padre Pio who had spent hours in the gallery, was asked: "Father, let us go to your room now so you can rest a bit." Padre Pio replied as he fixed his gaze on the tabernacle, "Where do you want me to go, my son! My place is here!" Only in paradise will we know the extent of the love of the Stigmatist of the Gargano for Jesus in the Blessed Sacrament.

One may get a glimpse of this love in the first volume of his letters. Padre Pio wrote to Padre Benedetto on September 8, 1911, confiding to him how the stigmata appeared intermittently on his hands and feet, and adds: "I have lots of things to tell you but find no words to adequately express myself. I can only say that when I am close to Jesus in the Blessed Sacrament my heart throbs so violently that it seems to me at times that it must burst out of my chest" (Letters 1).

Once when she was in the church of San Giovanni Rotondo, a spiritual daughter of Padre Pio, Luigina Sinapi, who died in the odor of sanctity, saw a beam of fire coming out of Padre Pio's heart, where he was situated in the gallery of the church. It was projected to the tabernacle. Luigina asked our Lord what this meant. Her Guardian Angel told her: "It indicates Padre Pio's great love for Jesus in the Blessed Sacrament."

Reprinted from the Voice of Padre Pio *magazine, San Giovanni Rotondo.*

Padre Pio Helps the Poor Souls

By Bro. Charles Madden, OFM Conv.

Although the Church in its funeral rites prays for the repose of the departed soul, a practice has arisen which tends to obscure the absolute necessity of praying for the dead. After Communion and before the final prayers for the deceased are said, members of the family, or the deceased one's friends go to the lector's stand to give eulogies about the deceased. While this can be praiseworthy and uplifting, too often these eulogies are done in such a fashion as to canonize the departed. Such eulogies can actually be a disservice to the deceased! One can easily leave Church with the impression that it is not necessary to pray for the soul of the deceased any more. Perhaps such extravagant eulogists no longer believe in Purgatory. But what is the reality?

Here is what the Catechism of the Catholic Church teaches about Purgatory (Nos. 1030-1032). "All who die in God's grace and friendship, but still imperfectly purified, are indeed assured of their eternal salvation; but after death they undergo purification, so as to achieve the holiness necessary to enter the joy of heaven.

"The Church gives the name Purgatory to this final purification of the elect, which is entirely different from the punishment of the damned. The Church formulated her doctrine of faith on Purgatory especially at the Councils of Florence and Trent. The tradition of the Church, by reference to certain texts of Scripture, speaks of a cleansing fire. (Cf. 1Cor 3:15;1 Pet 1:7).

"This teaching is also based on the practice of prayer for the dead, already mentioned in Sacred Scripture: 'Therefore (Judas Maccabeus) made atonement for the dead, that they might be delivered from their sin.'" (2 Macc 12:46).

Throughout his life Padre Pio had a special mission through his prayers to release souls from Purgatory. His life is replete with examples of souls in Purgatory appearing to him and begging for his prayers. To him these incidents were a normal part of his priestly life. He always spoke in a matter of fact manner about them.

Padre Pio described one such incident that occurred during World War I at the friary in San Giovanni Rotundo. He had been sitting alone in a guestroom absorbed in prayer one night when an old man entered and sat next to him. "I looked at him but never thought of how he had managed to get in the friary at that hour. I asked him: 'Who are you? What do you want?' The man answered: 'Padre Pio, I am Pietro di Mauro, nicknamed Precoco. I died in this friary on September 18, 1908, in room number 4, when this friary was still a home for the elderly. When in bed one night, I fell asleep with my cigar burning. My bed caught fire and I died. I suffocated and burned alive. I am still in Purgatory, and I need a Mass to free my soul from it. God has given me permission to come to you and ask for your prayers.' After I had listened to his story I said: 'You can rest assured that I will celebrate Mass tomorrow for your liberation.'" Padre Pio related that the Mass he celebrated the next day freed the man's soul from Purgatory. One of the other priests at the friary later on checked the village records and found that such an individual had indeed died under the circumstances described by Padre Pio.

On another occasion while the friars were at supper one evening Padre Pio abruptly left the table and dashed to the doorway and began a lively conversation with some people whom none of the other friars could see. They remarked to one another that he was going crazy. When he returned they asked him to whom was he talking. "Oh don't worry," he replied, "I was talking to some souls who were on their way from Purgatory to Heaven. They stopped here to thank me because I remembered them in my Mass this morning."

Padre Pio was particularly concerned that everyone should enter Paradise. A spiritual child of his, Antonietta Pompilo, said that Padre Pio told her: "I have made a covenant with God. After my soul is purified in Purgatory and is then worthy to enter Heaven, I will only stand at its gates and not enter until I have seen the last of my brothers and spiritual children enter before me." This points out Padre Pio's keen awareness and ever-present thoughts of life after death, and also his concern for those who have passed to the next life. We also have a particular duty to pray for our departed relatives. We should also remember that the holy souls are precisely that—holy. That is to say, if owing to our prayers and penances they are released from Purgatory, they are forever grateful to us and continue to pray and sing hymns of praise before the throne of God on our behalf. Their gratitude knows no bounds, and they take a particular interest in those who have helped them.

In his various letters which he wrote concerning the souls in Purgatory Padre Pio consistently made three points: 1) The importance of the Sacrifice of the Mass for the release of the souls in Purgatory; 2) the deceased still live spiritually among us and have not left us at all; 3) the importance of resignation to God's will on the death of a loved one, because this is extremely efficacious for the release of their soul from Purgatory.

The souls often forgotten by many of us had a very special place in Padre Pio's life; in fact they were consistently remembered in his daily prayers and Masses. On one occasion, while in conversation with some friars who were questioning him on the importance of his prayers in their favor, Padre Pio said: "More souls of the dead from Purgatory than of the living climb this mountain to attend my Masses and seek my prayers." What an amazing statement! During the fifty-two years he spent at San Giovanni Rotondo he was visited by multitudes of people; yet he made this statement, pointing out that his contact with the souls of the dead exceeded those of the living. Something to consider the next time you attend a funeral where the deceased is "canonized" before he is buried!

The above chapter is based for the most part on material excerpted from The Holy Souls: 'Viva Padre Pio' *by Fr. Alessio Parente, OFM Cap.*

The three means by which Jesus inspired such great love and deep commitment of Padre Pio — the crib, the cross and the tabernacle.

Love Our Lady and Pray the Rosary

After celebrating the Solemn Beatification Mass on Sunday, May 2, in St. Peter's Square, the Holy Father went to the Basilica of St. John Lateran to greet the over 180,000 pilgrims gathered in the square below who had followed the ceremony on large-screen televisions. Speaking from the Loggia, he urged the people to reflect on Padre Pio's love of the Blessed Mother.

"By his teaching and example, Padre Pio invites us to pray, in order to receive divine mercy through the sacrament of Penance and to love our neighbor. He invites us, in particular, to love and venerate the Virgin Mary. His devotion to Our Lady was apparent in every aspect of his life: in his words and writings, in his teaching and in the advice he gave to his many spiritual children. A true son of St. Francis of Assisi, from whom he learned to call upon Mary with splendid expressions of praise and love.

"The new blessed never tired of teaching the faithful a tender and profound devotion to Our Lady that was rooted in the Church's authentic tradition. In the privacy of the confessional, as in his preaching, he continually urged the faithful: "Love Our Lady!" At the end of his earthly life, when the time came to express his last wishes, he turned his thoughts, as he had done throughout his life, to the Blessed Mary: "Love Our Lady and help others to love her. Always recite the Rosary" [*The holy Father referred twice in his short talk to the atrocities being committed and the tragic plight of the many refuges in the Balkans and Africa which was uppermost in his mind.—Editor*].

"During this month of Mary may prayers be organized in every Diocese to implore the Blessed Virgin, Queen of Peace, with one voice in the Church so that in the Balkans, on the African continent and in every part of the world peacemakers may burgeon who will forget their own interests and be willing to work for the common good.

"May Padre Pio, a most loving son of the "Queen of Heaven," intercede for us and for all, so that sentiments of forgiveness, reconciliation and peace may flow from human hearts at the end of this millennium and the beginning of the new, third millennium, for which we are preparing." — *Pope John Paul II*

Why He Could Embrace Suffering

C. Bernard Ruffin

Padre Pio is famed for his supernatural gifts: for miraculous heal-ings, for bilocation, for prophecy, for the ability to discern the spiritual state of a soul. Monsignor George Pogany, who knew him for years, amused him saying, "When people read that book about you, they'll think that every twenty-four hours you work twenty-five miracles." He and other people who were constantly around him did not see him as a miracle man, but simply as a good holy man. Father Dominic Meyer, an American who served as his secretary for many years, was once asked if he found it "thrilling" to live with Padre Pio. "The thrill left me after two or three days," he wrote. "Not because I was disappointed, but because Padre Pio, as saintly as he is, was just as human as anyone else." Padre Gerardo di Flumeri told me personally, "You were most impressed by his spirituality, by his obedience, by his charity, but by nothing else."

One of Padre Pio's most important missions for our times was to teach people to cope with suffering. Suffering is a problem that people today do not want to think about. More than at any other time in history people use every means they can find to be free of sufferings. And when nothing works they blame God for suffering—whether it be physical or mental, poverty, loneliness, or any other trial. Many "pop religionists" try to convince us that if we are right with God we will have health and prosperity and avoid suffering. There are people who say if only people stopped eating meat and started the diet regimen they advocate people will never be sick and live to the age of 120. Padre Pio, who, incidental-ly, ate little meat, but (in addition to the *stigmata)* had the typical ill-nesses and operations that one would expect to encounter in a life of fourscore years, did not feel that way.

Some religionists would have us believe that if we suffer, it is be-cause we are sinful. Padre Pio, standing on nearly two thousand years of Christian tradition, taught that suffering is a part of life and not neces-sarily a sign of God's displeasure or of human weakness. He would have us believe that the important thing is not to attempt to escape suffering in this world, because we cannot, but how to deal with everything that comes to us from the hand of God—which includes suffering.

The Scripture passage most important to Padre Pio's approach to suffering is Colossians 1:24, in which St. Paul tells us, "I rejoice now in the sufferings I bear for your sake; and what is lacking of the sufferings of Christ I fill up in my flesh for His body, which is the Church." It is not that Christ's sufferings are insufficient and that He needs our help. But rather, we are given the privilege of joining our sufferings to those of Christ on the cross in order to share in His redeeming work, the salvation of souls.

This was Padre Pio's belief. In one of his many ecstasies, in which he was overheard conversing with Christ, he indicated that Christ does not need our works and that man cannot, through his own strength, help Jesus bear the cross, but, by the grace of Christ, we can participate in His redeeming work by sharing His sufferings. This theology is evident in the prayer card Padre Pio prepared when he was ordained in 1910. He had printed: "Jesus, my life and breath, today I timorously raise Thee in the mystery of love. With Thee may I be for the world the way, the truth, and the life, and through Thee a holy priest, a perfect victim."—A perfect victim. ...

When Padre Pio was a young man, the concept of "Victim of Divine Love" was well established: that there is a redemptive value in suffering which is offered to Christ in union with His saving sacrifice. There are some people who are called to a mission of extraordinary sufferings, whether they be physical, mental, spiritual, or all three. Padre Pio was convinced that he was called to such a mission. In his mystical life he experienced sublime sufferings. He also experienced sublime joys. But let us concern ourselves with what he had to say to ordinary Christians about dealing with suffering.

I first heard about Padre Pio when I was in college, during the last two years of his life. I wrote him that I wanted to enter the Christian ministry and I asked if I should be a Roman Catholic. I got a reply, *printed,* not signed, "The Superior." Then I lost the letter. For thirty years I thought it was lost, as I made two or three concerted efforts to locate it in vain. Just a few weeks ago, trying to organize my letters, I found it. It was in a stack of letters that I am sure I had been through more than once in the past, and I wondered why God would now permit it to surface. I read through the letter, in which the superior said that Padre Pio sent his blessing and told me to trust "entirely in the goodness of God." That phrase, I think, more than anything else, summarizes Padre Pio's theology: that we must commit our lives to the proposition that God is good. From this everything else follows.

176

Because God is good, we must trust Him. Yet, we suffer. If God is good, our sufferings must be necessary. C. S. Lewis, in his *A Grief Observed,* written after the death of his wife, said the same thing. He said that we must make a choice. Either our sufferings are necessary, or God is a "Cosmic Sadist." Padre Pio said that people in order to be cured of physical ailments, submit to "bloodletting [remember, he was writing eighty years ago], the lance, the razor, the probe, and the scalpel, and to fire and to all the bitterness of medicines. To be spiritually cured, we have to submit to the suffering of the Divine Physician." Suffering is necessary. Why could God not have created a perfect world where there is no pain or trouble? How could we possibly fully understand? From scripture we know that He did create everything "good." Then sin entered into the world through our first parents. We must trust in God, that He plans the greatest possible good for us, even through the original fall of mankind.

Padre Pio taught that suffering comes to Christians through the hands of God. Some people wonder about why "bad things happen to good people." There was a book by that title, by a Jewish rabbi. Padre Pio was no longer alive when it was published, but I think he would have been puzzled by the assumption that there are "good people" who somehow do not deserve suffering. He considered himself a miserable wretch, and, like all other orthodox Christians, insisted that God does not owe us anything, especially on account of our poor performance. We are all sinners cleansed and regenerated by the blood of Jesus, and, apart from Jesus, we are deserving of hell.

Padre Pio used to tell a parable: "A lady was embroidering a beautiful pattern. Her small son was seated beside her on a low stool. He saw her work, but on the back side. Seeing only the knots and the tangled threads of embroidery he asks, 'Mother, what are you doing? I can't make out what you are doing!' Then the mother lowers the embroidery hoop and shows the beautiful pattern of her work. Each color is in its proper place and the various threads form a harmonious design. So too, we see the reverse side of the embroidery of our lives because we are seated on a low stool." Things will look different viewed from heaven and eternity. "No suffering," Padre Pio wrote, "borne out of love for Christ, even poorly borne, will go unrewarded in eternal life. Trust and hope in the merits of Jesus and in this way even poor clay will become finest gold which will shine in the palace of the king of heaven." In other words, in heaven we will be paid back, recompensed for all the sufferings that we have offered to Our Lord.

Padre Pio said, "Let us refer everything to God and live and move in Him. Physical and spiritual ills are the most worthy offering you can make to Him who saved you by suffering." He added, "In all human affairs,

.... learn most of all to recognize and adore God's will in everything. Frequently repeat the divine words of our dear Master, 'Thy will be done on earth as it is in heaven.' This will be your anchor and your salvation."

Of course, if there were no heaven, this would all be meaningless. Heaven is very essential in Padre Pio's theology. He taught that heaven was a place where those who live in commitment to Christ will be reunited with family and friends to live forever in joy and love and peace in the presence of the Triune God. "Comfort yourself," he once wrote a bereaved woman, "with the sweet thought that your Daddy is not dead. He lives a life of joy that has no end. He lives in the company of his dearest ones." When asked if we will know each other in heaven, he replied, "What kind of a heaven would it be if we didn't have with us those whom we love?" He told a spiritual son, Pietruccio Cugino, "The joy of paradise will be enough to carry us all on. Every sacrifice we make on earth will be recompensed. Heaven is total joy, continuous joy. We will be constantly thanking God. It's useless to try to figure out exactly what heaven is like, because we can't understand it. But when the veil of this life is taken off, we will understand things in a different way."

Therefore, he taught that the believer must be patient in suffering. "Follow the Divine Master up the steep slope of Calvary, loaded with the cross," he wrote, "and when it pleases Him to place us on the cross by confining us to a bed of pain, let us thank Him and consider ourselves lucky to be honored in this way, aware that to be on the cross with Jesus is infinitely more perfect than merely contemplating Him on the cross."

"Keep your eyes fixed on Him who is your guide to the heavenly country," he wrote another time. "Why worry whether it is desert or meadow through which you pass, so long as God is always with you and you arrive at the possession of a blessed eternity?" We should not worry at all. "Our sweet Lord is deprived of giving us many graces solely because the door to our heart is not open to Him in holy confidence. Worry dries up piety and makes it sterile."

St. Gemma Galgani wrote that there are people who are called upon to be victims "who by their sufferings, tribulations, and difficulties make amends for sinners and their ingratitude." Padre Pio certainly believed that he had such a call, and at times, he seemed actually to seek out suffering. But he did not recommend this to other people. The object of the Christian life is to relieve the suffering of others in the world. His regard for suffering was the keystone of Padre Pio's great work, *La Casa Sollievo della Sofferenza* (the House for the Relief of Suffering), the large, well-equipped hospital he established in San Giovanni Rotondo (see the chapter on page 186). When people came to him troubled in body or mind, he prayed for them and, when possible, tried to put them in touch with those who could remedy their problems. However, he told us that we are not to go looking for suffering.

There once was a woman who came to him and said that she wanted to suffer, so she was going to eat some poisonous plants in hopes of contracting typhoid. "I will not permit any of this madness!" he roared. "There are many ways to do penance, such as offering to the Lord whatever trouble comes to us day by day. It is up to the Lord to give us our cross. If He has not sent you one, it is because He is not sure that you could bear it." We don't have to look for a cross. We can unite ourselves with Christ on the cross simply by offering to Him whatever comes to us each day. It is enough to bear each day's burden cheerfully. Even in the daily affairs of life, when God allows an absence of opportunities to suffer, there are occasions to make sacrifices to the Lord. Padre Pio used to talk about one of his deceased colleagues, whom he found quite annoying. "This blessed priest," he said, "when he was here in our family, almost every day, after lunch, when I was trying to get some rest, would come to talk about all his troubles with me. It took a great deal of sacrifice to listen to him. Now, every day, at the same hour, as a reward for the sacrifices he made me make, I say a holy rosary for his soul, even if I feel tired and exhausted."

We are saved, not by anything we do or anything that we are. We are saved by the grace of Jesus Christ. But, in order to grow in grace, we must accept everything that comes our way with thanksgiving, as from the Father's hand. Once someone asked Padre Pio how purgatory could be avoided, and he replied, "By accepting everything from God's hand. Offering everything up to Him with love and thanksgiving will enable us to pass from our deathbed to paradise." For Padre Pio, this was the key to Christian living: to commit one's life to Jesus as Lord and Saviour and, by the power of the Holy Spirit and through the intercession of Our Lady, to trust firmly and unshakably in the goodness of the Heavenly Father and accept everything that comes to us as from His hand, offering all to Him as a sacrifice, all that we find hard or unpleasant: both the great disasters of life as well as the petty annoyances.

As we approach the third millennium, there is cause for great pessimism if not despair as we look out over the world. Padre Pio, however, would have us "trust entirely in God's goodness." He would have us look, unfrightened by the lies and threats of the prince of darkness, through the gloomy fogs of a world cursed by sin and pain, to Our Savior, the Light of the world. He is the Lord of time, of space, and of history, who is forever on His throne, and who comes to us in the Blessed Sacrament so that we might take hold of Him and He of us, in a true and efficacious pledge that we are in His hands and nothing in this world or in the next can separate us from Him.

New Saint's Life, a Replay
of the Glory of the Cross

Rome, Sunday, June 16, after canonizing Padre Pio, before the Gloria of the Mass, the Holy Father gave the following homily based on the passage of the Gospel of Matthew 11:25-30 which summed up the life of the new Saint. In the life of Padre Pio, The Holy Father highlighted St. Pio's bearing trials patiently, seeking greater conformity with Christ Crucified, his prayer life ("I am a poor Franciscan who prays"), charity and generosity in administering the sacrament of penance. The Holy Father identified St. Pio's secret in his constantly seeking conformity with Christ Crucified, "Is it not, precisely, the 'glory of the Cross' which shines above all in Padre Pio? How timely is the spirituality of the Cross lived by the humble Capuchin of Pietrelcina. Our time needs to rediscover its value in order to open the heart to hope. Throughout his life, he always sought greater conformity with the Crucified, since the Franciscan friar was very conscious of having been called to collaborate in a special way in the work of redemption. Padre Pio's holiness cannot be understood without constant reference to the Cross." The translation of the Holy Father's homily, given in Italian, follows.

"For my yoke is easy and my burden light" (Mt 11:30).
Jesus' words to his disciples, which we just heard, help us to understand the most important message of this solemn celebration. Indeed, in a certain sense, we can consider them as a magnificent summary of the whole life of Padre Pio of Pietrelcina, today proclaimed a saint.

The evangelical image of the "yoke" recalls the many trials that the humble Capuchin of San Giovanni Rotondo had to face. Today we contemplate in him how gentle the "yoke" of Christ is, and how truly light is his burden when it is borne with faithful love. The life and mission of Padre Pio prove that difficulties and sorrows, if ac-cepted out of love, are transformed into a privileged way of holiness, which opens onto the horizons of a greater good, known only to the Lord.

"But may I never boast except in the cross of Our Lord Jesus Christ" (Gal 6:14).
Is it not, precisely, the "glory of the Cross" that shines above all in

Padre Pio? How timely is the spirituality of the Cross lived by the humble Capuchin of Pietrelcina. Our time needs to rediscover the value of the Cross in order to open the heart to hope.

Throughout his life, he always sought greater conformity with the Crucified, since he was very conscious of having been called to collaborate in a special way in the work of redemption. His holiness cannot be understood without this constant reference to the Cross.

In God's plan, the Cross constitutes the true instrument of salvation for the whole of humanity and the way clearly offered by the Lord to those who wish to follow him (cf. Mk 16:24). The Holy Franciscan of the Gargano understood this well, when on the Feast of the Assumption in 1914, he wrote: "In order to succeed in reaching our ultimate end we must follow the divine Head, who does not wish to lead the chosen soul on any way other than the one he followed; by that, I say, of abnegation and the Cross" *(Epistolario II, p. 155)*.

The ultimate reason for the apostolic ef-fec-tiveness of Padre Pio can be found in that intimate and constant union with God, attested to by his long hours spent in prayer and in the confessional. He repeated often, "I am a poor Franciscan who prays."

"I am the Lord who acts with mercy" (Jer 9:23).

Padre Pio was a generous dispenser of divine mercy, making himself available to all by welcoming them, by spiritual direction and, especially, by the administration of the sacrament of Penance. I also had the privilege, during my young years, of benefiting from his availability for penitents. The ministry of the confessional, which is one of the distinctive traits of his apostolate, attracted great crowds of the faithful to the monastery of San Giovanni Rotondo. Even when that unusual confessor treated pilgrims with apparent severity, the latter, becoming conscious of the gravity of sins and sincerely repentant, almost always came back for the peace?ful embrace of sacramental forgiveness. May his example encourage priests to carry out with joy and zeal this ministry which is so important today, as I wished to confirm this year in the Letter to Priests on the occasion of Holy Thursday.

"You, Lord, are my only good."

This is what we sang in the responsorial psalm. Through these words, the new Saint invites us to place God above everything, to consider him our sole and highest good.

In fact, the ultimate reason for the apostolic effectiveness of Padre Pio, the profound root of so much spiritual fruitfulness can be found in that intimate and constant union with God, attested to by his long hours spent in prayer and in the confessional. He loved to repeat, "I am a poor Franciscan who prays," convinced that "prayer is the best weapon we have, a key that opens the heart of God." This fundamental characteristic of his spirituality continues in the "Prayer Groups" that he founded, which offer to the Church and to society the wonderful contribution of incessant and confident prayer. To prayer, Padre Pio joined an intense charitable activity, of which the "Home for the Relief of Suffering" is an extraordinary expression. Prayer and charity, this is the most concrete synthesis of Padre Pio's teaching, which today is offered to everyone.

"I bless you, Father, Lord of heaven and earth, because ... these things you have revealed to little ones" (Mt 11:25).

How appropriate are these words of Jesus, when we think of them as applied to you, humble and beloved Padre Pio.

Teach us, we ask you, humility of heart so we may be counted among the little ones of the Gospel, to whom the Father promised to reveal the mysteries of his Kingdom.

Help us to pray without ceasing, certain that God knows what we need even before we ask him.

San Giovnni Rotondo, at the moment of the canonization.

Obtain for us the eyes of faith that will be able to recognize right away in the poor and suffering the face of Jesus.

Sustain us in the hour of the combat and of the trial and, if we fall, make us experience the joy of the sacrament of forgiveness.

Grant us your tender devotion to Mary, the Mother of Jesus and our Mother.

Accompany us on our earthly pilgrimage toward the blessed homeland, where we hope to arrive in order to contemplate forever the glory of the Father, the Son and the Holy Spirit. Amen.

May Mary place her motherly hand on your head

At the end of the Mass of Canonization of St. Pio of Pietrelcina, and before the recitation of the Angelus and the final blessing, the Holy Father greeted and thanked those who participated in the event and announced that the memorial of St. Pio is to be an obligatory memorial celebrated on September 23. The following is a condensation of a translation of his greetings in the language of the respective countries, French, English, Spanish, Portugese, and Polish, given on Sunday, June 1, just before the angelus.

"I want to thank in a special way all the pilgrims gathered in this square and in the neighboring streets, I must say with courage, especially those who have faced the sacrifice of having had to stand for a long

St. Peter's Square overflowing with people for the canonization.

time in this heat. I also greet the faithful gathered in prayer at San Giovanni Rotondo and all who are following the rite over television. As I urge each one to walk in the footsteps of St. Pio of Pietrelcina, I am pleased to announce that his liturgical commemoration will be inserted in the Roman Calendar to be observed as an obligatory memorial on 23 September, the day of his birth in heaven."

The Holy Father then greeted in French, English, Spanish, Portuguese and Polish the pilgrims who came from these countries for the canonization and were waving their national flags in response to the Pope's greetings.

"May Mary rest her motherly hand on your head."

The wish that Padre Pio once addressed to one of his spiritual daughters, he addresses to you today. Let us entrust to the motherly intercession of Our Lady and to St. Pio of Pietrelcina the journey of holiness of the whole Church at the beginning of the new millennium.

Text and illustrations on pages VIII, 180-184 Reprinted from English edition of L'OSSERVATORE ROMANO June 19, 2002.

PART VII

The House for the Relief of Suffering

Clementine Lenta

In the early part of the 1920's a man was seriously hurt in a mine accident near San Giovanni Rotondo. Bleeding profusely, he was rushed to Foggia for medical treatment, but a week later the unfortunate man was still waiting for assistance. He had been put on a cot in the hospital corridor as there was no other room for him, and the doctors had had no time to take care of him other than to stop the bleeding.

News of the poor man's plight deeply grieved the compassionate heart of Padre Pio. Though he himself had the gift of healing people miraculously, he knew this was not the real answer to his people's need for medical care. Foggia—about forty miles away—was too far away to treat the people of San Giovanni Rotondo, and others living in the Gargano district. Besides, the hospital at Foggia was antiquated and always overcrowded. Padre Pio saw that something had to be done to help his poor, suffering people. He began to envision a hospital at San Giovanni Rotondo.

Build a hospital? How could he, a Capuchin priest bound by a vow of poverty and with no money of his own, even dream of such an impossibility? But to the saintly priest "with God, nothing is impossible." And so he took his dream to the merciful Heart of Christ, relying completely on Divine Providence. Still, the years passed, and with the advent of the Second World War and the resulting devastation of Italy, it seemed that his dream would never be realized. The war moreover brought hundreds of thousands of casualties, hundreds of whom made their painful way to San Giovanni Rotondo. The sight of them made Padre Pio more determined than ever to alleviate their sufferings.

The first major step towards the realization of his dream occurred on the evening of January 9, 1946, when three friends, Dr. Carlo Kisnardy, Dr. Guglielmo Sanguinetti and Dr. Mario De Vico, gathered in his cell in the monastery of Our Lady of Grace. "We must do something for the sick," the priest said; "we must build a large home for them." The men understood he wanted a hospital and looked at each other in amazement. Build a hospital, now, when Italy was in shambles and its economy shattered? Padre Pio added that this was not to be called or be like an ordinary hospital. It would be a "House for the Relief of Suffering," where, as he said: "faith and hope will make their spirits well ... while science, if it can, will do the rest."

After they consented to support what seemed to them an impossible plan, Padre Pio turned to Dr. Sanguinetti and said: "You will come to live at San Giovanni Rotondo, and will be of much help." The good doctor was poor, as was everyone at the time.

Though he was entitled to a pension because of his many years' work for the state railroad, he could not afford to retire. Padre Pio answered his objections by raising his eyes to heaven and saying, "Well, ... there is the ticket! I am telling you that you will come to live here."

"Ticket? What ticket?" asked Dr. Sanguinetti. As he left for home to return to his practice in Borgo San Lorenzo, the question continued to bother him. He mentioned it to the father of a sick patient he was treating, the Marquis Sacchetti, and asked him for a donation. He received neither a solution to his question nor a donation. Shortly after he found out about the "ticket." The doctor was informed that one of the bonds he had bought from the State had won him a modest fortune in a bond number prize drawing allowing him to retire. When he told the Marquis of his good fortune, the latter's attitude changed at once. Sacchetti not only

The House for the Relief of Suffering was a miracle "house" from its inception to today's large medical complex situated on a barren, rocky mountain.

gave much of his fortune for the project but collected money from his friends.

On October 5, 1946, the project received its official status and was incorporated under the title, "House for the Relief of Suffering." The statutes of the new corporation declared that the principal object of the hospital was, "to receive any person who appeals for assistance and charity in the name of Christ." Although the funds available at that time were far from the amount needed, the founders imposed upon themselves one rule: not to ask anything of anyone but to seek only the help of God.

Soon offerings were coming in from many quarters. American soldiers, stationed in the nearby air base at Foggia, inspired by the priest's saintliness and grateful for his blessing and prayers, donated towards the erection of the hospital. Servicemen of other countries who had become acquainted with the Franciscan friar contributed, for they too had received many favors from him. Rich and poor from many nations, but most of all Americans, contributed to the building of this monument of Christian charity.

In 1947, Barbara Ward, the noted English author and economist, went to San Giovanni Rotondo. As a result of her visit and without any request being made to her, she was later instrumental in obtaining, through the influence of the late Fiorello LaGuardia, then mayor of New York and the Director General of the United Nations Relief and Rehabilitation Administration, 250 million lire from UNRRA funds for the hospital. A committee of experts in their particular fields was formed and work began. It was a tremendous undertaking, one which required prayer, sacrifice, skill, patience and hard work. It seemed as if it would never succeed. A prominent physician in nearby Foggia, publicly stated, "They're crazy! A hospital on a mountain."

The hospital was built about 2,400 ft. above sea level on a rocky, barren mountain. Many workshops had to be provided since there were no railways nearby. A kiln was built for making lime from stone dug out of the mountain side. An apparatus was set up for the manufacturing of cement slabs, tiles, etc. It was also necessary to provide water and electricity, all of which created many jobs for the unemployed. At the time there were four million unemployed in Italy, but there was no unemployment problem in San Giovanni Rotondo and nearby towns. The hospital was a bold enterprise which sparked the imagination of the rest of southern Italy. When northern Italy was turning more and more to Communism, the growth of Communism in southern Italy including neighboring San Giovanni was checked. Padre Pio's advice in this regard was: "If Christians were more Christian there would be no need for Communism."

Dr. Guglielmo Sanguinetti who came to live in San Giovanni to give his wholehearted support to Padre Pio's "wild" dream.

Besides the three faithful friends who began the great enterprise with Padre Pio, mention must be made of the builder and architect, Angelo Lupi, an eccentric genius. He not only served as architect but also recruited and organized local farm laborers, with group leaders and land surveyors. There was nothing the architect, inspired by the saintly priest, wouldn't do for him. He worked to the limit of his endurance, eating his lunch with one hand while he held a blueprint in the other.

"We must be quite forgetful of self ... in every poor man it is Jesus Himself who is languishing; in every man who is both sick and poor, Jesus is doubly present."

— *Padre Pio*

Little by little, the "House" began to take shape while the grounds were beautified. Because the stark hillside above the structure did not appeal to Dr. Sanguinetti, who had been accustomed to the wooded hills of his area of Italy, he ordered and supervised the planting of 10,000 trees. The interior of this "home for the sick"—at Padre Pio's express wish—was furnished in such a way as to soften the appearance of hospital rooms. The wards were small, the colors were soft and delicate, the lighting good and flowers graced the rooms.

Its high-tech hospital equipment is said to be among the best in Europe. The original building had 300 beds, later enlarged for 800; today there are 1200 beds. In 1956, 1998 sick came to the clinic; in 1967, 16,900 were admitted to the hospital. By 1972, the number rose to 19,462. For treatment the first preference is given to the sick people from the Gargano district, regardless of social status or economic condition. If there is still room, people from other parts of Italy and even from abroad are admitted. All patients, rich or poor, are treated exactly the same in accommodations, medical attention, nursing services, and food. No difference whatsoever is made between those who pay and those who cannot pay. The administration must raise the funds to cover the costs incurred by those who are not able to pay and/or those whose insurance is not adequate. And so, there is a constant need for special funds for the sick poor.

The medical and nursing care are of the finest. A Sister of the Congregation of the Suore Missionarie Zelatrici del Sacro Cuore heads each department and ward. Secular nurses, most of them graduates of a three year nursing course from the Red Cross training center in Bari, serve under the direction of the Sisters.

The House for the Relief of Suffering was officially opened on May 5, 1956, with Padre Pio offering Holy Mass on an altar set up at the top of the stairs, just outside the main entrance. Among the 15,000 people present were his Eminence, Cardinal Giacomo Lercaro of Bologna, and many bishops, priests, and religious, as well as government officials from the province of Foggia.

Padre Pio spoke briefly, stating: "I thank the benefactors of the whole world who have contributed to the construction of the House for the Relief of Suffering. ... May it become a center of the Franciscan spirit in action, a place of prayer and science where the human race finds itself in Christ Crucified as a single flock under one Shepherd. ... May our Blessed Lady of All Graces and our Seraphic Father, St. Francis in heaven and the Vicar of Christ on earth intercede for us that these wishes may be accomplished." The papal blessing of Pope Pius XII was given; the mayor of San Giovanni Rotondo thanked Padre Pio as the moving spirit of the hospital. Padre Pio cut the traditional ribbon; and he, together with Cardinal Lercaro of Bologna, entered the House and blessed the various departments.

The hospital is especially equipped for the study of heart diseases and shortly after its opening some of the most famous heart specialists in the world attended a symposium there on coronary diseases. Dr. Paul Dudley White, President Eisenhower's cardiologist was one of the speakers and he concluded his address with, "I go back to America deeply moved by the realization of this great project inspired by Padre Pio ... This clinic, more than any other in the whole world, seems to me to be the most useful for the study of the relationship that exists between spirit and illness; here more than anywhere else the study of the psychosomatic can make progress."

Before leaving the new hospital, the physicians went to the friary of Our Lady of Grace to express to Padre Pio their admiration for the wonderful work he had established. Dr. G. Nylen of Stockholm summed up their feelings nicely when he said: "This hospital is a tangible proof of the Good Samaritan." Padre Pio himself on an earlier occasion expressed beautifully the essentially Christian ideal and spirit of his hospital in these words:

"We must be quite forgetful of self. Rising above selfishness, we must bow down to the sufferings and the wounds of our fellow men. We must make them our own, knowing how to suffer with our brethren for the love of God. We must know how to instill hope into their hearts and bring back a smile to their lips, having restored a ray of light into their souls. Then we shall be offering God the most beautiful, the most noble of prayers, because our prayer will have sprung from sacrifice. It will be the very essence of love, the unselfish gift of all that we are in body and soul. In every sick man there is Jesus in person who is suffering; in every poor man it is Jesus himself who is languishing; in every man who is both sick and poor, Jesus is doubly present." — *From* Immaculata *magazine.*

How to be a Spiritual Child of Padre Pio

Padre Pio had many spiritual children in his lifetime. Today there are many who would also like to be his spiritual children. The following are the conditions and responsibilities. (1) live an intensely spiritual life of divine grace, (2) prove your faith by words and actions, (3) desire to remain under the protection of Bl. Padre Pio to enjoy the fruits of his prayers and sufferings, (4) imitate the new Blessed in his love for Jesus Crucified, for Jesus Eucharist and Our Blessed Mother, the Church and the Holy Father, (5) practice sincere charity towards all. Applications should be made in writing. Contact the National Center of Padre Pio, address on page 194.

Padre Pio's Prayer Groups

Wherever Padre Pio is known and loved, one will find his spiritual children. And wherever there are a number of his spiritual children gathered together, they will usually form a Padre Pio Prayer Group. To understand the phenomenal growth in the Prayer Groups one must first examine his spiritual paternity, which existed decades before the Prayer Groups were first conceived.

It wasn't long after Padre Pio arrived at St. Mary of Grace friary in San Giovanni Rotondo in 1916 that local people realized what an extraordinary confessor they had in this young priest. Two years later when the visible stigmata of Padre Pio became known, people flocked to him from all over Italy to put themselves under his direction. Thus in the early twenties, he already had many spiritual children, giving spiritual direction through the letters he wrote. Invariably his letters contained exhortations to prayer. Prayer to him was the very essence of life. His words on prayer are masterpieces of simplicity and colorful expression.

"The holy gift of prayer is placed in the right hand of the Savior. And in the measure in which you empty yourself of self, that is, the ridding of yourself of love of your own will and body, and rooting yourself in humility he will communicate it to you ... remember the graces of prayer are not earthly but heavenly waters and no effort of ours can make them flow." And again, "In books we search for God; in prayer we find him." Padre Pio points out that prayer is our greatest weapon, a key which opens the heart of God. "You must speak to Jesus with your heart as well as with your lips; indeed in certain circumstances you must pray only with your heart."

Later on in his life, we find few written words on prayer by Padre Pio as he was forbidden to write. But he continued to encourage his spiritual children vocally to a greater and deeper prayer life; his whole life was an example of the vital importance of prayer. Few saints in their lifetime have reached out and touched souls as did Padre Pio. These converted sinners would then ask him to guide them on the steep path to Christian perfection. He was ever on the lookout for another soul which he could draw to Jesus. His gaze would wander upon a group of pilgrims in search of the most afflicted or grieving one, and the significant meeting would frequently end in a lifetime of concern for that individual soul by Padre Pio.

So great was the love and commitment which he had for his spiritual children that he made this bold statement: "I shall stand at the gates of Paradise and shall not enter unless first all my spiritual children have already entered." Such an assertion came from either a madman or one enraptured with Divine Love. It is, so to speak, the Sacred Heart of Jesus speaking through the lips of his faithful servant, Padre Pio. To another spiritual child he said; "I possess your heart, just as you possess mine. Know then that when you are far away from me, that you are closer than the others. To be close to me doesn't mean to come to see me and to touch me, but to do my will in every detail: it is after all the will of God."

Since he was forbidden to write in the latter part of his life he discouraged letters but told his penitents and spiritual children to send their Guardian Angels and added, "I'll take care of everything." How he could take care of the needs of tens of thousands of spiritual children scattered throughout the world is hard to imagine. When asked, he again affirmed his paternity, "Those who come to me, I never again forget," but the mystery still remains. Even though the many thousands of souls who count him as their spiritual Father cannot offer an explanation, they are sure of his personal love for each one of them. Yet, even this does not express the whole truth for he said to one of his spiritual children: "You think you know my love for you. But you don't know that it is much greater than you can imagine. I follow you with my prayers, with my suffering and with my tears."

With such a spiritual father, it is not surprising that when Padre Pio appealed to his spiritual children to form prayer groups that the response was overwhelming. Actually the idea was not his. He merely fulfilled a wish of Pope Pius XII. In making an appeal for prayer groups in 1952, this saintly Pope, who is considered the Pope of Fatima, was no doubt prompted by our Lady of Fatima's words for more prayer and penance.

The idea of people meeting in groups at least once a month, under the direction of a priest, to encourage one another by word and example, and most of all by prayer to a deeper Christian commitment, had a great appeal to his spiritual children. They promptly named their groups, "Padre Pio Prayer Groups." The prayer groups offer prayers of thanksgiving to God for all favors received; they adore their God for his goodness and mercy; prayers of expiation for their own sins and those of the whole world are offered as well as prayers of petition to receive an increase in the Love and Life which Jesus pours out upon all mankind.

The monthly meetings usually take place on the first Saturday of the month, which is the day our Lady set aside for special veneration and reparation to her Immaculate Heart. Mass, Holy Communion, the Rosary and an hour of adoration are the usual devotions practiced on the First Saturday. Besides a spiritual director, each group must have two persons who assume the responsibility of gathering the group, planning the monthly observance, and who handle communications between the group and the official headquarters in Italy.

Each prayer group has its own particular characteristic, which leaves room for wide diversity among the groups. One promotes the scapular of Our Lady of Mt. Carmel and the daily Rosary in order to fulfill the requests of Our Lady of Fatima. Another group reports that many families having members who have terminal illnesses attend their Holy Hour. These families experience new hope and peace. Eventually they ask to join the prayer group. Padre Pio realized the great good that would be accomplished through the prayer groups.

Just before he died in September of 1968 he gave a special blessing to the prayer groups, the sick and his spiritual children. Representatives of prayer groups throughout the world were meeting at San Giovanni Rotondo to celebrate the fiftieth anniversary of the stigmata of Padre Pio. It was quite providential that they were thus present to receive this last blessing and to attend his funeral.

The great influence of Padre Pio in promoting prayer continues after his death in his prayer groups. It is a twentieth century response to the words of our Lord spoken two-thousand years ago: "Truly I say to you, ask and it will be given you, seek and you will find, knock and it will be opened to you." "Truly I say to you, if you ask anything of the Father in my name He will give it to you." "Truly I say to you, heaven and earth will pass away but my words will not pass away."

To form a Padre Pio Prayer Group, the names of the spiritual director and the two lay leaders, along with the name of the church where the group will hold its devotions, the dates and hours of services must all be reported to the official headquarters of the Padre Pio Prayer Groups, which is: Home for the Relief of Suffering, San Giovanni Rotondo, 71013 (Foggia) Italy. In the United States for further information:

National Center for Padre Pio, Inc.
2213 Old Route 100, Barto, PA 19504
TEL (610) 845-3000 FAX (610) 845-2666
www.padrepio.org & www.ncfpp.com

Padre Pio's Apostles

Among Padre Pio's spiritual children, certain ones were singled out to be his chosen apostles who would do much in furthering his many projects, and above all make him better known and loved. Three of these were American women: Mary Pyle, Elena Wenzel and Vera Calandra. Padre Pio could be quite hard on women at times, especially in the area of modesty in dress, yet like Our Lord who singled out women to minister to Him as close collaborators in His work of evangelization, he called these three to come "follow me" in furthering his work, and they were inspired to accept.

When the young, wealthy, talented American socialite, Mary Pyle, came to San Giovanni Rotondo in 1923 seeking spiritual counsel she was one of the first of many collaborators in the works of Padre Pio. The recent convert from the Presbyterian Church was invited personally by Padre Pio to remain at San Giovanni Rotondo and help him, and she did for the rest of her life. She became a Franciscan Tertiary and with a degree in music as well as a mastery of six languages, she helped Padre Pio and the friars in innumerable ways. She even built a seminary at his birthplace, Pietrelcina, using the wealth she had turned her back on in her desire to live a simple and poor life. She also built a hospice near the friary in San Giovanni Rotondo where many weary pilgrims experienced her gracious hospitality. It was here that Padre Pio's parents spent their last days on earth. She died a few months before Padre Pio and was interred in the chapel of the friars in the cemetery of San Giovanni Rotondo (More on Mary Pyle on the chapter L'Americana Collaborator pg, 129).

Elena Wenzel, a convert from Lutheranism, who originally came from Switzerland, relates how after reading a book about Padre Pio, *The City on a Mountain,* she had a great desire to confess her sins to the priest who had the gift of reading souls. She could not feel assured in confessing her sins to a priest that they were forgiven. She had a "dream" in which Padre Pio appeared to her looking deeply into her soul and assuring her that her sins were forgiven. After going to confession to

Padre Pio, who appeared just as in the "dream," and assured her that her sins were indeed forgiven, she was inspired to produce a film about Padre Pio. It was one of the first documentary films about him.

So impressed was she with the stigmatic priest that she invested her life's savings into this project with no assurance of ever getting her investment back. The film was a great success and is still, over twenty-five years later, being distributed as a video tape under the title, *Fifty Years of Thorns and Roses.*

At one point in the film's production Elena found she had exhausted her funds in the midst of costly editing. Fearful it would never be completed, she visited the Blessed Sacrament at St. Peter's in Rome to pour out her problems. On her way out of St. Peter's she passed by the altar of the Pieta. There, kneeling before the Sorrowful Madonna she saw a priest who looked familiar. She recognized Father Patrick Peyton. Waiting until he had finished his prayers, she approached the famous Family Rosary apostle and told him of her troubles. He offered to help, and told her on her return home to contact his film editor, John Fuller, at the Family Theater studio in California. With the professional help of John Fuller and the use of this up-to-date movie studio the film was finished and was made available in five major languages. She is presently working with St. Michael's Communication in Switzerland distributing their more up-to-date video releases.

Besides keeping abreast of recent developments of Padre Pio visual productions and promoting new video tapes on Padre Pio, her role as a spiritual child and apostle of Padre Pio has brought her many wonderful experiences and put her in contact with many souls whom she has been able to help. Some of these are related in the book, *Padre Pio of Pietrelcina.* Moreover this gracious lady, who is now in her eighties, has no thought of retiring as long as there are souls to be saved. So she continues the promotion of her former confessor and spiritual guide as she directs P. Pio Wenzonsky Productions of Parma, Ohio. On her last trip to see Padre Pio she confessed to him just the day before he died. A listing of video tapes that can be procured may be obtained by writing: P. Pio Wenzonsky Prod., Elena Wenzel, 8200 Spring Garden Rd., Parma, Ohio, 44120.

Probably the best known spiritual child and promoter of Padre Pio in America is Mrs. Vera Calandra. Her involvement with Padre Pio goes back to 1966. At the time she was a self-sufficient housewife and mother, without much time to get involved in outside religious organizations or activities. That all changed when her fifth child arrived. Little Vera Marie, as she was called, was a beautiful baby, but had such massive congenital defects of the kidneys and urinary tract that the doctors gave her no hope of living long. After two years and four major operations, her condition was still hopeless.

Advised by a friend to seek Padre Pio's help for a miraculous cure, Vera sent a cable to Padre Pio begging his prayers. Another operation was performed in which the child's urinary bladder was removed, for there was little hope—now that her kidneys were so badly damaged. Another cable was sent: "Please Padre Pio, continue your prayers. Little Vera is alive, but without a bladder. Implore God's mercy that she will be given a miraculous cure."

On August 15, 1968, the feast of the Assumption, praying to Padre Pio for his help, she experienced a delightful heavenly fragrance, like fresh roses (various scents are one of the charisms of Padre Pio, see pg. 27). What did it mean? She came to understand, as though Padre Pio were speaking to her, that if she brought the child to San Giovanni Rotondo immediately, everything would be alright. In two weeks she was on her way to Italy. It was an agonizing pilgrimage as she took, besides her sick child of two, her two-week-old baby which she was still

The National Center for Padre Pio is situated just a short distance from Philadelphia, at Barto, PA. A replica of the original chapel where Padre Pio received the stigmata, a gift shop and book store, as well as a large church to accommodate pilgrim groups are located on its spacious grounds.

nursing. Padre Pio laid his stigmatized hand on the head of little Vera and the little baby, Christina Rose. Four days later she was home. Shortly after her return she took Vera to the hospital to see if there was any improvement. In Vera's own words she relates what happened:

"On September 17, the feast of the Stigmata of Padre Pio's model, St. Francis of Assisi, little Vera's surgeon stated that where he had surgically removed little Vera's urinary bladder, there now appeared a remnant of a bladder. 'Surely, Doctor,' I said 'you are not saying that this child is growing a new bladder. Why that would be a miracle!'" Six months later, April, 1969, the doctor confirmed the existence of a "rudimentary bladder." It was a first in medical history. Thirty years later Vera Marie is a normal and healthy woman.

With much to be thankful for, Mrs. Calandra was ready to follow another little voice that prompted her to "shout from the rooftops" the extraordinary favor she had received. At first she worked off a kitchen table in her home in Norristown, PA, with magazines, books, holy cards on Padre Pio stuffed throughout the house. Later a special office was added to her house and came to be known as the "National Center for Padre Pio." Since that humble beginning, Vera who is a Secular Franciscan, has traveled thousands of air miles giving over 2,000 lectures on Padre Pio and distributing literature on the new Blessed. She organizes pilgrimages to San Giovanni Rotondo almost every year and works in close collaboration with the friars in Italy who recognize the Center as the National Center for the United States.

From a small family operation, the Center has expanded into a large 100 acre center with two churches, a book store, information center and offices with paid emploees as well as volunteers. The Center also serves to support tens of thousands throughout the country who seek further information on how to become spiritual children of Padre Pio and how to establish Padre Pio Prayer Groups. Now that the Center has spacious grounds and a complex of buildings, one of which is a replica of the original friary church of Santa Maria della Grazia in San Giovanni Rotondo, it has become a pilgrimage center.

The Center in Barto, PA, just a half hour from Philadelphia, offers the usual spiritual ministry to pilgrims: Mass, confessions, Benediction, and adoration of the Blessed Sacrament. During the first weekend of May and the day of the beatification, May 2, 1999, there were buses with pilgrims arriving from the East Coast and even from the Midwest. One priest summed up well the work of Vera, her husband Harry, and other members of the Calandra family thus: "This Center has become a spiritual oasis for souls hungering and thirsting for God."

A Worldling Becomes an Apostle

When Mario Bruschi accompanied his mother from where they were visiting relatives in northern Italy to San Giovanni Rotondo he did so reluctantly. He was having too good a time with new acquaintances going out to dances, night clubs etc. It was a long 12 hour drive to San Giovanni and he was in no mood to get up the following morning at 3:00 am to attend the Mass of Padre Pio. But mothers have their way as a rule. Spiritually, he was not prepared to see the Italian mystic; in fact he avoided eye contact as he was fearful that Padre Pio might point him out and ask him embarrassing questions. His mother wanted to go to confession to Padre Pio, but she had to wait her turn, which would be coming up in ten days. Again, mothers have their way and she even convinced Mario to go to confession to the famous priest who had the gift of reading souls. Four days later he found himself in a line of men going to confession. "I was hoping that he would end confessions for the day and I wouldn't have to face the priest who could reveal facts about my life that I was ashamed to reveal myself."

Padre Pio beckoned him to come forward and the man behind Mario gave him a shove. Padre patted his hand and asked him questions about his life which he answered with a yes or no. He didn't have to reveal his sins as Padre Pio was revealing them to him. Smiling he blessed Mario and said, "Let us pray." Prior to the confession he had befriended a Friar Giovanni, who asked him how everything went. After relating his experience, Padre Giovanni told him he had not received absolution but a blessing. He explained that for some reason known only to himself and God, Padre Pio did not always give absolution.

The American was shocked, annoyed and embarrassed. Padre Giovanni offered to take him to the small friary chapel where he heard his confession and gave him absolution. He even arranged for him to see Padre Pio before leaving for home. They entered the friary and Padre Giovanni knocked on Padre Pio's door. The door opened and there was Padre Pio. What follows is best described in Mario's own words:

"My eyes met his deep penetrating, dark eyes. Even today I see his eyes. As I stood outside his room, he asked me to state my business. I was too timid to enter. He walked towards me. I stepped back nervously, then knelt before him. I looked up into his saintly face and asked for absolution—by way of reminding him he may have forgotten to do so in the confessional. Padre Pio looked at me. He smiled, blessed me, and let me kiss his gloved hand. He said 'Go in peace, my son' but not '*ego te absolvo.*' He walked away a few feet and stopped. He turned around for a long look at me and continued on his way to the choir to join the friars at Vespers.

"Although Padre Pio did not give me absolution, he made me aware of the great spiritual distance which separated me from God and His graces to pursue my life according to His Will. I was also aware of Padre Pio's holiness, humility and goodness. I knew I had seen and touched a man who was close to God—a man who suffered joyfully for the sins of humanity to bring souls back to God." Mario credits Padre Pio for his coming back to God. He attends daily Mass now and goes to confession at least every two weeks. He met his future wife, Sarojini, through Padre Pio and they have four lovely children. In the past thirty years that he has been involved in the apostolate of Padre Pio he has shown films and lectured on Padre Pio in the tri-state area of New York, New Jersey, Connecticut and in eastern Canada.

When his wife, who originally comes from Sri Lanka, returned to visit her family, he accompanied her. He took the Padre Pio film hoping that he could also do some apostolic work during their visit. It actually led to a tour in both India and Sri Lanka and five subsequent trips in which he showed his film and gave lectures in Colombo, Bombay, New Delhi, Madras and many other large cities and towns in both countries.

He is presently the Director of the National Office of the Devotees of Padre Pio with Cardinal John O'Connor as Honorary Chairman and Bishop Francisco Garmendia as Spiritual Director. He is Group Leader of two Padre Pio Prayer Groups in New York City and lay director of a first Friday All Night Prayer vigil in honor of the Sacred Heart of Jesus and the Immaculate Heart of Mary. He led a beatification pilgrimage to Italy and organized a special beatification celebration at the Blue Army Shrine in Washington, NJ. Every August he has an annual Padre Pio Prayer Day at the shrine in Washington, NJ. Mario may be reached at: 1154 First Ave., New York, NY 10021 (212) 838-6549.

From these four examples, and there are many more throughout the United States and the world, we can readily see that Padre Pio inspires great commitment from his spiritual children which is given with joy and the understanding that they are merely following the "Way" of salvation as lived by the saintly Franciscan who so faithfully followed Christ without reserve.

For Further Reading

Biographies

Everybody's Cyrenean by Fr. Alessandro of Ripabottoni, OFM Cap. A biography in corrected edition.

His Early Years by Fr. Augustine Mc Gregor, O.C.S.O.A professional and well-documented study of the Padre.

A View of Padre Pio from Mary Pyle's House by Geraldine Nolan. Recollections connected with the Mary Pyle house (Friary Publication).

Mary Pyle by Bonaventura Massa, OFM Cap. A more complete study of the Franciscan tertiary composed of personal testimonies.

Padre Pio the Stigmatist by Fr. Charles Carty. One of the first English language books on Padre Pio and still one of the best. Many illustrations.

Padre Pio A Biography by Fr. John Schug, OFM Cap. By an American Capuchin who understands Padre Pio from the inside as a fellow Franciscan.

Padre Pio, the True Story by C. Bernard Ruffin. One of the best researched and most complete biographies on Padre Pio.

Roads to Padre Pio by Clarice Bruno.

Homage to Padre Pio by Gerardo DiFlumeri, OFM Cap.

Who Is Padre Pio? A good short introduction to his life.

From His Writings

Padre Pio of Pietrelcina, Letters I. These letters comprise the correspondence between Padre Pio and his spiritual directors.

Letters II. Spiritual direction for everyone through his writings to an individual.

Letters III. More letters of the Padre's spiritual direction to various persons.

Have a Good Day. Padre Pio's thoughts, arranged for every day.

Padre Pio the Great Sufferer. Brief meditations based on the letters of Padre Pio.

The Agony of Jesus. Meditation on Our Lord's agony in the Garden of Gethsemani.

Meditation Prayer on Mary Immaculate.

Other Titles

Mystery of the Cross in Padre Pio by Gerardo DiFlumeri, OFM Cap.

Send Me Your Guardian Angel by Fr. Alessio Parente, OFM Cap. All on Padre Pio's devotion to his Guardian Angel and St. Michael.

Humanae Vitae and Padre Pio. On his teaching regarding Faith and Morals.

Padre Pio's Mass.

The Holy Souls, "Viva Padre Pio" by Fr. Alessio Parente, OFM Cap. Padre Pio's relationship with the Poor Souls in Purgatory.

The Devil in the Life of Padre Pio.

IMMACULATA Magazine. Special issue on Padre Pio.

Thanks to Padre Pio by Karl Wagner. Beautiful testimonies.

Way of the Cross. A devotional booklet with an excerpt from Padre Pio's writings on meditations for each station, with color illustrations.

Voice of Padre Pio magazines, Back issues: great spiritual reading. A year's subscription to the monthly Voice of Padre Pio magazine.

Padre Pio: His Life and Mission by Mary F. Ingoldsby. One of the best biographies, much of it based on his writings, translated by the author herself. Ignatius Press.

The above books, with the exception of the last, along with a number of video tapes may be ordered at the address below.

National Centre for Padre Pio, Inc.
2213 Old Route 100
Barto, PA 19504
(610) 845-3000
FAX (610) 845-2666

Important Biographic Dates

1887   May 25: Francesco Forgione is born in Pietrelcina, near Naples to Grazio and Maria Giuseppa (di Nunzio) Forgione. Baptized the following day in the Church of St. Anne.

1899   Sept. 27: Confirmed by Bishop of Benevento and receives First Holy Communion.

1903   Jan. 6: Enters the Capuchin friary at Morcone.

Jan. 22: Receives habit and religious name, Fra. Pio (Bro. Pius in English); begins his novitiate.

1904   Jan. 22: Makes Simple Profession of vows for a three-year period.

1907   Jan. 27: Makes Solemn Profession in the friary of St. Elia a Pianissi.

1908   Dec. 19: Receives Minor Orders in the Cathedral of Benevento; ordained subdeacon two days later.

1909   July. 18: Ordained deacon in friary chapel at Morcone.

1910   Aug. 10: Ordained priest at the Cathedral of Benevento. His mother was present, while his father was working in America. The next day he celebrates his first Mass in Pietrelcina. Three days later celebrates first Solemn Mass. Remains in Pietrelcina to assist his pastor.

1910–1915   Sept. 20: Receives temporary invisible stigmata. After a few years they became permanent, but still invisible.

1915   Nov. 15: Drafted into the Italian Army. A month later assign to a Medical Corps in Naples. Shortly after, granted a year's leave of absence due to ill-health and returns to Pietrelcina.

1916   Feb. 17: Transferred to the friary of St. Anne in Foggia, whe he endures much from the attacks of the devil.

July 28: Visits San Giovanni Rotondo for the first time.

1916   Dec. 30: Given another six-month medical leave of absence from the Army.

1917   Jan. 6: Visits Marian Sanctuary of Our Lady of the Rosary in Pompei and returns to San Giovanni Rotondo.

May 16: Receives permission to accompany his sister to a convent in Rome where she is named Sister Pia.

July 3: Pilgrimages to St. Michael's Grotto.

Aug. 19: Returns to the military in Naples. In November he obtains another leave and returns to San Giovanni Rotondo.

1918	Mar. 16: Honorably discharged from the army because of ill-health; returns to San Giovanni Rotondo.
	Aug. 5: He experiences the "seraphic assault" similar to St. Teresa of Avila.
	Sept. 20: Receives the visible marks of the stigmata.
1919	May 15: Fr. Provincial has Professor Luigi Romanelli investigate the stigmata.
	July 26: Professor Amico Bignami examines him, gives negative report. Minister General of the Capuchins invites Doctor George Festa of Rome to examine Padre Pio on Oct. 9. Following year, July 15, examination by Dr. Festa and Prof. Romanelli.
1922	Apr. 18: Fr. Agostino Gemelli, OFM, attempts examination of stigmata and claims they are a fraud. His report impresses the Holy Father, Pope Pius XI.
1923	May 31: First decree of the Holy Office ordering isolation of Padre Pio. He can celebrate Mass only in the friary private chapel with no one attending. He may not respond to any letters.
1924	Jul. 24: Second decree of Holy Office against Padre Pio.
1925	Oct. 10: Dr. Festa operates without anesthesia on Padre Pio for a hernia. The pain is so great he passes out, affording Dr. Festa an opportunity to reexamine the wounds.
1926	Apr. 23: Third decree of prohibitions by Holy Office.
	July 11: Fourth decree of Holy Office against Padre Pio.
1929	Jan. 3: Death of Padre Pio's mother. He assists her to the end.
1931	June 9: All ministries are suppressed, with the exception of Mass celebrated in private.
1933	July 16: Pope Pius XI reinstates Padre Pio, allowing him to celebrate public Mass.
1935	Aug. 10: Simple celebration of the twenty-fifth anniversary of his priesthood.
1940	Jan. 9: Padre Pio presides at the first meeting of the committee for construction of La Casa Sollievo della Sofferenza. Same year formation of his first prayer groups.
1946	Oct. 7: Death of his father, Grazio, assisted by Padre Pio.
1947	May 19: Ground breaking for the construction of La Casa Sollievo della Sofferenza.
	July 6: Friary in Pietrelcina opens thirty-five years after Padre Pio predicts it.

1953	Jan. 22: Fiftieth anniversary celebration of Padre Pio's entrance into the Capuchin Order.
1956	May 5: Padre Pio's La Casa Sollievo della Sofferenza is inaugurated with Mass by Padre Pio before 15,000 people. Same year, cornerstone for new church is laid.
1957	May 5: Padre Pio announces need for enlarging the hospital, and is appointed Director of the Franciscan Third Order in San Giovanni Rotondo. He is also granted the privilege of personally guiding the Casa.
1959	July 2: Consecration of the new church, Our Lady of Grace. Cardinal Tedeschini crowns the statue of the Madonna. Aug. 6: The Pilgrim Statue of Our Lady of Fatima arrives by helicopter and is carried through town and brought to the Church of Our Lady of Grace. The following day Padre Pio, gravely ill at the time, venerates the statue, presenting a rosary donated to him by his prayer groups. That afternoon as the helicopter leaves he is miraculously cured.
1960	July 30: The Apostolic visit of Mons. Maccari begins, followed by new restrictions in January of the following year. Aug. 10: Fiftieth anniversary of Padre Pio's priesthood.
1966	May 3: At the tenth anniversary of Casa Sollievo, Cardinal Lercaro presides over the international convention of prayer groups.
1967	May 9: His brother Michele dies at San Giovanni Rotondo, followed by the death of his close American collaborator, Mary Pyle, April 27, 1968.
1967	May 25: Prayer groups convene for his 80th birthday.
1968	Sept. 20: The fiftieth anniversary of the stigmata. Sept. 22: At 5:00 A.M., he celebrates his last Mass, hears a few confessions, blesses the international convention of prayer groups, and blesses the first stone for the monumental Way of the Cross. At 6:00 P.M. he gives his last blessing to the people in church and, finally, waves to the crowd from the window of the friary before retiring. His crypt was blessed that afternoon.
1968	Sept. 23: Early in the next morning at 2:30 A.M. Padre Pio dies with the words "Jesus...Mary" on his lips. His body lies in state for four days in church.

1968	Sept. 26: At 3:30 P.M. the funeral procession winds through the streets of San Giovanni Rotondo. At 10:30 P.M. his body is laid to rest in the crypt.
1982	Nov. 29: Pope John Paul II grants his "nihil obstat" for the introduction of the Cause of Padre Pio.
1983	March 20: Archbishop of Manfredonia signs the Decree of Introduction of the Cause. On the same day the process of Beatification of Padre Pio is begun.
1997	Oct. 21: Cardinals and Bishops recognize the fact that Padre Pio lived the theological, cardinal and associated virtues in a heroic degree. Dec. 18: The decree on heroic virtues is promulgated.
1998	April 30: The Medical Board examines the miracle attributed to Padre Pio. The following June, theological consultants give their judgment.
1999	May 2: Beatification of Padre Pio at St. Peter's Square in Rome by Pope John Paul II, drawing a crowd of 300,000. After the Beatification Mass, Pope John Paul is taken to St. John Lateran Basilica to greet an additional 100,00 pilgrims who had watched the Beatification ceremony on large screen televisions.
2002	June 16: Canonization of Padre Pio at St. Peter's Square in Rome

Some Spiritual Counsels from Padre Pio

The following spiritual counsels of Padre Pio were gathered from the writings of Padre Pio before the year 1922. Amazing to relate, there are at least 12 printed volumes (300 pages each) of his writings from early childhood to the age of 35. In the year 1922 the Supreme Sacred Congregation of the Holy Office forbade him to write, and Padre Pio, as usual, obeyed.

His writings have the poetry and rich imagery of one who has lived close to the soil and understands human nature; he was once a shepherd boy. He had that touch of genius which made the most sublime truths understandable through concrete comparisons and rich figures of speech. Over and above these natural good qualities for communicating one's thoughts, there is the inspiration of the Holy Spirit. For one cannot help but be moved interiorly by a prayerful consideration of Padre Pio's sublime thoughts.

AGAINST TEMPTATION

The best means of guarding yourself against temptation are the following: watch your senses to save them from dangerous temptation, avoid vanity, do not let your heart become exalted, convince yourself of the evil of complacency, flee away from hate, pray whenever possible.

If the soul would know the merit which one acquires in temptations suffered in patience and conquered, it would be tempted to say: "Lord, send me temptations."

Temptations, discouragement and unrest are the wares offered by the enemy. Remember this: if the devil makes noise it is a sign that he is still outside and not yet within. That which must terrify us is his peace and concord with the human soul.

The field of battle between God and Satan is the human soul. It is in the soul that the battle rages every moment of life. The soul must give free access to the Lord so that it be fortified by him in every respect and with all kinds of weapons; that his light may enlighten it to combat the darkness of error; that it be clothed with Jesus Christ, with his justice, truth, the shield of faith, the word of God, in order to conquer such powerful enemies. To be clothed with Jesus Christ it is necessary to die to oneself.

That which comes from Satan begins with calmness and ends in storm, indifference and apathy.

We must know how to confide. There is the fear of God and the fear of a Judas. Too much fear makes one labor without love, and too much confidence prevents us from considering the danger which we must overcome. The one must go hand in hand with the other and proceed as sisters.

The sublime degree of humility is not only to recognize one's own abjection but to love it. "I have chosen," says the prophet, "to be abject in the house of God rather than to dwell in the houses of sinners."

Obey promptly! Do not consider the age or merit of a person. And in order to succeed imagine you are obeying the Lord.

Where there is no obedience, there is no virtue; where there is no virtue, there is no good; where good is wanting, there is no love; where there is no love, God is not there; where God is not, there is no heaven.

He who attaches himself to the earth remains attached to it. It is by violence that we must leave it. It is better to detach oneself a little at a time, rather than all at once. Let us always think of heaven.

Always live under the eyes of the Good Shepherd and you will walk unharmed through evil pastures.

The above treasures of wisdom are excerpted from the booklet, Padre Pio Counsels, available at "The Cause of Padre Pio, Inc." For further information see page 201.

Crypt of Padre Pio—the destination of many pilgrims to San Giovanni Rotondo.

The Academy of the Immaculate Books

All Generations Shall Call Me Blessed *by Fr. Stefano Manelli, F.I.* A scholarly, easy-to-read book tracing Mary's role in the Old Testament, through prophecies, figures and symbols to Mary's presence in the New Testament—a clear concise exposition (all Biblical) on Mary's place in the economy of Salvation.

Jesus Our Eucharistic Love *by Fr. Stefano Manelli, F.I.* A treasure of Eucharistic devotional writings from the Saints and their stirring examples. It is sure to inspire greater love and devotion to Jesus in the Eucharist. Valuable and inspirational reading for meditation before the Blessed Sacrament.

Virgo Facta Ecclesia *by Franciscan Friars of the Immaculate.* Made up of two parts: a biography of St. Francis of Assisi and the Mariological basis of the Franciscan Order in its long tradition of Marian devotion—from St. Francis to St. Maximilian Kolbe. Interesting insights on Mary's relationship with the three Divine Persons.

Not Made by Hands *by Thomas Sennott.* An excellent resource book and the only book of its kind on the two most controversial images in existence—the Holy Image of Our Lady of Guadalupe on the tilma of Juan Diego and the Sacred Image of the crucified Christ on the Shroud of Turin. Both give much scientific evidence for their authenticity.

Padre Pio of Pietrelcina *by Fr. Stefano Manelli, F.I.* The author is in more than one way the spiritual child of Padre Pio. He grew up under his spiritual guidance, and thus got to know him intimately. In fact, it was to Padre Pio that Fr. Manelli turned in order to help him in establishing a Franciscan community especially dedicated to furthering total consecration to Mary Immaculate.

Mary and the Priestly Ministry *by Fr. Emile Neubert, S.M.* According to the translator who was a student of Fr. Neubert, this book and the well-known title, *My Ideal, Jesus, Son of Mary* are two of the three most important works of Fr. Neubert—Mariologist, gifted scholar, holy priest and religious. The author encourages fellow priests to place themselves into Holy Mary's school, who is their mother and their teacher.

Special rates are available with 25% to 50% discount depending on the number of books, plus postage.For ordering books and further information on rates to book stores, schools and parishes: *Academy of the Immaculate, 124 North Forke Dr., Advance, NC 27006, Phone/FAX (888)90.MARIA [888.90.62742], E-mail academy@marymediatrix.com.* Quotations on bulk rates by the box, shipped directly from the printery, contact: Franciscans of the Immaculate, *P.O.Box 3003, New Bedford, MA 02741, (508)996-8274, FAX (508)996-8296, Email:ffi@marymediatrix.com. Website:www.marymediatrix.com.*

More books on *Marian Shrines & Saints* (Conclusion)

A Pilgrim Responds to the Book on Marian Shrines of Italy

I gave a copy of *Marian Shrines of Italy* to our friends who were with us in Rome. They were absolutely delighted! I can't express how much I have enjoyed this very special book. I want to hurry back to visit all the other Sanctuaries! — *Paul and Dolores Mulaire, Canada.*

Experiencing an "Astonishing Goodness" at Italian Shrines

I made a pilgrimage last year to Italy using as a guide your book, *Marian Shrines of Italy.* This remarkable book is to me, without exaggeration, a holy book and a treasure. Reverencing and praying at our Lady's shrines at Loreto and others around Rome has awakened such an astonishing sense of goodness. This is the only way I know to speak of it. These are miraculous places. It is an experience of the astonishing goodness of God, the astonishing goodness of Our Lady, and everywhere the astonishing goodness of our holy Catholic Church! Thank you for *Marian Shrines of Italy.* — *Anthony Pasquale, Catholic Adult Education Teacher.*

Pilgrimaging to Italian Marian Shrines Without Leaving the States

There are more than 1,500 Marian shrines in Italy, many located in Rome itself. Though this would be an indispensable book to consult before making a pilgrimage to Rome (or anywhere in Italy), one need not be planning a pilgrimage to benefit from reading this book. *Marian Shrines of Italy* covers 35 of these marvelous shrines, giving the reader a picture of the Marian shrine geography of Italy. Each shrine is a jewel in the heavenly crown of Mary. The book contains numerous pictures (many in color) of the shrines and images of the Holy Virgin.

Many of the better-known shrines to the Madonna are included: St. Mary Major, Our Mother of Perpetual Help, the Holy House of Loreto, and Our Lady of Good Counsel. However, many shrines, not as well known, at least outside of Italy, are also profiled. It is fascinating to read again and again about the mysterious designs of Providence, how and why they came about.

Reading the book presents the reader with a taste of the sumptuous Catholic banquet of devotion, art, architecture, and culture which is Italy's patrimony. — *John O'Connell, book reviewer for Catholic Faith magazine.*

Printed in the United States of America
POS Professional Office Services Waite Park MN